Selected Writings on Soviet Law and Marxism

By the same editors

PASHUKANIS
SELECTED WRITINGS ON MARXISM AND LAW

M. E. Sharpe, Inc.

N. I. BUKHARIN
SELECTED WRITINGS ON THE STATE AND
THE TRANSITION TO SOCIALISM
Richard B. Day, ed.

SELECTED WRITINGS OF A. R. LURIA
Michael Cole, ed.

E. A. PREOBRAZHENSKY
THE CRISIS OF SOVIET INDUSTRIALIZATION:
SELECTED ESSAYS
Donald Filtzer, ed.

E. A. PREOBRAZHENSKY
THE DECLINE OF CAPITALISM
Richard B. Day, ed.

P. I. STUCHKA

Selected Writings on Soviet Law and Marxism

Edited, annotated, translated, and introduced by
Robert Sharlet, Peter B. Maggs, and Piers Beirne

M. E. SHARPE, INC.
ARMONK, NEW YORK
LONDON, ENGLAND

Library of Congress Cataloging in Publication Data

Stučka, P., 1865–1932
    [Selections. English. 1988]
    Stuchka : selected writings on Soviet law and Marxism / by Piotr
Ivanovich Stuchka : edited by Robert Sharlet, Peter B. Maggs,
and Piers Beirne.
      p.   cm.
    Translation of selected essays, originally written in Russian.
    Bibliography: p.
    Includes index.
    1. Law—Soviet Union. 2. Law and socialism. I. Sharlet,
Robert S.   II. Maggs, Peter B. III. Beirne, Piers. IV. Title.
LAW <USSR 7 Stuc 1988>
349.47—dc19
[344.7]
                                           87-36773
                                               CIP

ISBN 0-87332-473-0

Printed in the United States of America

Contents

PART III

Socialist Construction and Soviet Legality

Preface and Acknowledgments

The Latvian-born legal theorist P. I. Stuchka (1865–1932) is generally recognized as one of the principal architects of modern Soviet legal theory and of the Soviet legal system itself. He was the prodigious author and editor of many treatises, textbooks, symposia, and a Marxist encyclopedia of state and law. In addition, he published an extraordinary number of essays, articles, and reviews in which his contribution to the Marxist theory of law in the 1920s was largely contained. The present collection is intended to make his writings more available to an English-language audience. The essays selected for translation in this volume illustrate both the development of his thought on Soviet law and Marxism and also the practical labors of a theorist who for a tumultuous decade was Chairman of the Supreme Court of the Russian Republic in Moscow. We have organized Stuchka's essays chronologically and grouped them into three convenient periods.

We were supported in this endeavor by the generosity of the National Endowment for the Humanities, and by grants from Union College and the University of Southern Maine. Peter Maggs was aided by a Ross and Helen Workman Research Grant from the University of Illinois. Jill Kendall, Ruth Manint, Barb Millazo, Rosy Miller, and Melanie Shunk provided various and expert secretarial assistance. Lana Eckhardt expertly proofread the translations. Elaine Shuman valiantly performed much of the time-consuming work of checking and updating many of the references and biographical material that Stuchka himself, for one reason or another, failed to provide.

Robert Sharlet, *Union College*
Peter B. Maggs, *University of Illinois*
Piers Beirne, *University of Southern Maine*

Editors' Introduction

Piotr Ivanovich Stuchka was born to a peasant family on July 27, 1865, near Riga in the Latvian province of the old Russian empire. Little has been recorded about his early years, but it is known that he completed the *Gymnasium* at Riga in 1884 and then entered the law department of St. Petersburg University. It was during his years at St. Petersburg that he began to immerse himself in the writings of the intellectual precursors of the Russian revolutionary movement, the writings of Marx and Engels and those of the Russian Marxist Plekhanov. Stuchka received his law degree in 1888 and immediately began work as a political activist and a progressive journalist on liberal Latvian newspapers. His recorded work on questions that concerned law and politics during this period consist of not quite two dozen newspaper articles and polemical essays in socialist periodicals. These include specialized articles on labor legislation, the many problems of judicial and criminal law reform in the Baltic provinces, and various essays on issues within the revolutionary movement.

For his activities Stuchka was exiled in 1897 to the Vyatka Guberniia. In 1904 he founded the Latvian Social Democratic party and led it into an alliance with the Russian Social Democrats; later, in 1914, this merged with Lenin's Bolshevik faction. He took part in the 1905 revolution and, following the severe military repression of the revolutions and his own move to St. Petersburg, he defended many revolutionaries in the Tsarist courts. In 1906 he resigned from the Central Committee of the Latvian Social Democratic Workers' party (Kalnins 1972: 136–39); his resignation doubtless stemmed both from his opposition to the Menshevik dominance of Latvian socialism and from his demands for stricter controls of Latvian anarchists. In 1907 he was appointed leader of the Latvian Bolsheviks.

Soviet historians record that Stuchka played a key role, during the disastrous Russian participation in the 1914–18 war, in politicizing the Latvian rifle regiments in the socialist cause. Indeed, these very troops later took an active part in the October 1917 revolution and because of their political reliability, became a sort of military vanguard for the Bolshevik leadership. Stuchka is known to have been a member of the Petrograd Committee of the Bolsheviks in February 1917, and then of the Bolshevik faction of the Petrograd Soviet. According to Leon Trotsky (1959: 440; see also Daniels 1967: 190–91), Stuchka was one of seven Bolshevik candidates for the Presidium at the Congress of Soviets of October 25, 1917. He was appointed Commissar of Justice (Stuchka 1922) in Lenin's first government of 1917 (he had been associated with Lenin as early as 1895) and took an active part in the drafting of the revolutionary decrees on the legal relations of the transitional period.[1] While working at the center of the revolution, Stuchka remained active in Latvian political affairs. Taking leave of absence from his responsibilities in the administration of revolutionary justice, he returned to the Baltic region in late 1918 to provide direction to the emerging political developments there. Shortly after, the German army was finally driven out and Stuchka was proclaimed as the first prime minister of the ill-fated Latvian Soviet Republic. However, his incumbency was short-lived: in January 1920, his government was overthrown in the course of the Russian Civil War and foreign military intervention against the Bolsheviks.

Stuchka then returned to Moscow, the center of Bolshevik power, and resumed his legal work. His major contribution to the law was carried out in the 1920s, a decade that was an unusually fertile one for the development of Marxist legal theory in the USSR. During the period that encompassed the New Economic Policy (1922–27) and the emergence and consolidation of Stalinism around 1929–30, a time that was then called the "transitional period" (i.e., the transition to full communism, when law and the state would have "withered away") some very able theorists investigated complex problems of law and the state. The names of Stuchka and his pupil Pashukanis, of Krylenko, Reisner, and Razumovskii— spring readily to the mind of the historian of the 1920s. Moreover, neither before this decade nor at any time after it have Marxist theorists of law occupied such strategic positions of political power. Stuchka himself held several positions in the Communist Academy, was a delegate to the Central Executive Committee of the Communist International, and leader of the latter's Latvian section (Sharlet, 1968: 41). He was appointed to a senior justice office in 1921, an office from which he guided the programs of relegalization and recodification as the Bolsheviks were forced to "retreat" to the limited capitalism of the New Economic Policy. His book *The Revolutionary Role of Law and State* appeared in the same year, and the origins of the Soviet Marxist theory of law can properly be traced to it. In January 1923, Stuchka was appointed chairman of the Supreme Court of the Russian Republic (and a member of the Control Commission of the Communist International), a responsibility that he was to retain until his death. For his dedication to the revolutionary cause and his immense achievements as a Marxist intellectual and public official, Stuchka was honored by the Party and decorated by the government on the occasion of his 65th birthday in 1930. Upon his death (by natural causes) on January 25, 1932, his ashes were interred in the Kremlin

Wall behind Lenin's Mausoleum on Red Square.

Stuchka adhered to the ill-fated "commodity exchange" school of legal theory, which took seriously the idea of "withering away of law," and thus in the late 1930s came into direct conflict with Stalin's and Vyshinsky's determination to expand the use of law for the enforcement of discipline and the creation of a stable incentive system. In common with Pashukanis and other members of the commodity exchange school of law, Stuchka's good name fell rapidly into disrepute. His efforts in legal theory came to be ignored and even vilified. According to Roy Medvedev, in 1937, he was declared "a propagator of harmful ideology and a deliberate wrecker in the field of jurisprudence" (1973: 202).[2] State Prosecutor Vyshinsky referred to Stuchka as an adherent of "the Bukharinist perversions of Marxism-Leninism" (1938: 53) and to his notion of the role of law in the transitional period as "a coarse perversion of the Marx-Engels-Lenin-Stalin theory of socialism" (ibid., p. 55; see further Sharlet and Beirne, 1984). He was not rehabilitated until the reforms of the post-Stalin era. In the USSR today, Stuchka is regarded as one of the main architects of Soviet legal theory and of the Soviet legal system itself. His work and career are the objects of considerable scholarly attention (Strogovich, 1960; Kliava, "Introduction" to Stuchka 1964; Plotnieks 1978), and an extensive, albeit censored, collection of his (Stuchka, 1964) has been issued. Indeed, a glowing tribute to Stuchka was recently published in the leading Soviet legal journal (Skripilev and Grafskii 1986: 137–38; see also Smirnov 1985: 24).

However, Stuchka's intervention in Soviet legal theory is still relatively unheralded outside the USSR. In part this is because his contribution to legal theory lay less in the realm of erudite abstraction than that of pedagogy, of polemics, and of the practical dictates of the building of socialism. Very little of Stuchka's work is currently available to an English-language audience, despite its recognition several decades ago by several prominent Western jurists (e.g., Schlesinger, 1945; Hazard, 1951; Kelsen, 1955) and his more recent rediscovery by authors in the Federal Republic of Germany (e.g., Loeber, 1965; Reich, 1969) and, very occasionally, by Western Marxists (e.g., Poulantzas, 1964). The only substantial segment of his writings in English translation is the first four chapters of his *The Revolutionary Role of Law and State*. Only a few pages of his voluminous essays have been translated into English (Jaworskyj 1967: 72–75, 87–92, 99, 240–43; Zile 1977; Rosenberg 1984: 223–28, 249–60).

The collection of Stuchka's writings in this volume intends to fill at least some of this void. The translations that follow display the important themes of the three major periods into which the changing thrust of his work on law can be partitioned. These periods include his critique of "bourgeois" jurisprudence (Part I— "From 'Bourgeois Law' to 'Revolutionary Legality'"); his positions in the complicated Marxist debates in the 1920s and 1930s about the proper content and objectives of Soviet legal theory (Part II—"The Marxist Theory of Law"); and his involvement in the actual practices of the Soviet state and Soviet law in the fifteen years immediately after the 1917 revolution (Part III—"Socialist Construction and Soviet Legality"). We begin with a brief, general introduction to these three aspects of Stuchka's work.

From "Bourgeois Law" to "Revolutionary Legality"

The immediate aftermath of the 1917 Bolshevik revolution provided an important illustration of the reciprocal relationships between law, legal theory, and politics. After the collapse of Kerensky's Provisional Government, the Bolsheviks found themselves in late 1917 with no explicit theoretical guidelines for the role of law during the transitional period between capitalism and communism. Russian jurisprudence was then dominated by foreign, non-Marxist, even anti-Marxist theories about the origins and functions of law. Although popular and widely read, neither the legal positivism of Hans Kelsen nor the social functionalism of the Austrian jurist Karl Renner afforded much of a basis for the development of a Marxist theory of law. Alongside this was the pervasive influence of German philosophical idealism; its ambassadors were numerous, but the names of Jhering, Laband, Jellinek, Windsheid, and Dernburg constantly recur as authoritative sources in Russian juristic treatises of the time. Following from the inauguration of the Pandectist Civil Code and the *Methodenstreit* debates within philosophical idealism, the legacy of late-nineteenth-century German social theory was a conception that the core of the social universe was the individual, volitional agent whose rights and obligations were expressed in legal rules. This message of the idealist literature was most prominently received in the psychologism of Professor Leon Petrazhitskii, a supporter of the conservative Russian Kadet party.

For erstwhile Bolshevik theorists of state and law these strands of legal theory presented, in concert, a formidable obstacle to the development of a Marxist theory of law. While Marx himself had written extensively about the complex articulation of law within different modes of production, his writings on state and law under socialism were sparse, polemical, and always utopian. Statements such as "the executive of the modern state is but a committee for managing the common affairs of the whole bourgeoisie" (Marx and Engels 1848: pp. 110–111), and [only under communism can] "the narrow horizon of bourgeois right be crossed in its entirety" (Marx 1875: p. 320), afforded considerable inspiration but little aid for those with a practical responsibility for the pressing dictates of socialist construction. The nihilism of this confused vacuum was exacerbated with the view, insisted on by Engels, that because law was the worldview of the bourgeoisie, it was only the most backward sections of the socialist movement that voiced their demands in legalistic terms.[3] Moreover, in *Anti-Dühring* Engels projected the additional view that when the state really is representative of the whole society, "the government of persons is replaced by the administration of things, and by the conduct of processes of production. The state is not 'abolished.' *It withers away*" (1878: 333). No indigenous Russian Marxist tradition existed in the analysis of law. The People's Will movement had been destroyed by 1887, and the Social Democratic writings of authors such as Kistiakovskii and Struve had been rejected and castigated as reformist by Lenin some twenty years before the 1917 revolution. The reception of classical Marxism in Russia had much in common with that long and tragic tradition of Russian anarchism that was opposed to state and legal power in any and in all of its institutional forms; even the first Russian edition of *The Communist Manifesto* had been translated into Russian by an anarchist, namely Michael Bakunin. Neither offered much guidance other than what amounted to the paralysis of legal nihilism.

This nihilist heritage pervaded the tumultuous days of the first Soviet experiment with *otmiranie prava* (the withering away of law). Between November 1917, and July 1918, the Soviet government, under the supervision of Lenin and the commissariats of State Control, Justice, and Finance, enacted some 950 decrees and other legislative devices. These included decrees for the abolition of the police, the standing army, and the civil service. One of the earliest decrees was Decree No. 1 on the Court, initiated by Stuchka and drafted by the People's Commissariat of Justice. This decree declared that "all statutes are recognized as repealed which contradict the minimum programs of the Russian Social Democratic Revolutionary Party and the Party of Revolutionary Socialism."[4] Much of the old legal system, including the Procuracy, the bar, and all but the most basic laws, was annihilated; in its place was set up a *de minimis* system of revolutionary tribunals, people's courts, and judges who had instructions to be guided by their revolutionary consciousness. According to Stuchka (in his essay, "Lenin and the Revolutionary Decree," translated below), Lenin supported the decree with great enthusiasm, and he facilitated its passage by releasing it solely through the Council of People's Commissars—rather than through the Central Executive Committee, where it would probably have met opposition from the Left Socialist Revolutionaries and the Internationalists.

However, beginning in 1918, the Civil War began to sweep through Soviet Russia with unexpected ferocity. The Bolshevik response to the subsequent chaos was "War Communism," a draconian set of policies intended to govern nearly every aspect of social life. The harsh realities of civil war quickly impinged on the Bolsheviks' stated objectives about the withering away of law. Decree No. 1 was followed by other decrees on the judiciary which added more layers to the appellate hierarchy and which reinstituted many elements of the discarded Tsarist legal system. This process culminated during the early years of the New Economic Policy in a fully articulated legal system that was based largely on the models of foreign (French, German, and Swiss) codification.

To our knowledge, before 1919 there was little if any serious debate about law among Russian Marxists. According to Stuchka himself (in his essay on "State and Law in the Period of Socialist Construction," translated below), before December 1919 there was no theoretical work on law from a revolutionary

Marxist perspective. It was at this date that the Collegium of the People's Commissariat of Justice—of which Stuchka had been commissar since March 1919—provided the first official Soviet definition of the concept of law. This appeared in the "Guiding Principles of the RSFSR Criminal Law," and declared the "law is the system or order of social relations corresponding to the interests of the ruling class and protected by the organized force of that class."

In 1921 Stuchka published the first edition of his text *The Revolutionary Role of Law and State*, which he wrote largely to serve a pedagogical function in the law schools that were then in the process of being reopened as part of the Bolshevik policy of relegalization prior to the New Economic Policy. It was widely read in jurisprudential circles and was used in law schools as an introduction to Marxist criticism of law. It was from this book that serious Marxist debate about law began, and it is to it that the apparent rupture with much of the earlier jurisprudence can be traced. While it is exceedingly difficult to summarize the contents of *The Revolutionary Role of Law and State*, we can identify three major arguments in it:

1. Law is the system or order of social relationships corresponding to the interests of the ruling class and protected by the organized force of that class. Law is of two types: (a) rules that stem from sectional, private interests, and (b) technical rules that are of a purely administrative nature.

2. Law is the product of class struggles. Class struggles occur in the processes of production and exchange.

3. Law has a vital role to perform in the transitional period between capitalism and communism. The law of the transitional period—Soviet law[5] or proletarian law[6]—is a temporary form of authority that primarily involves a simplification and a popularization of the new social order and which is supported by coercion and ideological persuasion.

In the four essays translated in Part I of this volume, Stuchka attempts to clarify several aspects of each of these arguments. The first two essays ("A Class Court or a Democratic Court?" [1917] and "Proletarian Law" [1919]) reveal Stuchka's practical involvement with new proletarian institutions such as the People's Courts. The central problem discussed in both essays is the relationship between the Tsarist legal system and the new apparatus of power: because the former was bourgeois in both form and content it must be discarded, but with what proletarian institutions should it be replaced? In trying to steer a path between the errors of anarchism (to which he was always opposed) and those of legal formalism, Stuchka points to two types of rules in the old Code of Laws of the Russian Empire: rules, presumably of a more or less technical nature, that "did not contradict revolutionary legal consciousness" and rules determining the very essence and direction of activity of the old regime. The initial phase of the proletarian revolution should seek to promote policies that encourage the "burning" of the latter and the retention of the former. "In general," he argues, "the charter for judicial procedure will henceforth simply be no more than an institution, or a guide, or a manual." In the next two essays ("The Marxist Concept of Law" [1922] and "Notes on the Class Theory of Law" [1922]) Stuchka attempts to insert the central problem of the forms of proletarian regulation, such as the "charter for judicial procedure," into an explicitly Marxist theoretical plane. He suggests that, although he agrees with Engels' dictum that legalism is the outmoded classical worldview of the bourgeoisie, nevertheless, the "struggle around law" must be a central feature of revolutionary class struggle. For this very reason it was wrong to suppose that Bolshevism was opposed to legality. Moreover, because all "legality" must be understood in the context of its material basis in specific relations of production, it was crucial that Marxists consider the forms of legality specific to proletarian organization. To this end, therefore, Stuchka urges his colleagues to develop a Marxist theory of law whose objectives would be to provide criticism of the individual branches of bourgeois law and guidance for the proletarian revolution.

The Marxist Theory of Law

We have seen that the New Economic Policy mandated and accelerated full-scale restoration of law in the early 1920s as a condition of economic recovery from the devastation of war and as a prelude to a concerted program of industrialization. Familiar legal institutions were revived. An elaborate program of codification was begun, based largely on foreign models. For the Bolshevik jurists the restoration of law involved the need for a Marxist critique of the USSR's essentially bourgeois legal system in preparation for the time when the Party could end the retreat and resume the process of the withering away of law. In this phase of the revolution Stuchka pioneered the Marxist critique of bourgeois jurisprudence and of the branches of bourgeois law; his efforts in these respects must be assessed both as speculative and preliminary and also as an incipient alternative to the radical wing of the emergent commodity exchange school of law advanced by Pashukanis. Stuchka's concern to develop a Marxist theory of law is the major theme of the first two essays of Part II of this volume ("A Materialist or Idealist Concept of Law?" [1923] and "In Defense of the Revolutionary Marxist Concept of Class Law" [1923]). In the former he attacks psychological and "will" theories of law, such as those advanced by Petrazhitskii and Reisner. Law, he responds, does not originate in ideology but in material social relations. Law, he asserts, has three aspects: it is a concrete form of a social relation and embodies a specific injunction; it is an abstract form of a social relation, the legal form of that relation; and it is an intuitive form, internal to consciousness. In the latter essay Stuchka attempts to reply to idealist criticisms of his *The Revolutionary Role of Law and State*. In so doing he emphasizes that law occurs in the economic base (rather than simply as a superstructural phenomenon), and that it is a real material object (rather than an ideological form) that derives from class relations in the processes of production and exchange.

By 1924 Stuchka had become a major figure in the Communist International, and his various political and legal posts were the tumultuous external setting for an intellectual life devoted to the development of the Marxist theory of law. An early member of the Socialist (later Communist) Academy, Stuchka organized and led its section on the general theory of law which, in the early 1920s, became the cynosure of the emerging Marxist school of jurisprudence and the spearhead of the "revolution of the law." He was also a professor of law at Moscow State University, a law lecturer in the Institute of Red Professors, and the first director of the Moscow Institute of Soviet Law. Through these strategic positions, Stuchka shaped the theoretical orientation of the new generation of emerging Soviet Marxist lawyers. However, in 1924 Pashukanis published his *General Theory of Law and Marxism*. Much that happened in Soviet jurisprudence and legal education in the next few years must be understood as an extension of, or a reaction to, the themes of Pashukanis's book and of the sections of the commodity exchange school that adhered to it. Let us briefly outline its importance. The *General Theory of Law and Marxism* represented a plea for the analysis of legal forms in their specific historical contact (see further Sharlet, 1968; Arthur, 1978; Beirne and Sharlet, 1980). Pashukanis argued that all cultures necessarily had social rules, but that not all rules are legal. If law is merely a system of rules that responds mechanically to the interest of dominant classes, then it cannot be distinguished from any other social relations that contain norms or rules. For Pashukanis, the task of Marxist theory, therefore, was both to provide a materialist explanation of legal regulation as a definite historical form, and to investigate the material content of legal regulation during definite historical periods. *Why* does the bourgeoisie rule by law (rather than by violence or naked coercion), and *how*, precisely, does it rule? Having defined the problem in this way, Pashukanis then asserted two fundamental claims. First, law is an inherently bourgeois phenomenon. It is only under developed commodity exchange that the capacity to have a right in general is distinguished from specific legal claims. Law is bourgeois because it reflects the form of this exchange. The logic of legal concepts corresponds with the logic of the social relationships of commodity exchange, and it is here—and not in the instrumental demands of domination, submission, or naked class power—that the origin of law is to be sought.

The argument that legal regulation is inherently bourgeois anticipates Pashukanis' second claim that there can never be a proletarian or socialist law. Relying on Marx's analysis of fetishism in *Capital* and his political concerns in the *Critique of the Gotha Program*, Pashukanis conceived of the socialist transition to communism not as a transition to new legal forms, but as the gradual extinction of the legal form in general. He stressed that the Soviet Union had two forms of economic regulation in 1924: the administrative/technical rules that governed the general economic plan, and the legal rules (such as civil and commercial codes, courts, and arbitration tribunals) that governed the commodity exchange which was the main feature of the New Economic Policy. Pashukanis therefore castigated the law of NEP, and even the new system of criminal administration contained in the *RSFSR Criminal Code* of 1922, as mere bourgeois law. He added that although the *Basic Principles of Criminal Legislation of the Soviet Union and Union Republics* had substituted the concept of "measures of social defense" for the concept of "guilt, crime and punishment" (Pashukanis 1924: p. 124), this amounted to a change in terminology rather than the abolition of the legal form. Criminal law was the sphere in which legal relations attained their maximum intensity and, as such, was the dominant bourgeois form of regulation. Only with the complete supremacy of administrative/technical rules, Pashukanis concluded, could Marx's description of social emancipation be realized.

It is clear that Pashukanis's argument contradicted one of the pillars of Stuchka's theory of law, namely, that law is a class phenomenon. Indeed, at several places in his *General Theory* Pashukanis explicitly takes issue with Stuchka. He pointed out (Pashukanis 1924: pp. 61–62) that Stuchka's definition of law was indistinguishable from social relations in general,[7] and that perhaps because it emerged from the People's Commissariat of Justice, Stuchka's definition, stemmed from the needs of the practicing lawyer. It "shows the empirical limit which history always places upon legal logic, but it does not reveal the deep roots of this logic itself" (Pashukanis 1924: p. 62). Stuchka's definition of law, in short, revealed the class content present in the legal form, but it failed to explain why this content appeared in such a form. Nevertheless, in the preface to the third edition of *Revolutionary Role of Law and State*, published in 1924, Stuchka noted the number of new works on the Marxist theory of state and law and identified Pashukanis's *General Theory of Law and Marxism* as the most outstanding. With a few reservations, he found Pashukanis' book "to the highest degree (is) a valuable contribution to our Marxist theoretical literature on law and directly supplements my work, which provides only an incomplete and greatly inadequate general doctrine of law." Stuchka thus helped raise Pashukanis from academic obscurity to the forefront of the "revolution of law."

By the mid-1920s the theoretical burden of prerevolutionary Russian legal theory and of foreign jurisprudence had apparently been removed, domestic juristic opponents had apparently been overcome through vigorous intellectual debate and political criticism, and the adherents of the Marxist school were extending their analysis beyond the general theory of law into civil, criminal, and other branches of law. In 1925 Stuchka provided (in "Lenin and the Revolutionary Decree") a brief but rare contemporary excursion into the legal history of early Bolshevik policy and Soviet regulation of the judiciary, and some interesting glimpses into the formation of Decree No. 1 on the Court. In the same year he launched a massive project, *The Encyclopedia of State and Law*. In retrospect this project can be seen as an intellectual monument to the Marxist hopes for the withering away of law. Stuchka served as chief editor of this two-year, three-volume undertaking and, in addition, he himself wrote most of the entries concerned with the principal concepts of Marxist legal theory. His contributions to the *Encyclopedia* that follow in this volume represent not merely Stuchka's "mature" work but also the distillation and consolidation of his most prominent work in the Marxist theory of law as it then existed. It is clear—surveying Stuchka's essays on bourgeois law, jurisprudence, the state, revolutionary legality, law, the legal relationship, legal consciousness, and the new concept of Soviet law—that the theoretical offensive against the bourgeois juridical worldview achieved its greatest intensity in this project, under the banner of the revolution of the law.

Socialist Construction and Soviet Legality

As part of the general "cultural revolution," the Marxist school of law, now based in the Communist Academy, launched its journal *Revolution of the Law* in 1927. This new periodical was intended to serve as a forum for the theoretical struggle against foreign bourgeois jurists and their domestic allies. However, within the Marxist school important intellectual and political cleavages were becoming apparent, and we should note here the conflict between the radical and moderate wings of the commodity exchange school, respectively epitomized in the writings of Pashukanis and Stuchka. The common public front of the Marxist jurists was seriously ruptured in Stuchka's article "State and Law in the Period of Socialist Construction" (Part Three) that appeared in the second issue of the *Revolution of the Law*.

While consistently praising the originality of Pashukanis's *General Theory of Law and Marxism*, Stuchka now felt the need to offer serious criticisms of it. First, he argued that Pashukanis was wrong to have identified the origin of law in the needs of commodity exchange and that to do so was to engage in a species of economism. Law, he countered, originates both in the appropriation of land and in the class struggles in the processes of production. Law reflects not the exchange of commodities but the authority and the power of economically dominant classes. Second, Stuchka suggested that Pashukanis correctly pointed out the similarity between economic fetishism and legal fetishism under capitalism, but that he erred in extending this parallel to law in general. Very real differences exist between feudal law, bourgeois law, and Soviet law. Bourgeois law, for example, can itself be divided into two types. In the first period of capitalism, property law (the private ownership of the means of production) determines the distribution of products. With the advent of monopolistic imperialism the anarchy of production is replaced by trusts, by syndicates, and by state imperialism. In short, capitalist development entails the "rationalization" of bourgeois law in the pursuit of profit for private capital. Moreover, precisely because Pashukanis had falsely equated bourgeois law with law in general he had proceeded to commit himself to another error, namely, to the utopian belief that the process of the withering away of law involved a direct transition from bourgeois law to non-law.

Third, Stuchka urged, against Pashukanis, that Soviet law should have a creative role in the period of socialist construction. "Soviet law," he asserted, "must be the political economy of the transitional period, *the economic policy of Soviet power laid out in paragraphs*" (Stuchka, this volume p. 186). Although Soviet law was "in general a reprint of bourgeois law," it was nevertheless a law that existed without a bourgeoisie. Soviet law was a necessary, temporary feature of the proletarian dictatorship whose object was socialist planning and whose Soviet character was protected by the class state of the proletariat.

The Fifteenth Party Congress of 1927 called for the construction of socialism and the end of the strategic retreat of NEP, and urged the spread of a "cultural revolution" throughout Soviet society. Stuchka took up the Party's call on behalf of the Marxist jurists in his article "Culture and Law" (1928). For Stuchka, the cultural revolution was an extension of the "revolution of the law" already underway since the mid–1920s. He synthesized both aspects of this revolutionary process into the "cultural revolution of the law" and criticized the two extreme interpretations—one for advocating the premature withering away of the law, and the other for urging excessive legal coercion. Stuchka saw as the task of Marxist jurists the need to the supersede the bourgeois legal culture of NEP and to forge a Soviet legal culture. The struggle to attain the latter would entail the recognition of the apparent paradoxical logic of the revolution—there was, on the one hand, the need to construct new apparatuses of state and law, but, on the other, the commitment to their imminent withering away. Stuchka's interim solution to this paradox was to advocate the simplification of existing law as a gradual step toward its eventual elimination, while retaining its capacity for coercion during socialist construction. In the spring of 1929 Stalin initiated the "revolution from above." The first Five-Year Plan was gaining momentum and collectivization had begun, with its crescendo of violence then only months away. Anticipating the Stalinist political tendencies that would emerge at the Sixteenth Party Congress a year hence, Stuchka ("Revolutionary Legal Perspectives") advocated the strengthening of the state as the dialectical path to its ultimate withering away. At the same time, he lamented the increasing bureaucratism of the Soviet administrative system—this he considered to be an unwanted bourgeois legacy, and he therefore proposed to counter it with the expansion of mass political participation through the local soviets. Only mass participation in policy, he reasoned, could lay the essential groundwork for the eventual elimination of the state. But the prescription for the withering away of the state should not, according to Stuchka, be applied to law. Because law was then a vital mechanism for carrying out socialist construction in the countryside, he concluded that the decentralization of law was not the correct path. Instead, he advocated the continued simplification of the legal process, making it comprehensible and accessible to the Soviet masses. Indeed, given the flood of complex legislation that was beginning to inundate the Soviet system, Stuchka saw the simplification of law as an especially urgent task.

After investigating the forced collectivization campaign against the peasantry during the winter of 1929–30, Stalin himself criticized some of the worst excesses of the cadres in his famous "Dizzy with Success" speech of 1930. Stuchka's essay "Revolution and Revolutionary Legality" (1930) was a variation on Stalin's theme and was addressed especially to the juridical cadres in the collectivization drive, some of whom were now, retroactively, deemed guilty of overzealousness. He specifically attacked the nihilistic and immature tendencies that sought to eliminate law and revolutionary legality. Only to overzealous leftism did revolutionary legality seem a constraint to the success of the revolution. Quoting Stalin, Stuchka insisted, to the contrary, that a nexus existed between revolutionary legality and the objectives of socialist construction. These two concepts, far from being in conflict with each other, in practice were complementary. Revolutionary legality, far from being a bourgeois concept, was both a mechanism for eliminating oppressive social relations—such as the domestic subjugation of women in households and families—and also a form for the inculcation of order and strict social discipline. This discipline was to be directed from the center against local excesses. Revolutionary legality, it transpired, was a crucial pivot for the continuation of the revolution.

The final essay in the present collection, "My Journey and My Mistakes," is Stuchka's answer to charges formally placed against him by his enemies on the left and right. As the editors' note following the article indicates, this is not the self-criticism that was demanded, but rather is a detailed attack on Stuchka's own critics, upon Pashukanis in particular. Stuchka repeatedly cites Lenin, and draws upon his own personal association with Lenin, to argue that it is his critics rather than he, himself, who are un-Leninist. Soon after this article was published, Stuchka died a natural death. One can only speculate what would have happened to his defiant spirit had he survived to era of the great purges of the late 1930s.

Notes

1. *Dekrety*, 1957–71.
2. See further, *Sovetskaia Latviia*, July 28th, 1960.
3. This theme recurs in Engels' writings, especially in the late 1880s and early 1890s. It is found most explicitly in Engels and Kautsky (1887).
4. *Sobranie uzakonenii i rasporiazhenii Rabochego i krest'ianskogo Pravitel'stva,* 1919, no. 66, item 590.
5. See P. I. Stuchka (1921); p. 66 in Hazard (1951).
6. See also P. I. Stuchka, "*Proletarskoe pravo,*" [Proletarian Law] pp. 210–220 in *Oktiabr'skii perevorot i diktatury proletariata: Sbornik statei* [The October Revolution and The Dictatorship of the Proletariat: A Collection of Articles] Moscow: (1919), pp. 210–20.
7. Pashukanis reiterated this criticism in the second edition of his book: "the elements which provide the material for the development of the legal form can and should be segregated in the system of relationships which are responsive to the dominant

class . . .," quoted in Sharlet "Pashukanis and the Commodity Exchange Theory of Law," pp. 69–70.

References

Arthur, Chris. 1978. "Editor's Introduction," in *Law and Marxism: A General Theory* (Evgeny B. Pashukanis). Trans. Barbara Einhorn, 9–31. London: Ink Links.

Beirne, Piers, and Robert Sharlet. 1980. "Editors' Introduction," in *Pashukanis: Selected Writings on Marxism and Law*. Trans. Peter B. Maggs, 1–26. London: Academic Press.

Daniels, Robert V. 1967. *Red October: the Bolshevik Revolution of 1917*. New York: Charles Scribner's Sons.

Engels, Friedrich [1878] 1975. *Anti-Dühring*. London: Lawrence & Wishart.

Engels, Friedrich, and Karl Kautsky. 1887 (1977) "Juridical Socialism," *Politics and Society*, 7(2):199–220.

Hazard, John N., ed. 1951. *Soviet Legal Philosophy*. Trans. Hugh W. Babb. Cambridge: Harvard University Press.

Jaworskyj, Michael, ed. 1967. *Soviet Political Thought: An Anthology*. Baltimore: Johns Hopkins Press.

Kalnins, Bruno. 1972. "The Social Democratic Movement in Latvia," in Alexander Rabinowitch, Janet Rabinowitch, and Ladis K. D.Kristof, eds., *Revolution and Politics in Russia*, 134. Bloomington, Ind.: Indiana University Press.

Kelsen, Hans. 1955. *The Communist Theory of Law*. New York: Praeger.

Loeber, Dietrich A. 1965 "Unbewaltigte Vergangenheit im sowjetischen Zivilrecht Zur Auseinandersetzung um das wissenschaftlichte Erbe von Peter I. Stuchka," in D. Frenzke and A. Uschakow, eds., *Macht und Recht im kommunistischen Herrschaftssystem*, 129–50. Koln: Wissenschaft und Politik.

Marx, Karl [1875] 1970. "Critique of the Gotha Programme," in *Marx/Engels Selected Works*, 315–31. London: Lawrence & Wishart.

Marx, Karl, and Friedrich Engels [1848] 1973. "The Communist Manifesto," in *Marx/Engels Selected Works*, vol. 1, 98–137. Moscow: Progress Publishers.

Medvedev, Roy A. 1973. *Let History Judge*. New York: Random House.

Pashukanis, E.B. [1924] 1980. "The General Theory of Law and Marxism," in Piers Beirne and Robert Sharlet, eds., *Pashukanis: Selected Writings on Marxism and Law*. Trans. Peter B. Maggs, 40–131. London: Academic Press.

Pashukanis, E. B. [1927] (1980). "The Marxist Theory of Law and the Construction of Socialism," pp. 188–199 in Beirne and Sharlet (eds.)

Plotnieks, A. A. 1978. *Stanovlenie i razvitie marksistsko-leninskoi obshchei teorii prava v SSSR, 1917–1936*. Riga: Zinatne.

Rabinowitch, Alexander, Janet Rabinowitch and Ladis K. D. Kristof, eds. 1972. *Revolution and Politics in Russia*. Bloomington, Indiana: Indiana University Press.

Reich, Norbert, 1969. "Introduction," in Peter I. Stuchka, *Die revolutionare Rolle von Recht und Staat*, 7–55. Frankfurt am Main: Suhrkamp.

Rosenberg, William G., ed. 1984, *Bolshevik Visions: First Phase of the Cultural Revolution in Soviet Russia*. Ann Arbor: Ardis.

Schlesinger, Rudolf. 1945. *Soviet Legal Theory: Its Social Background and Development*. London: K. Paul, Trench, Trubner & Co.

Sharlet, Robert. 1968. "Pashukanis and the Commodity Exchange Theory of Law, 1924–1930," Ph.D. diss., Indiana University.

Sharlet, Robert, and Piers Beirne. 1984. "In Search of Vyshinsky: the Paradox of Law and Terror, *International Journal of the Sociology of Law*, 12(2): 153–77.

Skripilev, E. A., and B. G. Grafskii. 1986. "P. I. Stuchka i aktualnie voprosi metodologii nauki prava," *Sovetskoe gosudarstvo i pravo*, 6:137–38.

Smirnov, V. V. 1985. "Law, Culture, Politics: Theoretical Aspects," in W. E. Butler and V. N. Kudriavtsev, eds., *Comparative Law and Legal System: Historical and Socio-Legal Perspectives*, 23–33. New York: Oceana Publications.

Strogovich, M.S. 1960. "K voprosu o postanovke otdel'nykh problem v rabotakh P. I. Stuchki, N. V. Krylenko, E. B. Pashukanisa," in *Voprosy obshchei teorii sovetskogo prava*. Moscow: Gosiurizdat.

Stuchka, P. I. 1921 (1951) *The Revolutionary Role of Law and State*. Pp. 17–69 in Hazard (ed.), *Soviet Legal Philosophy*.

Stuchka, P. I. 1922. "Five Years of Revolution in Law," *Ezhenedel'nik sovetskoi iustitsii*, no. 44–45.

Stuchka, P. I. 1924 "Foreword" to *Revoliutsionnaia rol' prava i gosudarstva*. 3rd edition. Moscow: Gosizdat.

Stuchka, P. I. 1964. *Izbrannye proizvedeniia po marksistsko-leninskoi teorii prava*. Ed. G. Ia. Kliava. Riga: Latviiskoe gosudarstvennoe izdatel'stvo.

Trotsky, Leon. 1959. *The Russian Revolution*. Garden City, N.J.: Doubleday.

Vyshinsky, A. Ia. 1938, 1948. *The Law of the Soviet State*. New York: Macmillan.

Zile, Zigurds L. 1977. *Ideas and Forces in Soviet Legal History*. 3d ed. Madison, Wis.: College Printing.

PART I

From "Bourgeois Law" to "Revolutionary Legality"

Introduction

Questions about the appropriate form and content of the regulation of social relations were an important aspect of Bolshevik discussion from the very beginning of the revolution. What relationship ought to exist between the Tsarist legal system and the new forms of Bolshevik power? Which aspects of social relations should be regulated by law, which by simple coercion, and which by propaganda and exhortation? Should the technical expertise of Tsarist lawyers be relied upon until a coherent system of proletarian law was enacted? To none of these questions did erstwhile Bolshevik legal theorists have any ready-made answers. No coherent program was provided either by prerevolutionary Russian jurisprudence or by classical Marxism itself. The confused, negative thrust of Russian nihilism merely exacerbated this vacuum. However, developed communism demanded the withering away of law and, therefore, the Bolsheviks set themselves the task of trying to identify temporary, democratic, and accessible legal structures appropriate to a transitional period of socialist construction. In the first two essays translated here Stuchka displays his practical concern with the character of new proletarian institutions, such as the People's Courts, and with the various elements of the legislation of the transitional period. In the next two essays Stuchka attempts to develop some of the major concepts within a Marxist theory of law.

In "A Class Court or a Democratic Court?" Stuchka reveals both optimism at the prospect of socialist construction and frustration at the pace with which it was proceeding. To a certain extent, in the very early phases of the revolution, the workers themselves had anticipated subsequent Bolshevik strategies. Immediately after the February revolution of 1917, for example, in Kronstadt and in the Vyborg side of Petrograd the workers had ignored the Tsarist courts and were in the process of setting up their own revolutionary courts. Stuchka himself admits that the revolution had acted very slowly with respect to the old bourgeois apparatuses of power. He complains, on the one hand, that courts remained bourgeois institutions in part because judges were not yet subject to democratic election and recall, and also because there still existed salary differentials based on such factors as the old division of members of the judicial magistracy. On the other hand, Stuchka reports, with seeming approval, that the provisional revolutionary courts were actually beginning the tasks of construction.

Prior to the passage of the first decrees on the court there was heated discussion among the Bolsheviks about the proper relation that ought to exist between the old court system and the objectives of the socialist revolution. One faction within the Bolsheviks urged the retention of prerevolutionary courts as necessary apparatuses for the period of socialist transition. Another faction was adamant that all Tsarist law and all existing legal institutions should be abolished because they were incompatible with socialism. Lenin himself effected a compromise between these two factions with the rules enacted in Decree No. 1 on the Court. This decree was intended to accomplish several objectives. First, it abolished large segments of the Tsarist legal system. These included the district courts, military and naval courts, commercial courts, court chambers and the departments of the Ruling Senate, the Procuracy, and the system of justices of the peace. Second, it was declared that all laws were invalid if they contradicted the decrees of the Central Executive Committee or the minimum programs of the Russian Social-Democratic party and the Socialist Revolutionary party. Third, a new court system was to be instituted. This system was based on a nationwide structure of local (later people's) courts and revolutionary tribunals. The former were to sit in judgment on civil cases and relatively minor criminal offenses; the latter were created to combat counterrevolutionary forces and to consolidate the gains of the revolution. Both were to be elected democratically, and their members were instructed to be guided by their revolutionary consciousness.

However, developments on the military and internal fronts rapidly edged aside (or pushed forward to the future) these early experiments with Soviet legal forms. Beginning in 1918 civil war swept through Soviet Russia with increasing ferocity. The Bolshevik response to the bloody chaos that ensued was a draconian set of policies that was intended to regulate all aspects of social life. It was found necessary to create more law. Decree No. 1 on the Court was followed by other decrees on the judiciary. Decree No. 2 on the Court both expanded the layers of the judicial system and also attempted to define the rules according to which the courts reached decisions. Old legal officials could now be elected to judicial and investigative institutions. The rules of court procedure of 1864 were henceforth to be operative in both civil and criminal cases insofar as they had not been abolished and did not run counter to the 'legal conscience' of the working class. There was to be a limited system of appeals from court decisions overseen by a Supreme Supervisory Authority in Petrograd. Decree No. 3 on the Court increased the jurisdiction of the local courts, and the Decree on the People's Court provided for appeal in cases of procedural error. Decrees such as these were part of an erratic program of legal regulation that initially culminated in a new Constitution (in 1918) and a set of guiding principles for criminal law (in 1919).

In his article "Proletarian Law" of 1919 Stuchka reasserts his commitment to the democratization of the law of the transition period. The composition of the courts, he insists, should be close to the people or coming from the depths of the people. Ordinary civil relations should be equally comprehensible to the citizen and to the lawyer; indeed, the courses in revolutionary judicial procedure that Stuchka was now teaching at the Socialist Academy of Social Sciences, were open to judges in the People's Courts. "Proletarian law," he argues, "is primarily a simplification, a popularization of our new social order." At the same time he discusses various aspects of the actual content of the Soviet law of the transitional period. These laws included a mass of new decrees on the abolition of estate and civil hierarchies, the separation of the state and the schools from the church, the eight-hour working day, abolition of the means of production and the bourgeois freedom of contract, and new rules of "social law" to do with the family, divorce, and prostitution. Finally, he suggests that the time was now opportune for the publication of a compendium of proletarian law. This compendium (to be published in a technical version for lawyers, and a simpler version for citizens) should include the laws of the new constitution, the rights and duties of the citizen, social law, property law, labor law, and international law.

In effect, these reforms instituted an incremental process of relegalization even before 1921 when the Bolsheviks declared the strategic retreat embodied in the principles and apparatuses of the New Economic Policy. Familiar legal institutions were revived and an elaborate program of codification was instigated based on foreign bourgeois models of law. The New Economic Policy mandated and accelerated full-scale relegalization in the early 1920s as an essential condition both to facilitate economic recovery from the Civil War and War Communism and to provide an institutional shell for the industrialization program. For the Marxist jurists relegalization implied the postponement of the withering away of the state and law. The task now became the development of theoretical analysis of the bourgeois legal system with a view to determining the conditions, within the constraints of socialist construction, for its ultimate dissolution. Stuchka played a prominent role in this early phase of Marxist legal theory. His work served, in an important but rather elementary way, as the nexus between Marx's, Engels', and Lenin's fragmentary writings on law and the sophisticated theoretical analysis engaged in by Pashukanis.

In 1921 Stuchka published the first edition of his noted text *The Revolutionary Role of Law and State*. Like many of his works, which were primarily produced either as primers and textbooks for pedagogical purposes or as treatises on specialized topics, this book was widely read in jurisprudential circles and was used in law courses as an introduction to Marxist analysis of law. At the level of general questions about the nature of legal rules, it was never Stuchka's intention to develop an integrated or coherent general theory of law. Rather, his intentions seem to have been both to criticize the major schools of bourgeois legal theory (especially those that had adherents in the Soviet Union during the New Economic Policy) and to develop some of the chief concepts within Marxist legal theory.

Both these intentions were evident in his essay "The Marxist Concept of Law" of 1922. This was written at the beginning of the New Economic Policy, and in it Stuchka articulated three themes. First, he stresses that it is important to remember Engels' dictum that law and legalism were the classical principles of bourgeois ideology. As such, a chief aspect of the New Economic Policy was to be principled communist struggle against legal ideology. Stuchka argues that the bourgeois-juridical perspective, with its notions of "blind justice" and the "nightwatchman state," must be rejected in favor of the recognition that law and state are essentially phenomena of class relations. However, as a second theme, he reminds his audience that revolutionary class struggle consists in part of "struggle around law," precisely because the distribution of the means of productions is expressed in and protected by the law of private property. Only under developed communism can law be dispensed with. Third, he attacks those who promulgated the slanderous view that the Bolsheviks were opposed to legality. On the contrary, Stuchka stresses, progress in the socialist transition must be based on revolutionary legality and class legal consciousness.

The final essay in Part I, "Notes on the Class Theory of Law," reproduces Stuchka's speech to the inaugural meeting of the Section of the General Theory of Law within the Institute of Soviet Law. In this essay Stuchka attempts to deepen the discussion of the class nature of law, and he argues that the material basis of law lies in the relations of production that are manifest in legal relationships. In addition, he analytically merges the concepts of revolutionary legality and proletarian legal consciousness into the more dynamic concept of revolutionary legal consciousness. Finally, Stuchka calls on his colleagues to undertake the development of the Marxist theory of law to provide guidance for criticism of the individual branches of bourgeois law. Toward this objective, he offers an inventory of twelve generalizations about the initial program of the Section of the General Theory of Law.

1. A Class Court or a Democratic Court?

While news is received about the widespread recognition accorded the new Workers' and Peasants' Government, the judicial branch, led by the Ruling Senate, continues to act in the name of the overthrown Provisional Government. Our judiciary thereby displays its independence from politics. So thinks our judicial personnel of Shcheglovite origin. [Shcheglovitov was a legal official in the prerevolutionary government and was the author of a leading legal handbook—Eds.]

We must concede that the Russian Revolution acts very slowly with respect to the old apparatus of power; except for the commanding heights, all the old apparatus is intact. The civil servants of the Republic have changed somewhat: they have joined trade unions based on the principles of *"Novaia Rus'"* [New Russia], *"Zhivoe slovo"* [Living Word], etc., or have introduced an electoral system into their milieu. However, although all socialist programs consistently demand the election of civil servants and judges as Commissars (including the Commissars of the former Ministry of Labor), within all socialist programs, nevertheless judicial officers are still appointed from above. The justices of the peace are exceptions to this, but even they are subject to indirect election through the city *dumas* and *zemstvo* meetings; moreover, the restricted right to vote (in these bodies) introduced no improvements, and the court has remained a purely bourgeois class institution. It is essential to eliminate this apparatus of the old authority and to subject the court to democratic elections, and elected judges liable to the right of recall. The first priority is to relieve the court of a series of cases that until now have encumbered the judicial system. The following cases will be transferred from the court: agrarian cases (to land committees), apartment house cases (to apartment house mediation committees, etc.), with the remainder, constituting three-quarters of all civil cases (to special workers' institutions). However, the overall volume of cases will significantly diminish with simplifica-

---

"Klassovoi ili demokraticheskii sud?," *Pravda*, No. 185, Nov. 10, 1917 (Old Style), Nov. 23, 1917 (New Style), p. 2, col. 1.

tion of the law because, all know legal ambiguities present for fifty years (even though early eliminable) have created very favorable grounds for casuistry and judicial red tape. These include defenses about jurisdiction, decisions, and separation of cases, etc. Finally, the removal of such obsolete institutions as tribal property or predetermined inheritance (subject to abolition), etc., will significantly shorten and simplify civil court procedure. The abolition of political and religious crimes, and the simplification of the penal system itself will also facilitate the work of the criminal court.

Every court must be elected from top to bottom. The old division of members of the judicial magistracy will disappear, because salary differentials based on the hierarchy of judicial officers will disappear (both a justice of the peace and a senator should receive the same salary). At the same time, we must coordinate this with the (salary) base for the personnel of the so-called procuratorial supervision and the bar. These institutions should be consolidated into a single elected, social institution. The old differential earnings of the bar (attorneys) and the magistracy (judges), and the political distinctions between the Procuracy and bar should therefore disappear. If not now, then very soon, we must dismantle these old legal institutions. But dismantling is not enough—construction is also needed. Provisional revolutionary courts have already begun to function in some places, and others must be set up under the aegis of all Soviets of Workers', Office Workers', and Peasants' Deputies. With the lists established for elections to the Constituent Assembly, we must next hold elections for an appropriate number of democratic judges. In turn, these elected judges should perhaps be allowed, for the first time ever, to elect from their own ranks the higher tier of judges which should of course be reduced in number.

These changes cannot be delayed.

2. Proletarian Law

The earth shall rise on new foundations
We have been naught we shall be all.

[From the "International"—Eds.]

I.

With a bourgeois conception of law, we cannot even speak of proletarian law, because the purpose of the socialist revolution is to abolish law and replace it with the new, socialist order. For the bourgeois legal scholar, the word "law" is inseparably linked with the concept of the state as a protective mechanism, a coercive weapon in the hands of the ruling class. With the fall, or more correctly, the *withering away* of the state, law in the bourgeois sense also naturally falls, *withers away*. We may speak of proletarian law itself only as the *law of the transitional period*, of the period of the proletarian dictatorship, . . . Alternatively, we may speak of law in the socialist society, using an entirely new meaning of the word. With the elimination of the state as an oppressive mechanism in the hands of one class or another, social relations and the social order will be regulated not by coercion but by the conscious good will of the working people, i.e., of the whole new society.

In this respect the tasks of bourgeois revolutions were much easier than those of the socialist revolution. The revolutionary words of Voltaire are well known: "If you want to have good laws, burn your old ones and make new ones." But we know how little these words were put into practice by bourgeois revolutions, even by the most decisive of them, the great French Revolution. That revolution mercilessly burned the castles of the feudal lords and cut the bonds of serfdom to these castles; it abolished both privileges and their holders, and replaced feudalism with the bourgeois system. But the actual oppression of man by man re-

---

"Proletarskoe pravo," *Oktiabr'skii perevorot i diktatury proletariata: Sbornik statei* (Moscow: Gosudarstvennoe izdatel'stvo, 1919), pp. 210–20.

mained, and the old laws remained intact and continued to be applied. The legal monument of the French Revolution, the Napoleonic "Code civile," was written more than 10 years after the revolution (of 1804), after the successful counterrevolution, not to mention the purely counterrevolutionary codes, such as the civil procedure and criminal codes (in 1808 and 1810).

In one of his first works, in 1843, Marx clarifies the basic difference between bourgeois and socialist revolutions:

> The bourgeois revolution undoes the old feudal forms of organization by the political liberation of the independent personality, but not giving a new form to the economic bondage and subordination of this personality. . . . All the presuppositions of this egoistic life continue to exist in civil society outside the sphere of the state, but as proper to civil society. When the political state has achieved its true completion, man leads a double life, a heavenly one and an earthly one. . . . He has a life both in the political community, where he is valued as a communal being, and in civil society where he is active as a private individual, treats other men as means, degrades himself to a means and becomes the plaything of alien power. [Marx 1843: pp. 93–94]

Private interests must be subordinated to universal interests, for whether or not a man is well fed in a bourgeois society, whether or not he must work through old age beyond his strength for a bare existence, whether or not he has time for the satisfaction of his spiritual needs, this is a private affair, the egoistic interest of each individual personality, which is no business of the state. "The state may turn into a free state *(Freistaat*, meaning also republic), without turning man into free man."

For the bourgeois revolution it was sufficient—judging by its decisiveness—to replace the power of one class or classes with the power of another class, and to change the form of organization of state power. But the means of oppression freely changed even without basic changes in the text of the law. The permanence of law seems to be the most significant feature of human society because it is based upon the principle of the exploitation of man by man. Thus, the Roman laws of slavery survive not only feudalism, but also all the phases of capitalist development right up to imperialism.

Es erben sich, Gesetz und Rechte
Wie eine ewige Krankheit fort.*

The bourgeois revolution did not always obey Voltaire's words and did not burn the old laws so decisively. Even when the old laws were burned, this was insufficient to eradicate them from the memory and habits of people. "The

---

*"Statute and law pass by inheritance like an eternal illness"—Goethe.

human mind is a secure storehouse in which Moses' commandments on the stone tablets are as factually real as the latest government decree about bread ration cards. In the mind ancient history is interwoven with the present in a single and equal reality'' (Renner). From this derives all the theories of the *divine* origin of such institutions as holy property, of the ''inborn'' nature of estate privileges, and of the ''natural right'' of the owner to the services of the worker, etc.

Socialist theory is a merciless critic of all existence, and so too the proletarian revolution is above all a merciless destroyer of every existing state and social order. It at once violates two articles of the Tsarist Criminal Code, Articles 100 and 126, and so frees the procurators of the counterrevolution from unnecessary decisions: whether to charge the revolution under Art. 100 (which provides punishment for bourgeois or political revolution aimed at ''overthrowing state authority''), or Art. 126 (planning a socialist revolution, ''the overthrow of the social order'').

In the field of law as in all else, it is the proletarian revolution that for the first time deliberately and irreversibly effects the demands for true democracy. It animates Voltaire's words and triumphantly casts on the bonfire all 16 volumes of the *Code of Laws of the Russian Empire* along with the empire itself and its imperialism. From the remaining, charred pages, some of our revolutionaries vainly began to fashion a ''Code of the Russian Revolution,'' instead of affirming in the articles of a revolutionary code the true achievements of the proletarian revolution or the principles of its development in order to make new, truly revolutionary laws.

The proletarian revolution demands creativity. It had to be bold both in destructive work and in the law-creation role. It would have been most inappropriate if the decrees of the Workers' and Peasants' Government had included citations to the former laws of the war period or peacetime, when such laws of former governments should be abolished.

But the socialist revolution is not a simple leap into the unknown. It is a long, more or less extended process of civil war by which bourgeois society, with its class division between oppressors and oppressed, is transformed into socialism. This transitional period requires a special law of the transitional period—partly because this system does not change in one stroke and partly because the old, traditional order continues to exist in consciousness. This is particularly felt by those strata of the proletariat recently awakened, while they still ''revolve within traditional ideology and are fed mentally with bourgeois meals.''

The Workers' and Peasants' Revolution has found a formula that has truly solved the problem. In the *Decree on the Court* (No. 1) we read that the new courts ''shall be guided in their decisions and verdicts by the laws of the overthrown governments only *to the extent that* they have not been repealed by the revolution and do not contradict revolutionary conscience and revolutionary legal consciousness.''

On the one hand this was the answer to all attempts to retain the old laws, even though they had been burned but nevertheless lived on in consciousness; "only to the extent that," on the other hand, was an answer to those who accused us of anarchic tendencies for the repudiation of the laws of the previous governments, just as our own Marxists (on the right) have accused us. I answered our opponents with the following quotation:

> But what do you understand by the maintenance of the legal foundation, gentlemen? The maintenance of laws which belong to a bygone social epoch, which were made by the representatives of extinct or declining social interests, and which therefore also convert interests contradictory to the general need into laws. However, society does not depend on the law. That is a legal fiction. The law depends rather on society . . . (laws) must necessarily alter in line with changes in the condition of life. The defense of old laws against the new needs and claims of social development is fundamentally nothing but a hypocritical defense of outdated particular interests against the contemporary interest of the whole. This attempt to maintain the legal foundation involves treating particular interests as dominant when they are in fact no longer dominant; it involves the imposition on a society of laws which are themselves condemned by that society's conditions of life, its mode of appropriation, it trade and its material production . . . this phrase, "the legal foundation," involves either conscious deception or unconscious self-deception. . . . [Marx 1849 pp. 250–51]

And so? There are Marxists who regard this as an anarchist citation. I have had to reveal to them the secret that this citation is taken verbatim from Karl Marx's famous speech before the Cologne jury. No, we are not anarchists. On the contrary, we give considerable, perhaps sometimes excessive significance to law, although only to laws of the new order. These laws correspond to the old laws to the extent that the new order can be reconciled with the old or withering order.

II.

"*All power now belongs to the Soviets*. The commissars of the former Provisional Government have been eliminated. The representatives of the Soviets shall communicate directly with the Revolutionary Government." This was decree (No. 5) of the Second All-Russian Congress, and it fully established a basis for proletarian law. For us there was no reason to dwell on the fact that during the eight months of the bourgeois government, both in its pure and revolutionary coalition forms, the Soviets repeatedly came to the fore, sharply presenting the question of taking all power in their hands. Of course, only the Soviets, representing the viewpoint of the proletarian dictatorship and socialist revolution, could seize power. No one had any doubts that either the bourgeoisie or its counterrevolutionary allies—the landowners led by Prince Lvov—would voluntarily, without a struggle, give up power: "This will be the final and decisive struggle."

If one recalls the days of the first revolution in February we see a clear similarity: then, local power was transferred to the commissars whom the Provisional Government mechanically named by one stroke of the pen as the representatives of the Zemstvo boards and as city heads. Thus, local power ended up in the hands of the bourgeoisie and the landowners organized in the Zemstvo-City Union with Prince Lvov, as the representative and head of the union. Only gradually were some of the local commissars, who were pressed by the revolutionary populace, replaced by pure bourgeois or even revolutionary elements. In July [1917] even Prince Lvov had to leave. The replacement of the Provisional Government by the Workers' and Peasants' Government, and, in the localities, the replacement of the power of the bourgeois commissars by Proletarian-Peasant Soviets removed the bourgeois class from power, replacing it with the proletariat and the poor peasantry. And this was everything! The *property qualification* [for voting] was replaced by the labor qualification. Capital in power was replaced by labor: "He who has been naught shall be all."

For a long time the whole *proletarian law of the state* consisted entirely of one decree (No. 5) of two lines. Only in January [1918] did the new name of Soviet Russia appear: "The Russian Socialist Federated Soviet Republic." Simultaneously, the *declaration* of the Congress established the famous basic principles of Soviet power. It was only at the Fifth All-Russia Congress of July 10, 1918 that *the Constitution* of *the RSFSR was adopted*. However, this Constitution repeats and confirms only what already exists and can be easily concluded from Decree No. 5 on the transfer of all power to the Soviets. This is just a written version of what the proletarian had created.

But the transfer of all power to the Soviets simultaneously destroyed not only the state but also the social order. The Workers' and Peasants' Soviet Republic, like every state, is also a class state. However, its task is not the oppression of the have-nots in the interest of the rich minority. On the contrary, the task of the dictatorship of the have-nots (i.e., of the huge majority) is the "suppression of an insignificant minority (i.e., the bourgeoisie), to eliminate the exploitation of man by man, and to establish socialism under which there will be neither class divisions nor state authority." In the Soviet republic the unification of the working citizen with the working man occurs anew.

Every proletarian revolution starts with destroying in practice Montesquieu's theory of the separation of powers. Look at the Soviet of Workers' Deputies in Petrograd, or at the Federated Committee in Riga in 1905: everyone was sent there for political advice, for advice about laws and government decrees, and even for judicial matters and civil disputes. The investigative commissions attached to the Military Revolutionary Committees in 1917 were the very agencies of power to which people turned even in divorce cases. After October 25, 1917, Soviet power in the RSFSR *is simultaneously legislative, executive, and judicial power*. This is not to deny the technical division of labor, but to reject the misleading theory of the independence of one power from another. The dictatorship of the proletariat and the poor peasantry is an indivisible, *mighty Soviet power*.

We know how the Paris Commune "wrecked and destroyed the whole bourgeois machine. Even the judiciary lost its apparent independence: in the future they had to be openly elected, accountable, and recallable."

The October Revolution continued the experience of the Paris Commune on an all-Russian scale. The standing army and police, as we know, were already destroyed before October 25. By its decree of October 28 on the transfer of all power to the Soviets, the October Revolution in principle destroyed the entire apparatus of the old civil service. In principle, but not in fact. A strike and sabotage by the bourgeois civil service were necessary to destroy it in fact as well. And the court. Despite the fact that the old court continued to render decisions in the name of the Provisional Government, wherever proletarian revolution had been victorious, much effort was needed to convince the comrades of the need to abolish the old court. I would say that our revolutionaries acted more decisively against the bureaucratic sabotage of the food ration councils, for example, than against the court. Perhaps because the court seemed alien for a whole month the revolution allowed open legal agitation in hundreds of its own courtrooms for the Provisional Government, against which armed struggle was then being waged.

Even before October the masses completely mistrusted the old court. This mistrust clearly appeared in the attempts to create their own revolutionary courts, e.g., on the Vyborg side of Petrograd, in Red Kronstadt, etc. But at the same time as the popular masses *abolished the old courts in practice*, the same logical, though daring, idea did not occur at once to the comrades who lead the Workers' and Peasants' Government. Only on November 24, 1917, did the Decree on the Court (No. 1) appear, *abolishing all the old courts without exception*. It was only on December 4, 1917, that the Ruling Senate was actually closed after it had just attempted to publish its edict-proclamation against the Bolsheviks. This edict was not published because the workers of the Senate printshop, and then the Senate typists, refused to reproduce it.

Although the Decree on the Court introduced a special judicial authority, this was only a technical division of labor. This authority was given not to a special class of judicial officers but to a people's court comprised of the workers themselves. Although we permitted an exception for chairman of the People's Court in the decree, calling old judges to these places (Art. 2 of the decree reads: "The former justices of the peace are not deprived of the right, if they give their consent, to be elected to the local (people's) courts." But the sabotage and a strike by the old judges saved us from their participation in the work of the people's proletarian court. On the basis of the experience in the provinces, where the old judges did not walk out everywhere, we had to conclude that the lawmaking role of the [People's] Court was significantly less in these courts than where they were absent. The formal aspect of their decisions was generally better than decisions in the purely Workers' and Peasants' Court, but decisions of the old judges are marred by citations to various articles of one volume or another of the Code of Laws intentionally burned in the great conflagration of October 25, 1917. Original thought is also absent.

Thus the proletarian revolution obtained a new force to participate in its creative work—the *People's Court*. There have been historical moments when even bourgeois jurists made law by judicial decisions. But they understood—or understand—this type of lawmaking to be the application of old precedents (remember Shchedrin's "Kashin Court in which precedent was established"), or as a reception, i.e., a borrowing of already existing (e.g., Roman) law, etc. But the People's Court of the Workers' and Peasants' Government had nowhere from which to borrow. On the contrary, every borrowing leads to conscious or unconscious counterrevolution. The People's Court justified our hopes, and we were correct in affirming that proletarian law would lead to the simplification of social relationships. We always considered it senseless to demand from citizens obligatory obedience to incomprehensible laws or, hypocritically, to speak of justice in a state where knowledge of all law is obligatory (for it is not permitted to plead lack of knowledge of them) while at the same time these laws are so complex that only legal specialists can understand and correctly interpret them.

I do not deny that the People's Court needs theoretical guidance, but it must be socialist not bourgeois theory. I therefore anticipate great success for proletarian lawmaking from the new "Socialist Academy of the Social Sciences," the people's universities, etc. A great task confronts us—to liberate proletarian consciousness from bourgeois thought, and to provide the proletariat with a general educational understanding. In the soviets and soviet institutions, the work of proletarian legal consciousness will then be liberated from the last vestiges of bourgeois tutelege.

III.

The proletarian revolution was at first presented with a very difficult task. It could not recognize the old laws, but it was difficult to create new codes. Let us assume that we will work faster than the French Revolution—their civil code was published over a decade after the revolution. In any event, months will pass before new laws are written. Moreover, the social relations of the transitional period are not distinguished by their permanence. Thus, it is only with significant qualification that one can speak of consolidating the law of the transitional period in writing.

I have already stated that the Decree on the Court introduced a well-known formula for the recognition of the old laws—"only to the extent that they have not been repealed by the revolution and do not contradict revolutionary conscience and revolutionary consciousness." But the note to Art. 5 additionally explains that objectively "all laws which contradict the decrees of the Central Executive Committee, or the Workers' and Peasants' Government, or the minimum programs of the Russian Social Democratic Party and the Socialist Revolutionary Party, must be considered repealed.'' This is not the time to enter into a polemic over the last phrase; factually, we can already verify its expedience and profound meaning.

The general minimum programs of the parties triumphant in the revolution contain demands for *the abolition of estate differences* and *the abolition of private ownership of land by estate owners*. Eight months of revolution passed and these demands, which were in themselves bourgeois-democratic, were not met. On the contrary, until July, Prince Lvov led the Provisional Government, and a peasant uprising against landlords was put down with military force by landlord-commissars. Then the October Revolution declared *landlord ownership of land abolished without compensation*, by Decree No. 3 and eliminated *estates and civil ranks* by Decree No. 31 (November 12, 1917). This was not simply a verbal declaration, but the actual liberation of the Russian countryside from serfdom. And of course the first decree (i.e., on land) is paramount, because no decree has yet been issued punishing the use of the abolished titles; it is not even known if such a decree will ever be issued. No one doubts that noble estates and Soviet power are irreconcilable concepts. The nobility has disappeared in Russia and can return only through counterrevolution, and then only for a short time.

In all socialist programs we find a demand *for the separation of church from state and of school from church*. Similarly, for the eight months of the first revolution all were silent on this demand. However, when a decree was published on January 23, 1918 (Decree No. 263), on separating church from state, and school from church, our fellow socialists tried to frighten us that this decree would lead to the downfall of Soviet power. And the supporters of the Constituent Assembly directly countermanded it where they held power. In fact, Soviet power easily survived the struggle with the church. Religious processions ceased to be threatening demonstrations, and from rural areas news more often came that the peasants themselves were driving out their priests; indeed, on this latter question Soviet propaganda has until recently been most listless. Of course, the main role here will henceforth belong to the Soviet school.

This is all from the political area, affecting man as citizen. But let us return to man as a private individual. For the first time, law undertakes the emancipation of man from serfdom in fact rather than in words. When they were emancipated the peasants received their personal freedom, but the landlords "drew the line" at their *right to land*. We have seen that the October Revolution corrected this injustice as a matter of first priority. But the revolution went further, introducing freedom from serfdom of another kind: *the eight-hour working day*, and then *nationalization of the means of production. From freedom of contract, the revolution* went to *labor service obligation*, and *wages* were transformed into *social support* on the principle of providing the minimum needed for survival. We know only too well that this has still not been achieved, and that before the revolution the extraordinary differential between the highest and lowest earnings was unusually onerous and probably caused temporary general malnutrition. We even allow the thought that *temporarily, but equally for all*, it may be necessary to extend the working day if productivity either does not rise or if it falls.

However, considering these questions from the perspective of bourgeois law, we lose all bearing. Where is freedom of contract? And with obligatory work, the *obligation to work* is confused with the *right to work*. And the ''right to laziness'' (wittily posed by Lafargue) in contrast to the right to work is turned into *obligatory* leisure (laziness) in the interests of national health. What support is there for the bourgeois legal theorists if a right is turned into an obligation and an obligation precedes a right?

Proletarian law has debunked the use of contract as a foundation and future generations will smile ironically when they read in a certain draft of the ''Criminal Code of 1918'' the attempt to place even the relations of the Red Army soldier to the Russian Socialist Federated Soviet Republic on a purely contractual basis, holding a Red Army soldier who has forgotten his proletarian honor criminally liable for early breach of contract.

Is the *abolition of freedom of contract* not a new crime of the Communist Bolsheviks? Read any page in Marx about the freedom of contract of the worker. The machine fundamentally revolutionizes the contract between worker and capitalist. . . . Formerly, the worker sold only his own manpower, which he freely disposed of as a free man. Now he sells his wife and children. He becomes a ''trader in living commodities'' (*Capital*). You will recall the bitter irony in Marx's words.

However, freedom of contracts is really undermined if, in case of any taking or voluntary acceptance of money, a question may be raised of need and financial position or of ability to work and of the source of the demand presented. These questions can all be raised freely under proletarian law not only by the court but also by the Commissar of Banks, or the Commissar of Labor, etc. A Shylock deal is no longer thinkable here.

Sacred institutions such as *the family and inheritance* fare no better with the decrees of the proletarian revolution than does sacred private property. Inheritance is abolished except for small items of property (not over 10,000 rubles); until the general introduction of social security, in case of their inability to work or lack of funds, the funds needed for the minimal essentials of life shall be provided from the remaining property for a spouse or nearest relative. Thus, the financial basis of the bourgeois family is destroyed, and [therefore] it would have perished even without the decrees on divorce and civil marriage.

But the holy family was destroyed even before this. There was no law whose introduction would have elicited so many petitions as the law on divorce. As People's Commissar of Justice, I received every day half-a-dozen letters and telegrams with requests to hasten the new decree. By the unilateral declaration of one spouse our decree *on divorce* finally removed any question of compulsion with regard to marriage, leaving mutual love as the sole motive for its existence.

By abolishing the concepts of "illegal cohabitation" and "illegitimacy," and by formally dividing marriages into those registered by the civil authority and those incorrectly or entirely unregistered, the proletarian revolution finally ended a shameful page of bourgeois hypocrisy. It was not from fear but conscience that the bourgeois defended two institutions equally sacred to bourgeois society—legal marriage and legalized prostitution, and rigorously struggled against all illegal cohabitation, i.e., neither registered in the church nor with the police.

We see how the proletarian revolution has directly or indirectly overthrown the foundations of bourgeois society one after the other. We have listed in this section a total of eight short decrees. As a result of them, stone by stone, nothing remained of bourgeois law.

IV.

I have before me the 71 booklets—778 decrees—of the Collection of Legislation and Decisions of the Workers' and Peasants' Government. This thick book seems like a thin little book compared with the 16 volumes of the old Code of Laws or the annual collection of decisions of the old government. However, if we discard those decisions relating to special cases (confiscation, nationalization, and organizational questions), then only a slender book of the basic provisions of the new proletarian law remains.

The time has come to begin systematically to codify a compendium of all proletarian law of the transitional period. This code must be accessible to the broadest masses. But will we succeed in compiling such a code in the next few months? If so, will it remain in force for long? By merely looking through the book of decrees, we can see how transient and changeable are the institutions and legal provisions created by the revolution.

We have been criticized for throwing out the Constituent Assembly that we ourselves sought and convened. Additionally, we have already thrown out or radically changed even the institutions that we first created. The proletarian revolution does not claim eternal and immutable achievements. The proletarian revolution is a process that develops through civil war. Less backwardness and more action are its slogans. When this revolution finally achieves victory, the withering away of the Workers' and Peasants' Government and proletarian law itself, in the traditional sense of law, will be completed.

Our *Soviet Constitution* will of course occupy the first place in Book I of our Code of Proletarian Law. These 90 articles of the basic laws of the RSFSR replace in short form several volumes of the former code. It is true that the Constitution provides for some instructions on the development of its basic provisions, but this refers mainly to specialized questions, e.g., the technical aspects of Soviet elections. These instructions will likely be printed in a separate book with the remaining instructions, orders, guidelines, etc., which in the old code were scattered throughout all the volumes. After the Constitution should come the rights and duties of *citizens*, both Russians and *foreigners*. In our country there will be no division into natives and foreigners, but in accordance with Art. 20 of the Constitution, only into *working people* and *non-working people*. Of course, this division is only temporary until the abolition of class differences in general, when all shall become working people. There will also be brief temporary articles on changing one's citizenship and perhaps also one's class. And this is all.

The most important section of Book I will be that on *Social Law*. Note that this book was previously included in Volume 10 [of the old code] and was called private or civil (i.e., bourgeois) law. But you will find it difficult to recognize this old friend: almost nothing of the bourgeois and very little of the private [law] is left in it. You will find in the opening pages on family law the holy family of the bourgeoisie, but you will find nothing holy here. This is the sole place where freedom of agreement triumphed, expelling all outside admixtures (in the form of church or civil sacraments or compulsion) from family law. Until the introduction of full social security, proletarian family law will still include preserved remnants of the [bourgeois family law] in the form of support payments (if someone is penniless or is unable to work). Social security will eliminate even this vestige of the old world.

Following the family law section will come "property law," or more accurately, the abolition and limitation of property rights. This section will include the abolition of private ownership of land, the socialization of land, the nationalization of the means of production and of urban housing, and the administrative procedures of nationalized property. Finally, authorization to use remnants of private property during the transitional period will also be included here.

Next will come the codification *of all the rules on labor*, both on productive labor and on labor in soviet or private service. This is the part of social law which in one form or another will continue into the new society. However, we have already seen that labor in the new society will be transformed from an obligation and duty into a right or, as Marx said, "labor will become not only a means of life but life's prime want" [Marx 1875: p. 19].

Following this section will come some survivals of contract law or, more accurately, limitations on contractual freedom. A new section on *international law* will be added. With respect to other countries, our Republic will maintain both exchange and contractual relations until socialism is introduced everywhere. In order to break once and for all with lengthy treaties of different types with different states, we will try to formulate those provisions that we unarguably recognize for all countries.

I do not know if all this will fit in one book, but it will be the basic and obligatory law for everyone. And it will not be an immutable obligation as before, for even the right to amend the Constitution is granted to the Central Executive Committee. Nevertheless, we shall strictly apply the principle of inflexibility with regard to Book I [of our law].

There is another matter for future legislation: these are technical instructions, guidelines, in which only the most general provisions are obligatory. Whether these are rules on court procedure, on postal and telegraph or railroad service or, finally, on Soviet agriculture, gardening, or bookkeeping—obligation everywhere will be equally conditional. The same will be true of the model instruction on criminal offenses and punishments, on serving punishments, and on public education and education in general. This will be a rather bulky volume, but meant merely for one or another group of people, for one or another special case, etc. I do not know how successful we will be in the strict application of this point, but we have adopted it in principle. We already have a number of such instructions in place of the former laws: instructions for the People's Courts, the Punitive Sections, and the separation of Church and State, etc.

But even if such a code existed—a code which it is now necessary to start compiling expeditiously—one task will still remain. This is to make the code accessible to all. Naturally, our code will be significantly smaller than the old ones—not one lawyer knew them or could read them from beginning to end. One part or another of it will of course be taught in a compulsory, general, or special school. Nevertheless, there will still remain the task of popularizing this new, albeit transitional law.

I have used the form of a catechism and have tried to compile a [primer on the] "People's Court" in questions and answers. This book, so essential, was given to the printer almost six months ago but, unfortunately, as a result of our disastrous printing situation it has not yet appeared. I also gave to the press in the same format our Soviet Constitution, knowing how prejudiced readers are against a paragraph by paragraph summary of this or that law. These guidelines were compiled as personal editions without obligatory force. But it is very possible that this more popular form will also be used for official editions. We find something like it in English and, especially American, codification. Then we will have two codes side by side: one with formal articles and one in a popular format. Perhaps the latter will become the future form of proletarian law once it has left the shadow of the bourgeois system. To us it is obvious that *proletarian law is primarily a simplification, a popularization of our new social order*.

On the one hand we are accused of issuing too many decrees, and on the other of lacking a whole series of the most essential laws. Both accusations are at once right and wrong. We do, of course, lack some of the most essential decrees, such as instructions on crimes and punishments. However, this is only natural given the lack of lawyers supporting our platform. But premature decrees are especially dangerous in this area. We can with complete justification blame the Provisional Government of Lvov and Kerensky for having lagged behind the revolutionary process by not having promulgated even a single guiding law in the course of eight months. However, this was clearly intended for counterrevolutionary purposes in the expectation of an imminent reactionary attack. However, no one can reproach us for lagging behind the revolution.

The decrees on land, on the eight-hour working day, on the family and inheritance, on separation of the church, etc., have not all been opportune because not all of them have yet been implemented. Even this opinion is wrong. We acted correctly: establishing these landmarks, that these basic decrees have steadily been implemented and that not one had to be repeated, are indicative of their expedience. Even so clever a bourgeois lawyer as Menger writes that "the eye of the present legislator is not aimed at the past but unerringly at the future." During the revolution this was the precise distinction between the consciously organized revolutionary leadership and a spontaneous or anarchic revolt. Despite all the weaknesses and shortcomings in our apparatus, any page of our collection of decrees and in no less measure any page of our code of proletarian law demonstrates that this is the superstructure of a serious revolution of substance and not a temporary accidental outbreak. The close relation between the proletariat and its law is clearly evident in the practice of the People's Court, and it runs like a red thread through the whole proletarian revolution. The revolution is not afraid of mistakes or of temporary setbacks; while the bourgeoisie *loses* hope with every failure, the proletariat, as the rising class, grows *one experience richer* with every mistake.

3. The Marxist Concept of Law

(Observations for Jurists and Others)

I would rather write on the Marxist concept of mathematics, astronomy, or religion, than present an essay on law in a Marxist journal. Who will read an article on law, and a theoretical one at that? We are evidently more interested in our relations with the distant planets, or the gods themselves, than in social relations. We know that law is a matter for lawyers, with the exception, perhaps, of Soviet law (i.e., Soviet decrees), but even these are probably better known by the bourgeois lawyer than by ourselves or even by Soviet lawyers. And, finally, ''Why do we need laws when the judges are our friends?'' We, you see, are communists.

Indeed, if we were subjected to a hostile examination—say upon re-registration [From time to time the Party required old Party membership cards to be turned in for new ones and used this occasion to weed out unfit Party members—Eds.]—about our Marxist concept of law, then I fear that it would be revealed that we have no such concept, that such a concept cannot exist, and that we think now, as on other matters, in a purely bourgeois manner. And I will say that this is fully understandable and natural.

In the introductory lecture to the courses for people's judges in 1918, I somehow said: ''*We now need fewer lawyers, more communists.*'' At that time, of course, I had in mind old bourgeois lawyers and contrasted them to communists with their revolutionary legal consciousness. But I did not then suspect that my comparison had once been anticipated by Friedrich Engels. When I began my work on the Marxist concept of law,[1] I considered among other things the interesting editorial against ''juridical socialism'' published in the journal *Neue Zeit* in 1887. From the 25-year index to this journal I found that this article was jointly written by Friedrich Engels and Karl Kautsky. In this article, we read: ''Religion was extolled for the last time in the seventeenth century, and barely

---

''Marksistkoe ponimanie prava,'' *Kommunisticheskaia revoliutsiia*, 1922, no. 13-14 (37–38), as reprinted in *13 let bor'by*, pp. 67–80.

fifty years later the new world view made its debut in France—the world view that was to become *the classical one for of the bourgeoisie, namely the juridical world view.* . . . This was the secularization of theology. Human justice replaced divine law, or God's justice; the State assumed the role of the church'' [Engels, 1887: p. 204].

Engels contrasts the *Christian* world view with the *legal* or *bourgeois*—equating these two latter concepts. After the victory of the proletariat, with complete justification, we must contrast the proletarian or *communist* world view with the bourgeois or *legal* world view. But in order to use such a new world view for comparison, we must develop it. For it does not exist in nature. Until we have internalized this new world view, the old (*bourgeois or legal*) world view will unconsciously prevail. However, the bourgeois intelligentsia will revert to Christianity, as is always the case in a time of great crisis. But what can we say of the bourgeois intelligentsia (see Bulgakov, Berdiaev & Co.), if, even in the Social-Democratic journal *Neue Zeit* in the article of the not-unknown Il'ia Gurvich, we read:

And with respect to it (i.e., Soviet justice against the Socialist Revolutionaries), we must come to consciousness and answer to this *class law*: ''Yes, there also exist *objective norms of law*, there exists *a non-party court*, and *the word of the holy writ* forbidding preferential treatment of the rich or poor,'' has turned out to be *a stronger truth than this class theory (Klassenlehre).* [Gurvich 1922: p. 418]

Before the revolution there were demands for ''back to Kant'' in the ranks of the Social-Democratic intelligentsia, and now there are demands for ''back to the holy writ.''

But jokes aside! The question is extremely important, although it initially seems uninteresting. We speak of our deeper understanding of Marx and Marxism, and this is most necessary if we are to avoid total shallowness. The question of law (the known order of human relations) must in this case occupy primary places in the theory of historical materialism next to questions of social classes, of the class struggle, and so on. This is particularly so at the time of our retreat, which we hope is ended when we *equate our ideology* in general with the so-called ''superstructure.'' But the whole danger of our ideological retreat must confront us if we are to remember Engels' words about the prevailing ''legal or bourgeois'' world view. Here surgical means of treatment alone are powerless, for with respect to the human mind and consciousness, more than anywhere, by virtue of the old law that ''nature abhors a vacuum.'' Until the old consciousness is replaced by the new, the old remains in effect. And if I read the wails in the White press of the whole world with respect to the remarkable speech of Comrade Zinoviev at the fall conference, and I see references from there only to measures of caution against evil persons, then I understand their silence toward the most important part of this speech: the ideological struggle of the communists against the old trends. I am very happy that, not long before this, in my essay "Revolution and Law" (in *Izvestia*—June), I arrived at the same point from the field of law: "*this will be a real class struggle*" between the lawyer of the bourgeois world and the truly Soviet lawyer, the new lawyer who, regretfully, is slow in coming into being. It must not be forgotten that there are serious barricades behind which our counterrevolutionary is solidly hidden. These barricades consist not only of the 16 volumes of the old Code of Laws and of *whole cartloads of bourgeois scholarly literature . . . but they are also in the minds of each of us* "legally thinking" people. Everyone should clearly recognize which side of the barricades he is on.

Class and law

I will deal first with the question of class, to emphasize that I am not dealing so much with legal questions as with class questions; in other words, with basic questions of the Marxist world view and, ultimately, of communism. Quite recently we still floundered about the nature of class and class struggle. If we start to explain the concept of class law and the class defense of this law (i.e., of class justice), then we must have a clear view of the concept of class and class struggle. Of course, it is no accident that Karl Kautsky, in trying to explain the concept of class, emphasizes that class "forms not only a communality of source of income, but also a communality of interests deriving therefrom and a communality of antagonism against other classes, from which each strives to serve as a source of income for the other, so as to enrich its own." But if class is determined by income distribution, then the class struggle is reduced merely to a struggle for the size of the income of one class at the expense of another, i.e., for the distribution of a product, which means to the economic struggle between classes, as groups connected by this common struggle. This explanation would be accepted by any follower of Scheidemann, particularly with Kautsky's reservation that the same opposition of interests exists even between separate subdivisions of these classes.

Marx definitely stated that the basic aspect of the division of people into social classes is *the distribution of people in production* and the distribution of the means of production between these people, and that the process of production, in its turn, determines the process of distribution of products. As early as 1906 Finn-Enotaevskii responded to Kautsky and proved with Marx's own words that "classes are determined by the distribution of the elements of production" and that "classes determine their role—their mutual relations—in the process of production."[2] This means that revolutionary class struggle is nothing other *than a struggle for a role in production*, for the distribution of the means of production. But since the distribution of means of production is expressed in and protected by the law of private property, this struggle for a role in production is therefore transformed into a struggle for or against the right of private ownership of these means of production. Thus, the revolutionary class struggle consists of a struggle *around law* because of a right, in the name *of one's own class law*; it is the goal of class struggle.

If we designate the concept of law as *the known order of social relations*, i.e., the mutual relations of people in production and exchange (and even bourgeois science, personified by the sociological school, arrived at this concept), then such an order indisputably cannot be eternal and immutable, but changes with the victory of one or another class. As the result of class struggle, law can only be class law. Bourgeois science could not reach such a conclusion, because even its best representatives always end up in a blind alley from which they cannot emerge. And following the bourgeois scholars, the socialists and Marxists also get lost. Thus, we became accustomed to speak of *class justice*. But even before the 1917 revolution we contrasted class justice with independent, unprejudiced justice[3] as even now socialists throughout the world do, forgetting or simply not knowing Marx's words ''What a stupid, unreal illusion in general is the non-party court if the legislator himself belongs to a party. What is the use of an unprejudiced judicial decision if the law is prejudiced?'' They spoke also of the *class state*, but contrasted it to pure or real democracy. And in recognizing the class nature of every state, even communists who contrast bourgeois class justice with proletarian class justice are left uncertain and in doubt, and show lack of understanding as to the concept of *class law*. Can even law and justice be of a class nature?

We will not argue here with the defenders of the idea of an eternal, holy, divine, etc. law. No danger threatens communists from this direction. But I will instantiate a Marxist scholar who has played an outstanding role in works on Soviet law. Comrade Magerovskii (*Sovetskoe pravo* [Soviet Law], no. 1) wrote as follows:

> In the totality of social and especially economic relations, relations are separated which are *fixed by the collective* with the aid of social norms as *externally obligatory* relations for each of its members, relations that *society* protects from violations; this *system of externally obligatory social norms, supported and protected by society from violations, is law*, and social relations regulated and organized by law *are legal relations*. [Magerovskii 1922: p. 26]

This definition of law resembles our own. He speaks of ''legal relations,'' of a ''system'' of social relations, supported and ''*protected*.'' But where we say: ''class state,'' meaning *class*, he has placed the word ''*society*'' or in another place ''*collective*.'' This means the ''will of society'' or ''the social contract'' is the source of law. *Law is not a class institution but a social one*.

We read further: ''To the extent that we study the law of class society, for us a *social class* viewpoint is established with unconditional necessity . . . and *law itself in this society* will be a system of externally binding norms, *supported and protected against violations by the economically dominant class of this society*''

[Magerovskii 1922: p. 26]. Something here is discordant. In one definition, law is the product of the entire society and the object of protection by society as a whole; in another it is protected only by a class. This means that Comrade Magerovskii has not found a coherent definition of law: *in one case* (true, in preclass or postclass society) it is *societal law*; in another, in that which relates to us (i.e., class society)—it is simply *class law*.

But there is another difference in our understanding of the class nature of law. Where we speak of the protection of this order simply by the *dominant class*, or more accurately by its organized authority (i.e., by a class state), Comrade Magerovskii uses the expression "the class *economically* dominant in this society." I do not know what nuance Comrade Magerovskii wanted to introduce by the word "economically," but it can cause a whole series of misunderstandings. For example, examine those groups who assert that in Russia *the capitalist class is already economically dominant*. They therefore understand law not in the "Soviet sense," but in a purely capitalist, bourgeois sense. Exactly this view is held by our bourgeois jurist or, more accurately, by our *jurist in general* (for we have almost no other jurists). This means that we have finally returned to the old legal or bourgeois world view. Of course, Comrade Magerovskii is far from such generalizations, but we can see how cautious we must be with *careful reservation*. It is necessary to say directly: either class law, or non-class (i.e., bourgeois-democratic) law.

Suppose we adhere to the great insight of the sociological school of bourgeois jurists (e.g., Prof. Muromtsev), namely, that law is not merely a simple totality of norms—we will not deal here with the question whether law is for "internal" or "external" use—but is the system itself, the very order of social relations. Then for we who have recognized the theory of revolutionary class struggle, this order can only be an object or result of class struggle or, more accurately, of victory in this struggle by one class or another. It means that for us law in this society can clearly only be class law. Thanks to Einstein the variable of time is simultaneously introduced into all concepts to which it relates (in the given case *to the whole period of the social division of classes*). We can therefore set aside disputes on the distant future or distant past and unanimously proclaim *law* in our sense of the word to be a *class concept*.

And if, contrary to expectation, during our lifetimes the *final disappearance* of all classes and class differences is attained, then the purely bourgeois concept of "externally obligatory norms" falls of its own weight, i.e., that *hypocritical obligatoriness* which is so characteristic of bourgeois society, its democracy, and its law.

Thus, the concepts of "class" and "law" are inseparable, at least at the present time. We define *law* as the distribution of people in production protected by the authority of the class state, i.e., the distribution of the means of production (private property) and the role of people in production. This is the society that is called a *legal* society, a *legal* state. Class struggle is now reduced to the protection of this legal order in every possible way on the one hand, and in the striving to overthrow it, to topple this state and social order, on the other.

The nature of law

In *The Revolutionary Role of Law and the State*, I explain in detail why the bourgeoisie found no scientific definition for law or without state a class perspective. But it could not adopt the class perspective because this would have been tantamount to recognizing the proletarian revolution.[4] But I showed in the previous section that law is purely a class concept.

We define law as follows: first, "a system or *order of social relations*; second, the determinative element of this order or this system is the *interest* of the ruling class; third, therefore, this system or this order of social relations is *conducted organizationally*, i.e., is supported and safeguarded against violation by the *organization of the dominant class*, i.e., by the state" [Stuchka 1921: p. 20]. In this way we divide law: into *its content—social relations* and into the form of their regulation and support or protection which includes state authority, laws, etc. This division already exists for Marx when he writes: "(1) property; (2) its *protection* by courts, police, etc." [Marx 1858: p. 87]. In the famous preface to the *Critique* he speaks directly of "relations of production or, what is 'but a legal expression for the same thing, property relations'" [Marx 1859: p. 509]. Elsewhere he indicates that every mode of production and, therefore, every society has its particular type of "property" (method of acquisition). Therefore, also relying on the achievements of the sociological school of "legal science," we define law as a system or order of social relations (i.e., of relations of production, or exchange or, in a word, of property).

After Marx stated this in such bold relief with respect to capital—which, also contrary to bourgeois science, he defines as a social relation—it seemed to us that the concept of law as a whole system, a whole order of social relations, remained undisputed among Marxists. But it must be recognized that this concept has encountered more serious obstacles than in political economy. Not without reason is legal science the last refuge for all idealist and ideological prejudices. Here, under various disguises, the *will* theory of law prevails. But prejudice remains prejudice even if it is colored red or provided with the protective label "Soviet."

While we *identify its content as the basis of law*—"the system of social relations"—a contrasting basis of the concept of law is presented to us, namely, *the form of law; the system or totality of norms*, or, more accurately, of social (also societal) norms, i.e., phenomena of will, not of society or people, not of class. In other words, we obtain the same thing bourgeois jurists have in mind when they speak of *law in the objective sense*, namely the totality of laws. Moreover, for the bourgeoisie, law in the *subjective sense* is represented by the relations regulated by this objective law. There is a definite boundary between us and the bourgeois world view, the world view of a society of commodity producers. We term social relations the *objective content* of law; the bourgeois jurist terms them the form of law, *an expression of will* or simply *will* (statute law, etc.). We call this *form*, this will, the *subjective element* of law, while the bourgeoisie, on the contrary, term the *content* of law (social relations) "*subjective.*" Bourgeois jurists declare the form or subjective element to be daily life, and the content or objective element to be the superstructure. Law is not exceptional here. This is why if we wish to remain Marxists, we must break decisively with the will theory of bourgeois science. In no way can this be transformed into a Marxist tool. However, in bourgeois legal science the theory of interest is a direct precursor of the Marxist concept of law; it is worth inserting the class perspective into this theory. However, as I already said, the sociological school of jurisprudence disintegrated as a science on the premise that this is impossible for bourgeois science.

In practical life it is difficult to accustom oneself to this concept, but in practical life economic categories such as capital, money, commodities, etc., are difficult to master as social relations. I will therefore try to explain our concept with two examples.

Depending upon the prevailing mode of production, ownership of the means of production (e.g., land) is quite varied: tribal, primitive-communist, semi-communist, private family, private feudal, private-capitalist, state-capitalist and, finally, socialist. Each form of ownership (distribution) of the means of production *has a corresponding relation of labor, acquisition, and distribution* (or exchange) *of the product, etc.* Each of these relations separately we term a societal (social) relation, but of itself it is not law. It is law only when it is made authoritative in connection with a whole system of all other societal relations. For instance, in the feudal period relations arose which we now call capitalist, but at first merely as an exception. Such social facts grew quantitatively until the quantity leaped into quality and the social fact turned into law, i.e., into a new system, a new order of relations.[5] This growth, this systematization, this ordering (or regularizing) might have been in fact an initiative from above, on the part of a new class that is victorious or is on the way to victory. However, it usually occurred from below, in a factual manner. The new class might in fact be transformed into the economically dominant class: capitalist institutions gradually, in fragments, penetrated the old "Code of Laws" in the form of new legislation of the old authority. A revolution came, the capitalist class won, destroyed the old system, the old forms, such as law and the state, etc. New legal forms arose, or old forms received an entirely new content. A new legal atmosphere was created in which all relations adopted the nature of the ruling system, crystallized in a capitalist manner. After its victory the proletariat transformed capitalist private property into state property, but for the use of the state of the proletariat, i.e., of its class, by way of nationalization. Only after nationalization does there follow socialization, i.e., transformation of this ownership for the use of the already classless society, of all mankind. With the advent of communism all law will finally wither away, including the most basic law of property.

How is all this expressed in law (i.e., in formal law) or in the legal form? Initially, this expression is in the form of factual defense by state authority of a given factual possession. Thereafter, it is expressed in the form of a law on reinstatement of violated possession; later, a law on length of possession; finally, on a formal legal act *(iustus titulus)*. Property is formulated as the full right of use, possession, and disposition of a thing (e.g., land). But what is private property in reality? It is the receipt, in one form or another, of the product of one's own or another's labor. Slave or serf labor, labor rent, in-kind rent, or monetary capitalist rent—all these are means of acquiring part of the product of another's labor by virtue of private ownership of land. But is all this fully described in law? While recollections of the former "communal law" were still alive, law was usually casuistic, i.e., by the individual case. More often, the new private right of ownership was supported by judicial decision. When private ownership became a matter of course, it stands to reason, on the contrary, that it was limited by the prohibition of outmoded types of exploitation such as slavery, serf labor, corvée, etc. The old land rent was abolished when nationalization of land was declared. But law never presents the whole system of legal relations in full. The articles of the statute are dead, "do not speak" on the one hand, and on the other hand, the law is broader than the statute. In other words, not every "economic relation has its legal jacket" and not every "jacket" has its "economic relation."

Another example is relations of purchase and sale. This method of exchanging one product (commodity) for another product (including also money) typifies a society of commodity producers. Gradually, purchase and sale is transformed into a special profession of a whole class of people—merchants—and becomes the sole method of the transfer of the product to the user, the monopoly of this class. Exchange (i.e., purchase and sale) becomes the basic relation and overshadows even property relations. But as Marx demonstrated, "in production, personality is objectified (made into an object); in use, an object is subjectified." Exchange is merely a method of individual distribution. It is obvious, therefore, why for the bourgeois jurist—as the ideologue of this society of commodity producers—the subjective aspect of relations (Marx calls this "formal-social movement") seems, on the contrary, to be objective, while the content of these relations is merely a subjective element.

If these considerations in favor of our definition of law seem purely formal, then the second part of our definition is decisive. *Class interest* defines the system or order of these relations. Class interest, as the material content of law, is contrasted to the old will theory of law. If will is the real creator of law then, of course, the essence of our definition is lost. Law, at first glance, may nevertheless continue to remain class law. But we are told, "will is the starting point of class struggle" and "will is the moving element[6] . . . the force of every societal process including production relations" [Veger 1922: p. 136]. This means that law is made by will. But whose will? Not of course of God, not of the monarch, and likewise not of the people ("*Volkswille*"). In class society this is the will of the ruling class. We agree on this. But what does the class will mean? Evidently, it is the manifestation (regardless at this point how) of *class consciousness*, or the manifestation by a class of consciousness of its interest, and as law in any event protects the interest of the ruling class (on this, it seems, there is no argument), then consciousness is determined by interest, and not interest (i.e., being) by law. Such is the logical conclusion.

Here lies the root of our disagreement. No Marxist denies the significance of the recognition of will, but he states that consciousness is determined by being, and that will is not free. Of course consciousness in turn influences being, incentive, and the economy, etc., but we assign the decisive role in the final analysis to being, to interest, to economics, etc. If this is effective with respect to separate persons, to individuals, then in much greater measure with respect to a whole class, society, or mankind. The words "collective will,"[7] "organized human will," etc. are no clearer in meaning than the long-discarded phrase "will of the people" and other such fictions.

In our definition we state that the system, the order of social relations that characterizes the so-called legal order, is supported and protected by the organized force of the ruling class, i.e., by the state. This support and protection on the part of the state takes very different forms: *planned*, organized forms of influence, such as laws; *one-time* forms of influence (police, administration in general); *indirect* forms of influence (tax systems) or *direct intervention* in economic life (as for instance, at the time of the implanting of capitalism), etc; finally, *ideological* forms of influence (persuasion with the aid of the school, church, the press, etc.). This influence on the "structure of social relations" may be very energetic and successful; to this "revolutionary role of law" I dedicated my entire book and also named one chapter for the "Law-Revolution" of one class, contrasting it to the "Law-Counterrevolution" of another class. But, for us the decisive role is played by an objective element—interest.[8] This determines the will of the individual and, to a still larger degree, class consciousness. In the totality of norms (both laws and customs, judicial practice, etc.) we see only one form of law—its subjective element—and to break finally with all survivals of idealism we propose breaking once and for all with the will theory of law.

The will theory had a real meaning when evidence was given either to the will of a higher being or to the creative power of some absolute idea. But when law was equated with statutes, the words "statute" and "law" lost all real content. We once had a legal journal *Pravo* [Law] that exhorted jurists under the banner of legality: in the name of the law of the Tsarist regime. It survived the February revolution but did not change the inscription on its banner. The law, this time, was the law of the first revolution; now there appeared in Moscow the professors' journal *Law and Life* which promised to fulfill the "obligation resting upon *Russian legal thought*" (?!), and continued: law is the banner under which it calls to Russian jurists. Assume here that the journal means the law of the Workers' and Peasants' Republic. What is included in the concept of the word law here? The real content of the law, in each of these three periods, connected with the specific relation of classes, is entirely different. Law is the will of the state authority of the moment, nothing more. By itself the word "law" is as lacking in content as the other fancy expression: "Russian legal thought." It would not be a bad idea if the students of these scientific luminaries asked their teachers to explain the profound meaning of this empty phrase. "Everyone goes in danger": this was the first law of Shchedrin's town governor. "Russian legal thought," having taken over the empty slogan "law," writes on its banner: within the limits of the law or "with respect" to the law, without regard to which, "it is dangerous to go." This is what, in the opinion of many professors, also is their (i.e., the bourgeoisie's) *subjective law* within the limits of *"objective law,"* i.e. the totality of laws (in the present case the laws of the Workers' and Peasants' State authority).

Is there a Marxist among us who understands the will theory of law as a kind of aggregate of the "letter" of the law? Of course not.

But the will theory is still connected with the "goal" theory (teleology). The goal of law, according to this theory, is merely [one?] part of the goals of the world and mankind. The goal set by a higher being, or determined fatalistically, is an absolute goal. Almost in the same category, for instance, is the final goal of Stammler. His elegant, empty words have had much success among us. His "unconditional final goal of human society—is the ideal unity, imaginable in general for all the goals of human joint activity." "This will be a society of people with freedom of will" (*"frei wollender Menschen"*). But Stammler was true to the precepts of his old friend Bentham; he at once explains that this goal is the idea of human society in which each, striving to achieve his own goal by this same act, also fulfills the goals of another. In other words, the goals of another are turned into his own, and vice-versa. It is true that as Social Democrats we contrasted the *final goal* to short-term goals, but by this we intended Marx's concept that *only then will the history of human society begin.*

Nevertheless, we do recognize goals. In promulgating statutes, we strive toward the achievement of these goals. This is why it is said that our class will—the totality of our decrees—is our class law. However, this argument can lead to an opposite conclusion. The totality of our decrees least of all embraced or now embraces the whole area of legal relations: it is not for nothing that we have introduced the concept of revolutionary legal consciousness. When we threatened black marketeers with our most severe punishment, they were conducting orgies of their speculative exchange relations at Sukharevka and in all the economic administrative departments. And when we now legalize part of these orgies, this hardly corresponds with the free will of the proletarian class. No, the will of statute law is not the sole creator of law, and this will is helpless *against* the economic "laws of nature." Shchedrin's Pompadour meticulously issued edicts to stop the flow of river water. Insofar as we issued our own decrees, guided by the laws of economic development, we pushed all history forward. But why then speak of will as the decisive element when it was only *the expression of the true recognition of class interest*?

We cannot be accused of scorn toward laws in general. On the contrary, we have sometimes believed too strongly in our decrees. And our critics from the journal *Law and Life*, for example, vainly try to seem to be accusing us of having no faith in law in general, rather than to be accusing us of having overturned their laws.[9]

We will be on the true path if we master our scientific definition of law, recognizing law as a system or order of social relations or, in other words, *a system of the organized defense of class interest*, and relegating statutory law, which performs the function of regulating this system, to an extremely important, but nevertheless formal significance. After this we must conceive law anew in our minds, and so revise it in the curricula of our schools, courses, etc.

Economics and law

We have seen that there are communists who distinguish between a class ruling *economically*, and a class ruling *legally*, or *politically*, or simply ruling. This problem is more important in speeches and writings of the counterrevolution and especially of the so-called loyal opposition. The basic position of economic materialism on base/superstructure relations has been drummed into the ears of these literati by both the Second and Second and a Half Internationals and the purely bourgeois and trite phrase, compared with which even the Stammlerite doctrine on law—form and function—could be called profound or deeply conceived. For a long time now we have been "hit over the head" with quotations from Marx. This began when Kautsky, and then all the bourgeoisie, argued that the October Revolution could not be recognized as a proper revolution; apparently it contradicted Marx because the economic base was not developed enough in Russia for such a superstructure. After we had to retreat, in the economy, to the New Economic Policy, the Mensheviks and all those around them (both the *Socialist Revolutionaries and the Constitutional Democrats immediately became convinced "economic materialists"*!) affirmed: "Communist dictatorship under the New Economic Policy, i.e., simply speaking, with the strengthening of the bourgeois-capitalist order, is such a historical absurdity, such an embodiment of meaninglessness, that it is equally . . . insupportable, for the new bourgeoisie of all sizes, for the proletariat, and for true communists."

Of course we could limit ourselves to the simple conclusion: "When at war, be at war. There is no time to argue with you now; for the winner *to surrender to the defeated*, in any event, is a *still greater absurdity than to win*. But we will deal with the theory when we are finally convinced who will hang whom." Such an answer would free us from theory but it would also lower our class consciousness, based on the correct (i.e., revolutionary) concept of Marx's theory.

We answer them, but it is necessary to recognize that we answer sometimes rather thoughtlessly and our concept of Marxism often seems rather primitive, particularly when we use the comparison of the base and the superstructure. Following Stammler, serious people often say that "every economic relation has its legal covering." (One would like to be even more colloquial and clear, correcting this to: pillow-case [This is a play on the Russian words for "covering" (*obolochka*) and "pillow-case" (*navolochka*)—Eds.].) In his speech at the conference, Comrade Zinoviev, sharply argued with the *Changing Boundary Markers* group and to pacify the Mensheviks. [*Changing Boundary Markers* was the name of an anthology published in Prague in 1921 by émigrés who advocated renewed cooperation with the Soviet regime on the ground that NEP made it capitalist.—Eds.] He stated that "Marxists must realize that economics and politics never, with a wave of a magic wand, proceed in unison; that the transformation of political forms *is always somewhat behind the development of economic phenomena.*" He landed "right in the face" of some of our comrades as well who placed all their hopes on a certain *slowing* of the destruction or *reconstruction* of what they considered to be foundationless, baseless superstructure, taking hope that the newly acquired base—the Western European revolution—would arrive in time. (I even found somewhere an outside limit of 10 years.) Consequently, it is highly relevant again to return to the old question of economics and law.

This is necessary both for theoretical considerations and for purely practical purposes. Even in Marxist publications we encounter the idea that we are returning somewhere, and in the opinion of some have never gone anywhere. If the terminology of jurists (and particularly of Marxist jurists) were not often incomprehensible for the ordinary mortal, such an idea would strike one much more boldly. The Council of Peoples' Commissars is merely a cabinet of ministers, the All-Russian Central Executive Committee an ordinary Parliament but with unusual electoral rights, etc. And when I accidentally saw in a window all 50 volumes of the cassational decisions of the Ruling Senate, I very clearly recalled Heine's words: "What is the point of this? The earth is round (*Die Erde ist rund*) and therefore we will return to the beginning." Here we must nevertheless give a theoretical answer, not confining ourselves to a statement in the incomprehensible expressions of old bourgeois reflections.

I have dealt with the question of Marx's concept of base and superstructure in another place,[10] in the following issue of the journal of the Institute of Soviet Law, where I try to show that this reference has simply been incorrectly interpreted: by base Marx understood *law*, as a relation of *production*, for at the same place he terms a "relation of property" merely a *juridical* expression for a "relation of production." For Marx, the superstructure is a *"form of consciousness"* of relations such as *law*. This means that the base is social reality, and the superstructure is consciousness! We have merely returned to the basic problem of dialectical materialism, and all the Stammlerite explanations are a simple tautology.[11]

Marx explains in *Capital*:

> [I]f the laborer wants all his time to produce the necessary means of subsistence for himself and his race, he has no time left in which to work gratis for others. Without a certain degree of productiveness in his labor, he has no such superfluous time at his disposal; without such superfluous time, no surplus labor, and therefore no capitalists, no slave-owners, no feudal lords, in one word, no class of large proprietors. [Marx 1867, 1:511]

This refers to a society still without classes. But when "the productive forces have also increased with the all-around development of the individual, and all the springs of cooperative wealth flow more abundantly—only then can the narrow horizon of bourgeois right be crossed in its entirety and society inscribe on its banners: From each according to his abilities, to each according to his needs!" [Marx 1875: p. 19]. This will again be a classless society. Between these two periods lies an endless class struggle. The class struggle is determined by the development of productive forces and the development of class consciousness. If the victorious proletariat did not have the strength to support or raise labor productivity, then its state authority alone would turn out to be superstructure without foundation, without basis. But, on the other hand, without this victory of the proletariat, the productivity of labor would be directed not at the satisfaction of "to each according to his needs," but to the means of mutual annihilation. Objectively, productivity is already sufficient in a number of capitalist countries to satisfy "to each according to his needs."

Economics thus determines the class structure of society, the interest of each class, its role in production, and its class consciousness, i.e., its consciousness of its class interest. All else depends *upon the outcome of the class struggle*. A victorious class maintains and protects its class interest, *its law*. The victorious proletariat is no exception to this rule. Having won, it strives not only to preserve its authority but also to act reciprocally by means of this authority upon the economy, and with all its efforts to raise labor productivity and simultaneously, the productive force of the country. The outcome of this struggle depends upon its successes. Every other mechanistic interpretation of revolutionary Marxism, and the interrelation of economics and law, must be discarded as an unscientific and counterrevolutionary conclusion.

Class consciousness and revolutionary legality

It happens that at historical moments a phrase is spoken and is very accurate and apt, but time passes, the moment is forgotten, and the phrase becomes an empty sound or is disproportionately exalted. The latter occurred with the phrase "revolutionary or socialist legal consciousness." After the October Revolution, when we were compelled (literally compelled) to discard the old court and, in principle, to declare all old laws abolished inasmuch as they were not confirmed by our decrees, we did not become anarchists. Instead, we expressed ourselves very carefully, and included even the minimum programs of the parties victorious in the revolution among a number of sources of law. But what could fill the vacuum left by law? We went the way of initial emergence of all law, granting this role to the *class court*. In antiquity it was the Roman praetor, then the feudal judge, and today the English class court that rejects precedents, i.e., makes new law. And we gave to our own proletarian-peasant court the inspirational phrase: *revolutionary legal consciousness*.

We did not yet say: class consciousness. *We did not have this concept then.* The phrase "legal consciousness" was itself brought in by bourgeois scholarship (by Petrazhitskii's psychological school) and in fact, and only later in theory did it assume a class character. The revolutionary way of the People's Court was the path of revolutionary force along which, however, every proletarian revolution will have to go. At the beginning, in a burst of enthusiasm, we did not notice the shortcomings. But when this situation became most difficult it became the object of exaggerated praise! The phrases about "creative genius," and "the depths of the proletarian soul," etc. threatened to turn this very important concept into an empty sound.

What do we now understand by the phrase "class legal consciousness"? If for us class consciousness is consciousness on the part of a class of its interest, then the *legal consciousness* of a class can be termed *the class consciousness of the victorious class*. But if even class consciousness is acquired by a class only slowly, then legal consciousness, as law itself, is always infused with diverse traditions and old prejudices, as we have already seen above. And since the legal world view is the bourgeois world view in general, then there is no reason to be surprised at the fact that instead of a *systematic* means of extending the new order, the People's Court made only more or less successful individual decisions and then only due to the revolutionary atmosphere. But the court lacked the ability to conduct an organized retreat to determined and limited boundaries. If before this, coherent laws were extremely *desirable* for the revolution, *in retreat* they became positively *necessary*.

But this does not mean that with the appearance of the various necessary codes, class consciousness became an excessive item of luxury! On the contrary! These codes were edited by a lawyer who saw only a return to the old. Here there are only two aspects: the foreign professor considers that "something *will continue* to exist *from our* law" (Nol'de); our professor recognizes "the revolution that has been lived through . . . *never* and under no circumstances *will return* us *entirely to the beginning, etc.*" (Prof. N. Totskii). But they, and after them Soviet jurists, "reversed themselves." Is not a danger created that in practice *all kinds of problems*, all kinds of "unclear and incomplete points" and generally the "exact meanings" of the new laws, will be supplemented for certain by the old charred remnants of the 16 volumes of the Code of Laws of the Russian Empire and the 45 volumes of the cassational decisions of the Imperial Senate?

Such a practice in class consciousness must be limited. The laws of the NEP period are a *retreat* but not a *return* to the old. And all gaps, unclear points, and exact meanings must be explained *from the perspective of the revolution* rather than *the counterrevolution*. The People's Court, the class jurist, must firmly remember that the laws of the Workers' and Peasants' Government, and the workers' parliament (the All-Russian Central Executive Committee), are obligatory for them. They are not merely *externally obligatory*, but are obligatory as the reflection of the consciousness of the present stage, in the form of part of the class interest, namely concessions in the interests of *further victories* of the class, and no more.

Elsewhere I said that only in this way can legality be turned into revolution. On the one hand, this legality will be conscious, for it is based on revolutionary legal consciousness, as the consciousness of class interests—this is its internal characteristic. On the other hand, the word "revolutionary" indicates our forward direction, while professors' legality ("legal thought") is counterrevolutionary because its position is directed (regardless of whether openly or secretly) backward. Even without knowing its destination, still backward!

It was slander to state that we were allegedly against any "legality." In conducting such a well-organized revolution we demonstrated our adherence to an *organized method* of regulating our social relations. But "when in a revolution, act as in a revolution." To reduce chaos by statutory law, even revolutionary law, is not a task for one day. And the laws of the revolutionary period are extremely unstable, particularly if a class without a defined class ideology is victorious in the revolution.

In my work on law I showed that centuries before the great French Revolution, the legal consciousness of the emerging bourgeois class was gradually developed under the term "natural law" until it became positive law (the Declaration of Rights, and later the Civil Code). Nothing like this happened with the proletariat. In the legal sphere (and not only in the legal sphere) they were ruled by bourgeois ideology. Only the *revolution itself* destroys these bourgeois foundations, is destroying them slowly, but basically only where the proletariat has been victorious. In the rest of the world the proletariat must carry out the same struggle independently. *Law is the last refuge of bourgeois ideology!* In this area it is therefore easier for a conscious proletarian to tear himself away from the claws of the bourgeoisie than for a communist with a legal background. Here lies the assurance of revolutionary success. Here, proletarian "social reality" also determines legal "consciousness."

Notes

1. P. Stuchka. *Revoliutsionaia rol' prava i gosudarstva; Pervaia chast: Obshchee uchenie o prave* [The Revolutionary Role of Law and the State. Part One: General Theory

of Law] (Moscow: Gosizdat, 1921).

2. See Lenin's definition of class in "Veliki pochin" [A Great Beginning] [Lenin, 1919: p. 421].

3. The new program of the United Social-Democrats in Germany loudly proclaims a "court from all strata of the population" as socialist.

4. An exception is scholars of a feudal bent: they label bourgeois capitalist law as class law, but in the name of a return to their "classless" law—feudal law.

5. For example, gradually the initial taking of land or occupying it, the defense of this de facto occupation from violations, and long or ancient occupation turns into ownership. In German this terminology is even clearer: *besetzen, Besitz, ersitzen,* i.e., obtaining it by simple [mere] occupation of the land: occupied, continuously occupied, and permanent occupation.

6. This quotation is from Comrade Veger's review in *Sovetskoe pravo* [Soviet Law], no. 1 [Veger 1922]. In place of the elipses in the text there is the word "transmitting." This is obviously a slip of the pen, for the moving force is not transmitting, and transmitting is not moving.

7. I do not refer here to the conscious classless society of the future where this fiction may become reality: this will be the "kingdom of freedom."

8. Even the bourgeois scholar Jhering states: "Logic is subordinated to interest."

9. For example, read Professor Nol'de's words in the foreign edition: "legal chaos reigning in Russia makes it impossible to identify exactly what of our law has disappeared and what will continue to exist." NEP, according to this, is not a retreat but a continuation of existence.

10. [In "Notes on a Class Theory of Law."]

11. Here is excluded a paragraph, the thoughts of which are stated more fully in other places. [Note from *13 let bor'by*—Eds.]

4. Notes on the Class Theory of Law

Our Task

The Section of the General Theory of Law is today opened in the Institute of Soviet Law. What should be its basic task? Until now the general, and indeed every theory of law, usually functioned to render legal questions inaccessible for the masses interested in them. It was either the domain of an "estate" (if not a caste) of lawyer-jurisprudents or the work of professional philosophers. But whether this was concrete law in the hands of the estate of lawyers, or abstractions of legal philosophy, both in content and in form it was equally inaccessible even for the members of the lawyers' class.

When actual law now embraces the broadest masses and relates to ordinary relations of people, law in theory and in general has remained incomprehensible in published analysis and incomprehensible to all. It has reached the point where people who have seriously approached legal questions have openly expressed doubt whether it is even appropriate to speak of the theory of law; in effect, can there be general discussion of law as a subject of science? Legal theorists sometimes described actual law as a phantom, an illusion, and devoted themselves to the cult of their internal, intuitive law which was not obligatory for anyone else.

The October Revolution tried to put law "on its feet" in life, first driving the caste of "priests of holy truth and justice" from the temple of justice and then allowing the "boor" himself to judge his own legal affairs. This was a simple supplement to the substantive revolution, the revolution of authority relations. Having destroyed all estates at root, having deprived the privileged within them of their ranks, titles and their economic basis (nationalization of every type), the revolution could not then ignore the privileged estate of lawyer-jurisprudents. It seemed enough to "burn" (figuratively, of course) all 16 volumes of the Imperial

---

"Zametki o klassovoi teorii prava," *Sovetskoe pravo*, 1922, no. 3, pp. 3-18.

Code of Laws of the Russian Empire and the 40 volumes of cassational decisions of the Imperial Ruling Senate, to destroy this age-old hold over the ignorance of mankind on the questions closest to it.

The separation of the state from the church (of course a specific church—the religion of feudal or bourgeois society), in the person of the clergy, still does not mean the eradication of religiosity itself. So too, the separation of state and law (bourgeois law, of course), in the person of the estate of jurists, far from signified victory over the legal world view. Not without reason did Engels identify the legal world view with the bourgeois world view in general. And just as the bourgeoisie only prevailed with its new, legal world view, and forced out the feudal-religious world view, so also the proletariat will finally prevail only by introducing its new proletarian or communist world view into mass consciousness. In fact, any edition or work on Soviet law usually instills utter disillusionment in us. The cover is Soviet; but inside, so to speak, the pages reveal the old, the bourgeois. I will not talk about the authors, other than to say: "do not worry, gentlemen, although the color is 'Bolshevik,' the goods are still from the old stocks, a French brand"; or about the conciliatory public, other than that never under any conditions would we return to the "beginning," that the overthrow had been made irrevocably," that therefore they stand on a Soviet base but peddling the same old goods, even without a Soviet coloration. I refer to the completely honest "Soviet jurists" who have in fact remained jurists. They are not personally guilty, since the concept has remained unexplained until now, so I will not talk of Soviet law, but of law in general. Until now Kant's words retained their significance: "jurists still argue about the concept of law." But so long as they *merely argued* over the concept of God, belief in him was not destroyed; and so long as they are only arguing about the concept of *law*, then the legal, bourgeois viewpoint will prevail.

This is why it is time for us to think about the theory of our own Soviet law, or rather about our own theory of law in general. After what has been said, this is not simply idle or unnecessary talk. Another danger is that law might remain a term not accessible or understandable by anyone. Our first task is to return legal questions (which are soaring in the clouds) to earth. If, and to the extent that, law in general relates to the most real relations of people and, moreover, of all people without exception, it must be understandable to all. And I say openly, that behind our incomprehensible, abstract tirades, besides old and bad habits, conceptual unclarity is often hidden—a lack of understanding of the question, a poverty of thought. In the new section we must emphasize the question of a theory of law understandable for all, of the lowering of the holy, divine concept of law to earth, of its transformation into a purely proletarian concept.

Our first task in the age of intensified class struggle must be the merciless criticism of all old concepts. This is unavoidable, for no easy task confronts us: to show first of all that it indeed is old, has outlived its time, and is headed for destruction. You cannot erect a new building where unsuitable ruins are located—until you turn the old into a pile of trash and have picked it up—so you too will build a new legal theory in vain if you have not destroyed the old; such a new theory either will be parallel, and so superfluous, or will be reduced to a new front for the old decrepit building.

This criticism cannot be limited to old works. We must not ignore any works with the label Soviet, or even those of our closest comrades. Constructive and sharp polemicism is, of course, the best and most lively method of explicating differences of expression and clarifying thought. I was not merely turning a phrase when I wrote in June in *Izvestia*:

> There will be a real class struggle between the jurist of the bourgeois world and the truly Soviet jurist. The latter is a new jurist, and regrettably only emerges slowly. Our counterrevolutionary jurist, it must not be forgotten, has significant barricades behind which he is firmly hidden. These barricades consist of the 16 volumes of the Old Code of Laws, whole cartloads of bourgeois scholarly literature . . . and of the brains of all legally minded people. We should all clarify which side of these barricades we are on.

The task of our section, incidentally, is to prepare young theorists of Soviet law. We must give youth the full opportunity to set out on a new road free from those old prejudices with which we must still struggle at the level of consciousness. This does not mean a refusal of all that is good and useful, all that the old world bequeathed to us. Bourgeois political economy gave (and gives) much of value to Marxism; so too, of course, in incomparably smaller amounts, we receive something from the old legal world. It is not easy to find one's way in these piles of materials.

We do not reject cooperation with old legal scholars; on the contrary, every serious scientific work will be most valuable for us. If our class struggle is lengthy then I am convinced that we will also teach our opponents to speak in our language, i.e., class language. Let them openly conspire in the language of their class, but let them discard today's false, pacifying language that has become unscientific. Until this occurs we must uncover both the strong and the weak features of bourgeois law. There is no reason to be silent; victory is possible only against an open, and not against a hidden, enemy. But in order to reveal the falsehood and duplicity of all law in bourgeois society (a society based upon general wage slavery), we must contrast it with our own open class law of the transitional period. This is not an eternal but a changeable, transitional category.

But if we contrast the communist with the legal or bourgeois world view, then do we not excessively broaden the limits of the general theory of law? Recall the disputes of our bourgeois legal science about the limits of the general theory of law. This encyclopedia of law (as the heir of the philosophy of law) in Russia was at its time something almost revolutionary but inadvertently indulgent. The communist world view, of course, is not limited to bringing clarity just to legal questions other than the general theory of law (nor was the bourgeois legal world view so limited in its time, cf. the encyclopedists) and still more important, there is the theory of historical materialism, or as Comrade *Bukharin* calls it, Marxist sociology. Questions of law constitute only part of this sociology, albeit a most essential part inseparably connected with the basic concepts of historical materialism. Until historical materialism has clarified all of the basic questions of its theory, the general theory of law must therefore devote much time to the fundamental general questions of historical materialism.

The practical goal of the general theory of law is to provide definite criteria, a certain standard, and some direction to the specialized branches of Soviet law, and to find quantitative and qualitative distinguishing characteristics of the Soviet nature of these branches of law. We must mercilessly castigate Soviet jurists who try to develop theories about the convergence of our law with bourgeois law: "Well, Bolsheviks in general are not such dangerous people; they say the same as other, 'regular' jurists, only in different words, such as: Council of People's Commissars instead of Cabinet of Ministers, All-Russian Central Executive Committee instead of parliament, Regional Committee Chairman instead of Governor, right to use instead of ownership, etc.'' But we are also going too far in another direction. For instance, I have read (citing from memory) that our civil law allegedly introduces much that is new: "Soviet," allowing judges to annul contracts contrary to the laws, usurious, etc. Such boasting is dangerous, because as any lawyer will respond: "These are all old, valuable principles of bourgeois law (particularly of the Ruling Senate practice!).'' He will be correct. Comrade Goikhbarg went significantly deeper into the question when he noted certain peculiarities of our NEP civil law, for example its relation to former confiscations and nationalizations, etc. (also citing from memory). However, it was first necessary to say simply that we *actually used the old principles or bourgeois law* because we left the court in the hands of the working class. However, these principles were generally only false declarations for the bourgeoisie.

I am very sorry that I have to say such elementary things in a serious speech. But I am not breaking down an open door if I show that the general theory of law must be of interest to every conscious communist and not merely the jurist. This truth must still be often repeated. We must deal with very, very old questions. On the essence of this general theory of law, our first attempts in this respect will not even be much better than the first words pronounced so long ago on natural law. But from these first words was born the revolutionary *Declaration of the Rights of Man and the Citizen* and the grandiose edifice of the bourgeois world view.

Class or social (democratic) law

Of all the phenomena of social reality, law has until now very likely remained the least open to criticism from the class perspective—even less so than the church, the state, the court, etc.

Initially there was the fact that the socialists declared the state to be a class state, but they contrasted the classless and all-class democracy with the concrete class state of the bourgeoisie. They also struggled against bourgeois class justice, but contrasted it with the independent democratic court. None of them mentioned the class nature of law; among them prevailed a bourgeois or, more accurately, chaotic understanding of law. The October Revolution, in words and in fact, transformed this problem into the replacement of the bourgeois class state (i.e., bourgeois or pure democracy) with the proletarian dictatorship of the Soviet republic. Somewhat later it also transformed the problem of justice, contrasting proletarian class justice with the class "independent" court of the bourgeoisie. This contrast was most evident in the historic trial of the Socialist Revolutionaries, where this perspective, officially proclaimed from the dias, met no opposition or objections from the communists.

But the problem of the class nature of law was put only timidly after the October Revolution, by individual comrades, and no earlier than 1918. It received its official formulation in the Collegium of the People's Commissariat of Justice only in 1919. But even after that the problem was quietly bypassed or silently avoided. Particularly now, when we are partly returning to apparently abolished institutions, and when it is as if a position is being created where to speak of proletarian class law would be like speaking of a rope in the house of someone who had been hanged. We still meet direct objections to the theory of the class nature of law.

But this is not all. In those instances when the little word "class" has been added to a given concept, some undefined, unrevolutionary sense has been injected into it. When I wrote my general theory of law in 1921, I did not find a ready revolutionary definition of the concepts "class" and "class struggle" in our Marxist literature. I had to gather the material necessary for this myself, dedicating a small chapter to the necessary clarification of these concepts. Now we have, with respect to class, in addition to the observations of Finn-Enotaevskii, in his *Education* (1906), Comrade *Bukharin*'s valuable book on the theory of historical materialism, where he repeatedly deals with this concept. Previously we avoided Kautsky's explanation that "individual classes form not only a communality of sources of income, but also a communality of interests deriving therefrom and a communality of their opposition to other classes, of which each strives to serve as a source for the income of another, in order to enrich the source of its own income." This means that the basis of class struggle, according to Kautsky, consists of the struggle for the distribution of the product, i.e., it goes no further than reformism, bourgeois democracy. Now we contrast to this definition, in Marx's own words, the definition of class, as a category of persons "joined by a general role in the process of production" in dependence upon the distribution of the elements of the means of production; for the distribution of the means of production also determines the distribution of the product. I already added that the role in production and distribution of the means of production was supported in property relations and in bourgeois society in the law of private property. Class struggle continues today around this private property, i.e., its abolition; I drew the following conclusion. From Marx's revolutionary teaching about class struggle I concluded:

> The class of exploiters can never strive for the elimination or destruction of the class exploited by them. In those cases when it renounces this principle it perishes itself along with the exploited class. From this derives the adaptable and conciliatory nature of the class of oppressors, which sometimes makes concessions it does not itself understand to the class of the exploited. This development inevitably leads to the dictatorship of the proletariat, but the proletariat, as an oppressed class, *cannot fail to hope for* the destruction of the class of its oppressors. [Stuchka 1921: p. 29]

Understanding class struggle in this sense, as a struggle for a role in production and as a struggle for the very right of private ownership of the means of production, or for its elimination, we simultaneously have adopted the *viewpoint of the class nature* of law.

I will mention but one objection to this concept, namely, that of Comrade Magerovskii. His definition of law casually mentioned:

> In the totality of social relations and especially economic relations, those relations are separated which are *fixed by the collective with the aid of social norms, as externally binding relations for each* of its members, which society protects from violations; this *system of externally binding social norms supported and protected by society from violations is law.* [Magerovskii 1922: p. 26]

while "social relations regulated and organized by law are legal relations" (*ibid.*). Further, there are arguments about the problem of the conditions on which "depend the proclamation by society of particular relations among its members as *externally binding,* etc."

We will not deal today with the question of whether law existed before *class* society or whether there will be law *after* it. The concept of *society* is introduced here into the very definition of law as the regulator and protector of law. Does this mean that in a society that is "divided into social classes," where the ruling class also constitutes the "collective," where this ruling class protects and supports its own social norms, there is no law?

Comrade Magerovskii objects to this: "*To the extent that* we study the law of class society, for us (by whom?) with unconditional necessity the social-class viewpoint or the social-class methodological principle of the study (and only that) of law, and *law itself* in this society will be a system of externally binding *social norms*, supported and protected against violations by the *economically dominant class of this society*" [Magerovskii, 1922: p. 26].

What is this? The second definition *categorically contradicts the first*. If law is the totality of norms dictated by the *entire* society, supported and protected by the *entire society*, then these norms are clearly promulgated and protected only in *part*, perhaps by an insignificant part of this society, then *there is no law*. Here the logic is inescapable: 2 x 2 = 4 (part is not equal to the whole).

Or perhaps *several systems of law* coexist in the same society? Petrazhitskii suggests that with positive law there is intuitive law. Comrade Magerovskii has added limiting words: "the economically dominant class." When we speak of the dominant class, we have in mind the dominant political class, i.e., the class holding state authority. Or perhaps it was thought that under Tsarism one class ruled economically, and this means that it dictated and protected law, while another or no one class held political power. The question becomes still more timely if you talk to "NEP-men" who are now saying that the *capitalist class* rules in Russia. Are *their* "social norms" considered law here? No, they themselves are still awaiting, but will not get this "superstructure."

Such definitions will not do; they are too careful, and therefore undefined and directly untrue. We simply erase the word "economic" and note that in class society, according to Magerovskii, there is *class* law but no *social* law. From this definition it is unclear what sort of collective it is that "fixes" or promulgates these norms, but presumably it is the same class that also supports it. I will not try to settle this question definitely because I later read that the "October Revolution . . . overthrew *the entire system of legal relationships which supported and organized the class rule of Russian landlords and capitalists*" [Magerovskii, 1922: p. 29]. This means that it was not ruling class authority that supported legal relations, but legal relations that supported the ruling class. But a little later, new Soviet law is declared to be "engendered in the words of the proletarian spirit." (*ibid.*, p. 94) Although poetic expressions are not very useful for work in legal science, it is nevertheless permissible to conclude that this creative proletarian spirit is a class spirit. The law of a class society is *recognized as class law* and he who said "A" must also say "B".[1]

Thus, either we have the concept of social law, an abstract and undefined concept capable of standing alongside any definition from bourgeois science, or it is a concrete concept, a class concept, and is applicable only to class society. *Law cannot be one and the other* at the same time.

In my work on law I briefly showed, with the example of the philosopher's "natural law," how the new class law of the bourgeoisie prospered under this name. This law had dual meanings because it existed in parallel with positive law. With the victory of the bourgeoisie, natural law was transformed into positive law and the category of natural law disappeared. But within this new bourgeois law, its basic character, its duality, its characteristic internal hypocrisy and inconsistency—these were preserved because its self-proclaimed future role was as *natural, social* law. In relation to the oppressed majority of society it is in fact *purely class* law. However, Comrade Magerovskii has reserved this characteristic of duality (in an honorific sense) for our Soviet law:

In studying Soviet law, we note, before anything else, its dual nature. On the one hand, it is still directed toward the past, toward bourgeois society; it still comprises elements of bourgeois law. On the other hand, it is directed toward the future, toward a socialist society, and owing to this it comprises elements of socialist law. [Magerovskii 1922: p. 30]

In my opinion, this is an incorrect and deeply unjust accusation. Soviet power, as the dictatorship of the proletariat, means power that is definitely class power and, therefore, its role is the elimination of bourgeois law. But, as a system of social relations, law cannot be eliminated with one blow; on the contrary, it has been necessary to retreat and to tolerate something from the past which had already been abolished.[2] But what is the duality in this?

There still is no talk of socialism. We speak openly of *state capitalism*, but with the state power of the proletariat, and we even speak about permitted *private* capitalism. Here one can perhaps speak of parallelism; such parallelism is a thing that is natural and ordinary in history. *We are against any dualism*; we openly and clearly say which of our social relations (relations of production, exchange, acquisition) are permitted and which are not. But we reach this compromise *consciously* and *in the interest of the politically ruling class of the working people*. Our revolution has introduced this certainty because it has also openly adopted *a class perspective in the question of law*. It is therefore impermissible to speak of our law as *"externally binding"* norms." The general division of norms into norms for *"internal"* or *"external"* use is mocked even by some of the bourgeois scholars, but it is entirely inappropriate for proletarian law. For us it is entirely sufficient that decrees (norms) are binding in general. But for the class that enacts and enforces them, they are simultaneously *internally binding*. This fact is very important because for us the best means of coercion has always been *persuasion*, i.e., propaganda, agitation—means of *"internal"* influence.

System of relations or totality of norms?

As is well known, in my work *The General Doctrine of Law* (*Obshchee uchenie o prave*), I chose to begin with an extant definition of law, created not by myself, but adopted (with my participation and signature) rather hastily by the Collegium of the People's Commissariat of Justice. I stated that I recognized shortcomings in the formulation of this definition. But I insisted that it was correct in principle.

I understand law as a system or order of social relations that correspond to the interests of the ruling class, etc. This is contrasted with law as "the totality of norms of conduct" or "norms of external regulation," "the system of externally obligatory social norms," etc., in a word, the totality of positive laws or so-called law *in the objective sense*. Among these obligatory norms there are usually many dead "silent norms," so an intermediate explanation is also therefore created: that "law in the objective sense is the sum of abstract (universal) obligatory norms of external conduct (the word "external" also figures here but it has jumped from norms to conduct itself), to the extent that such norms in general *are subject to coercive execution (regel mässigerzwingbar).*" The question is therefore whether law is a system or a structure of *relations* determined by the *interests* of the ruling class and brought to life by the authority they have organized, by the state (not only by statutes, but also by all other measures and simply by economic or even moral pressure); or whether law is merely the *totality of norms*, but does not entirely exhaust the full regulation of legal life. I read in a polemic (against me) by one of the adherents of the second opinion the *terrible* idea that in such a case "it is necessary to take *production* relations for *legal* relations, to declare the superstructure to be the base."

In fact, this sin stems from Marx; he truly allowed this "mixture" when, in his famous *Preface to the Critique of Political Economy*, he speaks of "*relations of production*" or,—what is but a legal expression for the same thing—"property relations . . . " [Marx 1859: pp. 503–4]. Would anyone deny that "relations of ownership" are "legal relations"?

What is the essence of this dispute? The decisive element in the concept of law is its content: namely, the protected, supported interest (of the class). Our opponents support the old, will theory, giving chief, if not exclusive, significance to the formal side or, still worse, to will: *will defines interest* (and not the contrary?), i.e., "*consciousness defines life*"! But in the understanding of law in the sense of the *process* of "external" *regulation*, we recognize the form of law as the content and the interest (and the relations deriving from this interest) merely as the object of this regulation. This answer to the problem recalls the old picture, drawn by Marx, that bourgeois science has placed human relations on its head. Can these human relations abide long in this awkward position?

The will theory of law assumes the most varied forms—such as the will of God, of a higher being, of a king, of the people, and ultimately the social contract as the result of a multitude of wills—and rules in legal science to the extent that one can speak of a ruling theory in this chaos of opinions. Seeing destruction from the theory of interest, it finds its last refuge in psychology. In fact is it not characteristic for political economy, sociology, and law to seek salvation almost simultaneously in pscyhology? It would be very interesting to follow this phenomenon in more detail: the individualism of bourgeois society and individualist-psychological theories; the democratic theories of "social contract" and the attempts by Petrazhitskii and others to construct a separate theory of *dual* pscyhological experiences; finally, the crisis of collectivism in the prism of bourgeois individualism and the form of theories of social psychology. But this is the same as the notion of the *primacy of consciousness over life with which we are struggling and must struggle.*

We contrast our "one-sided" theory of historical materialism with this tendency. It is not "economic fetishism"; it is not an "absurd thought that everything happens mechanically,'' that will does not play a role. Nor is it a denial of will and its significance or a belittling of the significance of the science of psychology. It is simply correctly understood Marxism and, to those who state that ''will is *the starting point of class struggle*'' and that ''will is the *moving force* of every social process, including *production relations*,'' we reply that this is poorly understood or undercooked Marxism. None of this is said by way of reproach. In the process of the world revolution, when communism attracts masses of the most diverse leftist elements to its ranks, with their former ideology, idealistic or near idealistic, so when ''revolutionary will'' demonstrates marvels of energy and initiative, it is hard to fit in the cold, at first glance, limits of historical materialism. But the main cause of this phenomenon must be recognized as ignorance about the nature and *content* of revolutionary Marxism, which places at the basis of its theory ''the revolutionary class struggle''—*class interest and a correct revolutionary consciousness of this interest.*

If it is possible to blame our definition of law, then it can only be blamed for underemphasizing *the role of ''class interest.''* According to this definition—the system of relations only ''*corresponds*'' to class interest, while this interest must have *the determining role*, of course, through the prism of *consciousness*, i.e., state authority of the same class. With respect to this formulation we will work things out but we will remain *intractable* with respect to the meaning of ''interest'' and ''will,'' i.e., ''*reality and consciousness*.'' If we spoke of *the order or system* of social relations, then these words emphasized the participation of human will, and its significance.

In order to overcome this disagreement, which is one of *deep principle*, a correct formulation of it is necessary. If we attain two such formulations, of which each expresses the controversial point of the definition in one or two words: ''*determining class interest*'' or ''*regulating acts of will, norms*,'' then we will reach either agreement or disagreement. The first formulation will be based upon objective, the second upon subjective characteristics. Bourgeois theory, in contrast, assigns the definition of law in *the subjective sense* to the former, and gives the name ''law in *the objective sense*'' to the latter. But this *confusion of ideas* excludes *base and superstructure*.

Base and superstructure

I do not know if Marx would have used the graphic and accurate expression of base and superstructure if he had foreseen how often his pupils would abuse it; the question of ''primacy,'' the question of base and superstructure, as is well known, received from the German professor Stammler, the banal solution of economy-content and law-form. This unfortunately also penetrated the simplified everyday usage of many Marxists. Who has not been struck in the eye by phrases such as ''for every economic relation there is a corresponding legal covering''? But what is this if not Stammlerism?

But reference to "base" and "superstructure" was very fashionable for our opponents after the October Revolution. At first, Kautsky & Co. (and then all the Marxist-thinking bourgeoisie) argued that the new superstructure (the proletarian dictatorship) did not *correspond* to its economic base, that it therefore was without foundation and would fall; that the base had still not matured and that "the little birdie had broken into song too early." The "Marxist bourgeoisie" has therefore begun to affirm (and after it Kautsky and all Social Democrats— especially Russians) that the old base has returned in the form of the New Economic Policy, and this means the restoration of the old superstructure after it, and so on.

To calm my critic who shrieked that I was "declaring the superstructure to be the base"—I pointed out that Marx himself terms the "property relation" simply the *legal expression* for the "production relation."

What did Marx in fact understand here by the words "base and legal and political superstructure?" In his *Foundations of the Critique of Political Economy*, Marx distinguishes the concept of "property" from the concept of *protecting* property through justice, the police, etc., and explains the concept "protection of property" by the words: "every form of production creates its own legal relations, forms of government, etc." [Marx 1858: p. 88]. Again in this work, Marx wrote of his intention to study "*forms* of the state and (*forms*) of property with respect to relations of production and circulation," and also "legal relations" (i.e., institutions), and he refers to the task of studying "uneven conditions of development (*unegale Verhältnisse der Entwicklung*) of material production and legal and political forms."

"But the really difficult point (in comparison, for example, even with art) to be discussed here," he says, "is how *relations* of production develop unevenly or legal relations (*in ungleiche*[3] *Entwicklung treten*). Thus, e.g., the relation of Roman private law (this less the case with criminal and public law), to modern production" [Marx 1858: p. 109]. Marx never finished his *Foundations of the Critique*, and likewise the tasks set by him remained unfinished. Only in connection with this thought can we understand his famous words in the *Preface*: "*the immense superstructure is more or less rapidly transformed*" [Marx 1859: p. 506], starting "with the transformation of the economic base" (*ibid.*).

This almost shows that all the interpreters of the relation between base and superstructure have overlooked something. Marx's contrast here can simply be reduced to that between social *reality* (the base) and *consciousness* (the superstructure).

> In considering such transformations a distinction should always be made between the material transformation of the economic conditions of production, which can be determined with the precision of natural science, and the legal, political, religious, aesthetic, or philosophic—in short, ideological forms in which men become conscious of this conflict and fight it out. [Marx 1859: p. 506]

"Forms" here are certainly the *phenomena* of consciousness, which means production relations or, which are the same as (but just expressed legally) the relations of ownership. The *most basic legal right*—that of ownership—is therefore contrasted with *those forms* in which people "fix" ownership (statutes), protect it (justice, police, religion), and propagandize it (philosophy and ideology in general). But the conflict itself is already played out between *law* (ownership) and *its fixation*, to use the expression popular among our Marxists, and *the forms of its protection*.

Marx was also sure here of his dialectic. For him the important element everywhere was motion, conflict, struggle. If we speak of the relation between economics and law (or more correctly, legal forms), then also here we must consider this relation in the stage of struggle. This struggle is nothing other than the struggle between classes for the realization of their interest. Classes, in turn, are only an expression of the distribution of the means of production, i.e., ultimately, relations of acquisition and the right to property. Every society, every means of production, has its form of acquisition and property. Social classes— defined by the distribution of elements of production and by their role in production—constantly (consciously or unconsciously) *struggle for this role in production*. Seeing, therefore, how and to what extent their class interests are reflected in their consciousness: they loot, for example, factories and machines—in the first stage they struggle for improvement of their role in production for distribution of the product—in the second, they struggle for the right to property itself, as defining 'their role, in the third stage, i.e., in the stage of social revolution.[4]

Corresponding to the course of this struggle, consciousness appears, changes, and develops. So too do the superstructural forms in which this consciousness is "determined." It is determined neither by society nor by its collective, but simply by the ruling class in the person of its organized authority, of the state in the interests of this same class, which, however, does not exclude compromises and concessions on its part.

Such an approach simultaneously simplifies and complicates the question. The base is material reality; the superstructure is consciousness, the form of consciousness of this reality. Take the concrete example of the October Revolution. Note the changes it made in the relations of production. The proletariat in fact and in rhetoric nationalized the land, the large factories, etc. for the use of its state, i.e., of the working class. These "changes in property relations" were material reality. For the working class, in granting certain political concessions or in making certain political retreats in favor of the capitalist class (but not by the landowners), to have also surrendered its authority, the proletariat would have had to come to *the consciousness* that it had to *give in*, or the capitalist class would have *had to defeat it* by force. Who? The capitalist class! But in practice it is helpless without the aid of the proletariat or the peasantry. One cannot therefore speak of any *automatic transformation in the superstructure*. Everything depends upon *the outcome of the class struggle*!

A very important role here falls *to working class consciousness* both about its interest and about the need for *partial retreat*. *The power of our revolution* also consists of the fact that it *consciously knew how to make such a concession* while retaining economic and political *power*. We will see that the problem of base and superstructure therefore lies on another plane.

Class consciousness and legal consciousness

If we speak of workers' consciousness, then we have in mind class consciousness. This concept is taken from the practice of German Social Democracy of the glorious past, where there was also talk of *"Klassenbewusst,"* i.e., "a worker with class consciousness." But the content included in this concept is quite undefined. The workers' movement began with the fact that the workers, in Lassalle's words, had first to be shown that they were workers: that the English word for worker, "poor," i.e., impoverished, is not a derogatory word. From this it is still far to the consciousness that worker is a title of honor. This consciousness is produced only by proletarian victory.

We must define the concept of class consciousness more precisely. By this term we understand the consciousness by a class of its class interest. In Marx's *The Poverty of Philosophy*, we read: "This mass is thus already a class as against capital [unconsciously—P.S.], *but not yet for itself*. In the struggle . . . this mass constitutes itself as a class for itself. The interests it defends by it become [now consciously—P.S.] *class interests.*"

Engels paints a rather cheerless picture of class consciousness:

> Furthermore, when by way of exception the inner connection between the social and political forms of existence in any epoch comes to be known, this as a rule occurs only when these forms have already by half outlived themselves and are nearing extinction. [Engels 1878: p. 109]

And in fact, so the ruling class achieves consciousness of its inevitable destruction. The most farsighted of its members either go over to the ranks of the future class or undertake a desperate struggle against this socially "rising poor" or, finally, degenerate into powerless, cheerless pessimism and disillusionment. The remaining mass believes in the immortality of its state. The rising class is another matter. Its consciousness grows in the struggle, and in proportion to the struggle, passes through a series of phases. But its growth is extremely slow. Today's victory of the basic truths of revolutionary class consciousness—truths discovered by the genius of Karl Marx—required seventy years and grandiose revolutions (1871, 1905, 1917). Nevertheless, this consciousness does not extend to the whole proletariat, but only to the vanguard of the world proletariat.

But if this is the situation with class consciousness, then what can be said about *legal consciousness*? This is a popular phrase in general use today. But what is its content? For the bourgeois, for the ruling class, there is at least a famous *elemental* concept of law: plunder according to law, using the eternally youthful expression of Shchedrin. If it is true that "law is born from the depths of the class soul," then paraphrasing Linguet, it can be said that "this spirit is simply property." This bourgeois legal consciousness, as I already indicated, has actually turned into a whole legal world view and has assumed the all-embracing significance of the bourgeois world view.

But what about the concept of proletarian class consciousness, i.e., the class consciousness of the proletariat? In the summer of this year, in a German Social Democratic paper, I happened to read the words "about Western European legal consciousness." This Western European legal consciousness was contrasted with Eastern European, more accurately Asiatic, or in other words, with proletarian legal consciousness. Spengler, on the contrary, contrasts "eastern" with western. In essence these contrasts are idle talk. Until now we have only confronted simple bourgeois legal consciousness. This has played, and will continue to play, a role in the form of tradition for a long time after the victory of the proletarian revolution. If Bauer called nationality our historical element, then legal consciousness may properly be called the main element of the *historical prejudices* of classes. As such, it is the most difficult of all to subject to criticism! This is why it is the last area to be penetrated by the class perspective.

Of course, our first formula for proletarian class justice (in the decree on the court) responded to the wide range of "revolutionary class consciousness." But we confined it within certain limits, namely, the decrees and the minimum political program of the victorious parties. Later, when these limits expanded unchecked, there was talk of the creative spirit of the proletariat, even of the creative genius of the working class in the area of law, etc. Aside from the fact that such florid words are in sharp dissonance with the modest, worthy language of our revolution, they also do not correspond to reality. If we describe laws almost literally copied from bourgeois codes as "this formulation is crystallized from five years of socialist legal consciousness," then this is the result of a total misunderstanding.

In the editing of Decree No. 1, the phrase legal consciousness was probably given the content infused by Petrazhitskii's theory (see Comrade Lunacharskii's article in *Pravda*). In fact a significant role was played by bourgeois legal consciousness, and moreover in the decree's "underground" edition. But one should do it justice: where the people's court consisted of quite conscious proletarians, it actually contributed something new. The class composition of the court, at first glance a purely quantitative change, also brought into its deliberation something qualitatively new. An old jurist wrote of this reform that instead of one judge it seated three workers—*nothing more*. We could have replied: but also *no less*. In the court, proletarian class consciousness was originally transformed into *proletarian class legal consciousness*.

Class *legal consciousness* is one part of general class consciousness; it is narrower than the latter and relates to the strengthening, the support, the protection of class interest or to the whole system of these interests. In an article on the Decree on the People's Court we included a citation to the minimum political program. We then unconsciously formulated this thought and almost *accidentally established the basis for the new and only correct theory of law*, namely *the class theory*. We resolved the question in this way *not because of the theory but despite it*. The victory of the proletariat actually demonstrated that *class legal consciousness* is *the class consciousness* (i.e., the recognition of the class interest) *of the victorious class*.

With the transition to the New Economic Policy, the idea of *revolutionary legality* became extremely popular among us. This time it was openly victorious. At first, we added the word "revolutionary" by accident, or simply to distinguish our legality from bourgeois legality, thereby emphasizing the essential difference between the content of pre- and post-October laws even though the language of the latter excessively recalled the former. The word "revolutionary" in this legality was to emphasize the rule that the law will be applied and interpreted *looking forward and not backward*.

Later we assigned the word "revolutionary" here sometimes simply a mystical sense, and in such a manner, it seems to me, that only what has been stated in this chapter can give us a true significance for this word. In fact, where decrees or codes deviate from revolutionary decrees or measures, they have a counterrevolutionary content. However, as I indicated, the strength of our revolution lies in the fact that it was *consciously able to make necessary concessions*.

All these concessions were *in the interest of the revolution* and, therefore, of the working class. *This consciousness* also transforms the compromise made in the interests of the final victory of the revolution into revolutionary interest, because through it *state authority*, as the means for the revolutionary transformation of society, remains in the hands of the proletariat. Only by understanding revolutionary legality in this way can we make it more or less stable. Seeing in the decrees containing this retreat only *externally obligatory* norms of conduct both for citizens and for People's Courts, we hardly can count on the firm conduct of such "revolutionary legality." In combining revolutionary class consciousness and revolutionary legal consciousness, in accordance with the laws of logic, we both provide positive content to this legal consciousness (in the absence of statutes in the first period of our offensive), and find accommodation between revolutionary class consciousness and retreat compelled in the interests of the revolution. In such a form of compromise, law does not cease to correspond to the class interest of the proletariat. Legality is and will remain revolutionary.

Conclusion

I have limited myself here to the urgent problems of our legal theory. It seems to me that we must reach a definite decision about these problems, and this decision is possible only through complete openness and the defining of disagreements. The history of our understanding of law after the October Revolution has shown us that life was more clever than the theorists, and that theory only found *post factum* the correct motivation and formulation of the basic answer to the fact that *all law in class society is class law* in the interests of the ruling class, i.e., the class in power. It follows that in the future we must maintain a proximity between the revolutionary theory of law and the bearer of the revolution, the broad masses.

The class nature of law consists in the fact that it has as its content the protection of the interests of the ruling class. This content of law is therefore a system of social relations, and the well-known structure of such relations; and the totality of norms is only *a form of conduct* or *the support for this structure*. The first, social reality, determines the second as consciousness, which does not exclude the influence of consciousness upon reality itself: "it can shorten or alleviate the pangs of birth."

The area of law is a refuge where all the remnants of idealist and ideological survivals and traditions are hidden. It is now time to "turn" the science of law upside down. This goal is attainable only in the general theory of class law. This theory is the first to have transformed jurisprudence into a truly scientific doctrine—not a lifeless doctrine, but one capable of having a maximal and positive influence upon practice. This latter, incidentally, applies to all the reality of our scientific doctrine.

But the theory, having revolutionary class struggle as its object, cannot of course win without a struggle. Neither by compromise, nor ambiguous formulas, nor eloquent silence, will the Marxist concept of law be achieved as part of the revolutionary Marxist world view, but only by merciless struggle for its basic principles.

Impotent academic science has no banner other than empty phrases about the tasks of "Russian legal thought," or "statute law" regardless of whose statute, i.e., *about the letter of the law*, as the slogan for the struggle. We must formulate precisely those fighting thoughts which now must unite revolutionary Marxist jurists for a difficult extended struggle *for a revolution in the sphere of legal understanding, for revolutionary legal consciousness*.

In view of the fighting significance of disputes on the Marxist concept of law, I have drafted a brief addition to my paper in the form of the following points of our initial program:

1. Law, like the state, its authority and justice, can only have *a class nature* in a class society. The debatable academic question of whether law existed in pre-class society and whether it will exist in post-class society, I leave untouched.

2. The basic characteristics of law are: class interest and the protection of this interest by the organized power of the class, i.e., by the state.

3. Whether to recognize law as a system or structure of social relations (the content of norms), or the system or structure of norms itself (the form of the system of relations), depends upon the viewpoint from which

one approaches this problem.

4. For *the bourgeois jurist, law in the objective sense* is a form, i.e., a totality of norms. On the contrary, for the Marxist it is a system of relations as *the content* of law.

For the bourgeois *jurist*, law in the subjective sense is the relations themselves. For *the Marxist* it is just the opposite—the totality of norms as acts of will.

5. The core of the revolutionary-Marxist theory of law is thus the *theory of interests*; *the will or goal theory*, which includes all psychological theories of law, is rejected.

6. The world view of the ruling class in the area of law is termed legal consciousness; the class consciousness of the proletariat is therefore consciousness of class interest in the minds of the *victorious* working class. Just as Engels contrasts the legal or bourgeois world view with the Christian world view, so we contrast the proletarian or communist with the legal or bourgeois.

7. Because class interest is recognized very late by the respective class, and because class consciousness is the product of a long process, thus class law also slowly penetrates the consciousness of a given class because the task of the revolutionary jurist is to deepen with all his abilities the legal consciousness of his class.

8. In revolutionary class law, an enormous role is played by the masses. The energy of the revolutionary Marxist must therefore be toward popularizing law both in practice and in theory rather than distancing and alienating law from the masses.

9. The revolution consists of the seizure of state power for the purpose of *organized* realization, or the putting into practice of the class interest. This is apparent from a whole series of important laws in the first days of the October Revolution. But the revolution is also a class struggle in fact, as well as words, and all unorganized, "anarchical" (or arbitrary) applications of private initiative appear strongly in those branches where the former ideology is especially strong. This explains the very bitter struggle against prerevolutionary law in the proletarian revolution, and the necessity of temporarily limiting oneself to "revolutionary legal consciousness" instead of general laws.

10. Revolutionary legality intended to dislodge these "arbitrary" actions of private revolutionary initiative, declaring from the very first days of the revolution the obligatory nature of every revolutionary law of the victorious class.

11. With the inception of the "New Economic Policy," revolutionary legality maintains its power and achieves great importance, because the concessionary laws of the revolutionary government are obligatory both "externally" and "internally" ("not by fear, but by conscience"); from its internal side, it must be based largely on revolutionary legal consciousness (persuasion, and not just coercion).

12. Revolutionary legality from the "external" side consists of the fact that the extent of retreat in the resolution of legal questions is interpreted *strictly* by

looking to the future of the revolution. Every *extended* interpretation of the *retreat*, in the sense of return to the old, must be rejected as a contradiction of revolutionary legality.

Notes

1. In the "classical" collection on legal science of Moscow University, in the journal *Law and Life*, Trainin writes "Each social-political system has its own legal form, *each class its own law*. This means it is merely a question of the qualitative evaluation of a given class law." This recognition, using Trainin's expression, is a fact of "deep social meaning and *legal significance*."

2. This is clearly expressed by Professor Nol'de, in a foreign publication, where he states that "the legal chaos reigning in Russia makes it impossible to distinguish what of *our* law has finally *disappeared* from what *will continue to exist*."

3. The editor, Kautsky, placed a question mark after the word "*ungleich*," but Marx here transposed for the word "*ungleich*" the word "*unegal*" used by him earlier in the same passage.

4. The teaching of Marxism in the purely "abstract" form of the doctrine about the development of economic forces up to the breaking of the membrane, unrelated to the class struggle taking place during this period and leading to the *breaking* of the membrane, gives sad results.

PART II

Marxist Theory of Law

Introduction

The New Economic Policy attempted a concerted program of economic reconstruction in the wake of the Civil War. Relegalization was a major mechanism of this program. Familiar legal institutions were now employed alongside the apparatus of proletarian law, and the Bolsheviks promulgated a new system of codification based largely on foreign bourgeois models. In this retreatist phase of the period of socialist transition Stuchka continued his criticisms of bourgeois jurisprudence and of the substantive content of bourgeois law and, at the same time, began to develop the major concepts of a Marxist legal theory. These two primary concerns are the themes of his first two essays in Part II.

In "A Materialist or Idealist Theory of Law?" (1923), published in the most prominent Soviet Marxist philosophical journal of the early and mid–1920s, Stuchka entered the lists against natural law philosophy, the historical school of law and, especially, the psychological theory of law of Petrazhitskii and his principal Soviet adherent, Reisner. He inveighs against those jurists who presumed to find the origins of law in ideology, in the "heads of people," rather than in real, socioeconomic interactions or the material relationships of people. In searching for the source of law, he avers, "being" must take precedence over its "consciousness." He then explores the ideological formation of law by tracing transformations in the idealist notion of the origin of law in popular will—from the will of a deity, an absolute idea, the popular masses, the parties to a contract, the social collective, to the contemporary notion of the will of the individual. He attacks those (such as Cunow) who believed that the legal order is a purely mechanical adaptation between social structure and a given mode of production. Following Marx's first chapter in *Capital* ("On Commodities"), Stuchka suggests that law has dual forms. On the one hand, law is the concrete form of a social relation, and embodies a specific injunction; on the other, it is also an abstract form of a social relation, the *legal* form of that relation. Addressing himself to the thorny problem of base and superstructure, Stuchka argues that the concrete forms of the property relation coincide with production relations. Finally, he argues that law has a third aspect, namely, the intuitive form which "with respect to a given social relation, occurs within a person, his evaluation of this relation from the point of view of justice, internal legal consciousness, etc."

In his 1923 article, "In Defense of the Revolutionary Marxist Concept of Class Law," Stuchka criticizes Reisner for attacking the materialist approach to law from the point of view of the psychological conception of law. In response, Stuchka recapitulates and clarifies the fundamental positions taken thus far, and he delineates the differences between them and the Reisner-Petrazhitskii perspectives. This entails making the following distinctions between (1) law as a material object and law as ideology; (2) class law and intuitive law; (3) social class as the source of law and the individual as the source of law; (4) the actual legal relationship and the form of law; and (5) law as a part of the base and law as a superstructural phenomenon. Stuchka reiterated that his little book *The Revolutionary Role of Law and State* merely intended to pose the correct questions about law from a Marxian perspective rather than to provide definitive answers. Hence, some new terrain was entered as he refined further the concept of "system" as the system of social relations grounded in the processes of production and commodity exchange.

In 1925, the first issue of the journal *Revolution of the Law* appeared as a collection of essays under the editorship of Stuchka. The impressive list of contributors included Bukharin, Pashukanis, and the philosophers Adoratskii and Razumovskii. Stuchka's own contribution on "Lenin and the Revolutionary Decree" was a combination of his personal recollections of Lenin and a brief excursion into the legal history of Soviet power just after the Bolshevik revolution. As such, it sought to impart a Leninist history to the Soviet Marxist theory of law. Stuchka set for himself the task of reconciling Lenin's hostility to jurists with his own belief in the importance of law and legality for achieving revolutionary objectives. He provided a number of quotations from Lenin affirming his strong belief in the efficacy of law, and even suggested that Lenin had an *"excessive belief"* in governance by decree during the years of Civil War and the policy of War Communism. However, Stuchka then proceeds to soften his criticism by outlining, with approval, Lenin's pragmatic approach to the early Bolshevik decrees.

According to Stuchka, Lenin viewed the resort to law and even bourgeois parliamentarianism as appropriate instruments, under certain circumstances, for the revolutionary tactician. He also regarded the governmental decree as an essential legitimizing mechanism for statements about Bolshevik policy, a way of communicating policies to the masses in a more formal, politically secular, and hopefully, persuasive manner. Finally, Lenin saw the decree as a vital medium for the "translation" of abstract policy into the more practical language of implementation. In the course of sketching out Lenin's views, Stuchka provided a rare (for this period) but brief excursion into the legal history of early Bolshevik policy and Soviet law on the judiciary, and some interesting glimpses into the struggles to enact Decree No. 1 on the Court.

The Marxist school had by the mid–1920s extended its writ well beyond the "commanding heights." The ties between prerevolutionary Russian legal theory and bourgeois German and foreign jurisprudence had been ostensibly severed, domestic juristic opponents had been bested in intellectual debate, and the adherents of the Marxist school were extending their critical work beyond the general theory of law into civil, criminal, and other branches of law. At this juncture Stuchka launched a massive project, *The Encyclopedia of State and Law*, which in retrospect stands as an intellectual monument to the heady years of Marxist hopes for the withering away of law. Stuchka, as the elder statesman and organizational leader of the Marxist jurists, served as editor-in-chief of the two-year, three-volume undertaking. In addition, he himself wrote most of the entries on the principal concepts in the Marxist theory of law. Stuchka's contributions to the *Encyclopedia* that we have selected and translated represent not merely his own mature work but the distillation and consolidation of the most prominent work in the Soviet Marxist theory of law. To the reader of his essays on "Bourgeois Law," "Jurisprudence," "The State," "Revolutionary Legality," "Law," "Legal Relationship," "Legal Consciousness," and the new concept of "Soviet Law," it is clear that the Marxists' theoretical offensive against the "bourgeois juridical world view" achieved its greatest intensity under the banner of the "revolution of the law."

In the first two *Encyclopedia* entries ("Bourgeois Law" and "Jurisprudence") Stuchka attempts to compare the hypocrisy of bourgeois jurisprudence with the new science of class law developed by Soviet jurists. Both essays seem, in retrospect, pedestrian, repetitive, and unenterprising—no doubt reflecting, by his own admission, the lack of serious Marxist analysis both of legal history and of the history of ideas.

In "The State" Stuchka inserts a brief discussion of the proletarian state into a summary of the historical forms of state power, on the one hand, and specific theories associated with specific states on the other. There are two small, albeit interesting and important, features of this essay. Firstly, Stuchka suggests that the concept of the proletarian state will only become unnecessary with "the uniting of the whole world in a *single* Union of Soviet Socialist Republics." It is tempting to regard this pithy statement as a rejection of the doctrine of socialism in one country; whether Stuchka subscribed to such a rejection it is impossible to know. Certainly the statement suggests a basis for Stalin's theory of the strengthening of the state as developed in the 1930s. Second, while reiterating his opposition to anarchism and to utopianism, Stuchka resigns himself, as Lenin also had done on several occasions just before his death, to the fact that the project of socialist construction engaged in by the dictatorship of the proletariat was likely to be "extremely long." This view turned out to be not only historically correct; it also insulated Stuchka from much of the Stalinist criticism of the leftist "red professors" of the radical wing of the commodity exchange school of law.

Stuchka distinguished "Revolutionary Legality," from the *Rechtsstaat*, whose basic meaning he defined as the self-limitation which a bourgeois "state authority imposes upon itself." Revolutionary legality in contrast involved not the limitation of state authority, but the insurance of uniform enforcement of Soviet law from one end of the huge country to the other. Stuchka's definition was the forerunner of the current Soviet concept of socialist legality. Stuchka tempers the extreme centralist nature of this definition with a call for allowing a reasonable amount of discretion to the officials actually enforcing the law.

In the article on "Law," Stuchka clearly differentiates his position from the "Commodity Exchange" approach of Pashukanis. Stuchka's theory of the class nature of law provides the necessary theoretical basis for the continuation of law on a broad scale during the construction of socialism. The officially decreed definition of law adopted in the 1940s rests basically on Stuchka's theory. His theory of the interaction of superstructure with the base also provides a way to give a Marxist justification for the active use of law as an instrument for the molding of society.

Stuchka returned to the differences between himself and Pashukanis in the article on "Legal Relationship." He again argues that the "commodity exchange" theory is insufficient to explain legal relationships, but that rather one should seek a "class" explanation, by looking at the class wills of the persons entering into the legal relationship. In an approach that eventually became the sole orthodox approach in the Soviet Union, he defines legal relation as a social relation that is protected by the organized authority of the ruling class.

Stuchka gives a historical interpretation to "Legal Consciousness." He argues that immediately following the revolution, when change was moving faster than legislation, in accordance with Decree No. 1 on the Court, the court had to be guided by "revolutionary legal consciousness"—the understanding of the will of the victorious proletarian class. With the limited retreat to NEP and the accompanying development of detailed Soviet legislation and of instruments for enforcement, legal consciousness was replaced, for the law enforcement agencies, with "revolutionary legality."

The article on "Soviet Law" is of considerable importance, because it clearly states an ideological basis for considering the law in force in the USSR to be "Soviet law" and hence by implication legitimate and worthy of respect. The article was written for the third volume of the *Encyclopedia of State and Law*. This volume was published in 1927, toward the end of the NEP period. In the article Stuchka defines Soviet law as the law of the transition period from class society to classless society. He contrasts his view to two other views. Under one of these views, what was in force in the Soviet Union were remnants of bourgeois law, retained as a temporary measure until the eventual withering away of the state and law. Under another of these views, bourgeois law and Soviet law coexisted, but the term Soviet law was limited to the law regulating peculiarly Soviet institutions. Both these other definitions, by labeling part or all of the legal system as "bourgeois," threatened its legitimacy. By calling the whole legal system "Soviet," Stuchka emphasized its legitimate, positive role in carrying out of "class" (i.e., Party) policy. In this, as in many other cases, Stuchka's practical views prevailed.

The difficulty Stuchka faced in pressing this viewpoint was the well-known passage from Lenin's *State and Revolution* which, quoting Marx, seems to say that postrevolutionary law will still be bourgeois law. Stuchka passes over this passage quickly and seems obviously uncomfortable with it. He then moves to justify his own position by arguing that the revolution had rapidly superseded the laws of the old regime, that Soviet law had placed strict legal limits on the degree of bourgeoisification of the law under NEP, and that an "attack in the direction of socialism" had begun.

For the extreme anarchist elements in the Bolshevik revolution, the phrase "Soviet law" must have appeared to be a contradiction in terms. For Pashukanis, the law in the Soviet state was merely a continuation of bourgeois law applied to the shrinking and doomed area of commodity exchange. Stuchka admits that the idea of Soviet law arose only after the revolution. However, he states that it has become an accomplished fact with the elaboration of detailed Soviet legislation in all areas. Once again, Stuchka provided the theory that by the mid–1930s would win out over that of Pashukanis and become part of the standard Soviet ideology of law. As decades passed from the time of the revolution, it would have been exceedingly difficult to muster ideological support for a law that was branded as "bourgeois" in nature.

Thus, while the *Encyclopedia* entries are often cryptic and dogmatic, they served the important purpose of providing a theory of law that could support the Soviet legal system not for the brief transition period envisioned by the more radical communists, but for decades, indeed for the indefinite future. Their logic in fact suggests the abandonment of the idea of the withering away of law.

5. A Materialist or Idealist Concept of Law?

I ask for your attention, even though it has to do *only with matters of law*. Because jurisprudence, the science of law, is the last refuge for all sorts of idealistic and generally ideological survivals.

Of all the so-called humanitarian sciences, the science of law is the most deeply resistant to materialist views. But of all the sciences it has also suffered most from the absence of such criticism. How helpless is the lawyer who, *qua* lawyer, has political power over the whole world when he declares himself a scholar! Until now he cannot even provide a true definition of his impression of law. The most candid of lawyers openly asks: is it possible to speak of a science of law in general?

But jurisprudence as a science did not enjoy good fortune in its own bourgeois environment. However, it doubtless enjoys great success among various socialists including, sometimes, even . . . communists. Renkers, Radbruchs, etc. are considered not only political but also scientific luminaries. What do their scientific works provide? In the best cases they provide the old themes of "juridical socialism" (cf. [Engels and Kautsky, 1887]) sired by the late Professor Anton Menger. On what do they base their teaching? The best of them base it on psychology, with an additional "economic factor." At root, all this is a purely ideological construct.

We have experienced great upheavals everywhere both in real social relations and in the ideal, intellectual world. But only now—in the fifth year of the proletarian revolution and having actually burned all 16 volumes of the laws and not having stopped before the Ruling Senate itself—have we begun to debate problems of law. Until now the only disputes about law have been about the old understanding of law where the previous legal *Weltanschauung* is alive, and bourgeois legal ideology is still in power.

"Materialisticheskoe ili idealisticheskoe ponimanie prava," *Pod znamenen Marksizma*, 1923, no. 1, 160–78.

I.

When our disputes on law arose, one could observe a very different attitude toward these "discords" on the part of comrades who had not participated in them. Some definitely sympathized with the disputes, even if from habit they did not read articles on law. But some comrades were most unhappy with these disputes. Do they not smack of anarchism, they thought? Are not these disputes directed against our decrees (in brackets: written even in the majority of cases by old lawyers), others argued? Why touch this idyll of law, this romantic little corner in our heads, grumbled others. But on their faces was malicious joy: "Well, it serves Stuchka right! Why has he thought of bothering with systems such as law? Who and how does it bother if a small amount of idealism remains in our heads?"

Here, I ask: is it a romantic little corner or a hostile fortress? I reply directly: a fortress! What role does the "romantic little corner of idealism" play in our heads? Either it must disappear or it will rule over our world view. For "human consciousness always reveals its inner unity; the inner unity leads to the fact that everything taken in by consciousness is immediately combined with all that went before, and consciousness always remains unified." The modern science of psychology teaches this. This is the very "striving of the mind toward the systematization of phenomenal relations" described by Engels in *Anti-Dühring*. Engels himself defined the legal *world view* as *the classical world view of the bourgeoisie*. A clear danger exists that our future world view will structure the most ordinary social relations in terms of legal idealism. And if something like Peter's edict, that all communists should state their Marxist view of law—"so that," speaking in the words of Peter the Great, "every evil would be revealed,"—then a most varied bouquet of opinions would be received.[1]

It is one thing that there are now no serious battles on the ideological front, although the almost uniform view of law among communist lawyers shows the real significance of this romantic corner. The French communists had to be forcibly removed from the Masonic lodges; will we not have to take such coercive or threatening measures against legal romanticism?

I will not linger on the concept of a "practical idealist." This means a fighter for an idea, simply a man with an idea, a man dedicated to an idea. To confuse such concepts would be an unworthy play on words. The concept of idealism derives its world view from the primacy of ideas, absolute or relative, objective or subjective, and is fully defined. Every step forward will be ruthlessly toward that Rome, toward the idealistic world view for which "the spiritual is the first and the basic." All still remember the disputes about Dietzgenism. Comrade Lenin seriously warned about it in his "Materialism and Empiro-Criticism." In the latest work of Josef Dietzgen we read:

We, accordingly, are neither materialists nor idealists, *but both one and the other*. From the point of view of critical understanding we are obligatorily *both idealists and materialists*. [What nonsense!] However we always call ourselves critical natural monists.

This was written when the idealistic world view had launched a serious attack against materialism. The whole bourgeois sector of the International Congress of Peace in the Hague [which created the "Amsterdam International of Trade Unions" whose goal was to oppose war] belongs to the sect of "idealists."

But the legal idyll is more dangerous than the others. Law is naturally disposed toward idealism. Nothing further need be said now that the Bulgakovs, Berdiaevs, Franks, and others have opened their religious-philosophical society in Berlin. When the bourgeoisie first flourished in Rome (of course, not in the modern sense), religious priests were replaced by laymen, by lawyers. The caste of priests was "secularized." The lawyers with the sunset of the bourgeoisie are now converted back to the bosom of the church. The estate of lawyers is "canonized," but they retain their worldly manners and desires. They have not abjured the old world; no, they are ready for new battles. This is why we are right to affirm about this fortress: *"Ceterum censeo, Carthaginem delendam esse."* "This fortress of Carthage must be destroyed to its foundations" in civil war, for before us is a civil (or rather a bourgeois) fortress!

II.

It is well known that before the 1917 revolution, the whole Social Democratic world, having forgotten the words of its teacher Marx, criticized the class state of the bourgeoisie, but contrasted it with a classless democracy. October 1917, the October Revolution, and Comrade Lenin's book *State and Revolution*—all put forth the proletarian dictatorship as the class state of the oppressed classes. Social Democracy had long condemned the class court of the bourgeoisie, but it believed in the extra-class court of democracy. (The program of the combined German Social Democrats even terms this court, with the participation of all social strata, "socialist.") November 1917, created a class "people's court" of the proletariat, and in the summer of 1922, the chairman of the Revolutionary Tribunal, Comrade Piatakov, with the approving roar of the proletarian masses, proclaimed himself the bearer of the class justice of the proletariat. At the Congress of Functionaries of Justice in 1918, we began to speak timidly about *class* law (which many thought an internal contradiction). The People's Commissariat of Justice needed to reply officially to the question: "What, according to us, is law?" We quickly replied: "Law is a *system* (or what is almost the same—a structure) *of social relations* corresponding (i.e., the system) to the interests (rather, the interest) of the ruling class (and everywhere) protected or supported by the organized power of the ruling class" (i.e., as a general rule, by the state).

On whose toes did we then tread? Primarily, all those who sought the essence of law not in real social relations, but in fantasy (both the jurist and the baron, have their own fantasy, and as yet there is no unified concept of law), in ideology (in various "ideas" of justice), in psychology (in a will or a goal) or, simply, in statute. However, the latter (the "statutizer") most closely approached the truth because the *system* of social relations is really now regulated by statute. Or at least in words. But from this law is made neither the general expression of all law nor the exclusive and all-powerful regulator of law. All our opponents lack a common view. But all have one general feature uniting them against us: they seek the content of law in the heads of people and not in real, mutual relations.

The most basic disagreement occurs over the *class aspect*. We could settle for a definition of law as a "system (so-called) of rules that protect a given system of social relations, etc., which is enforced by the state, and which is an organization of a class," although we would dispute this definition. But on the class aspect we will fight with anyone who thinks otherwise.

III.

"For class law! For the working class—the proletariat"—this is a slogan: "for the revolution." For the capitalist class, the bourgeoisie"—this is the slogan of counterrevolution. But the slogan: "just for law"—this is an antirevolutionary slogan (i.e., in the time of revolution also counterrevolutionary), at best replacing revolution with *obligatory* evolution.

What is a class? In his "A Great Beginning," Comrade Lenin wrote:

Classes are large groups of people differing from each other by the place they occupy in a historically determined system of social production, by their relation (in most cases fixed and formulated in law) to the means of production, by their role in social organization of labor, and, consequently, by the dimensions of the share of social wealth of which they dispose and the mode of acquiring it. [Lenin, 1919: p. 42]

To my deep regret, I was without this definition when I wrote my small book, *The Revolutionary Role of Law*. Comrade Bukharin evidently also did not have it when he wrote his theory of historical materialism, and we both concluded that "classes are determined by their role in the process of production," "the distribution of the means of production," "the protection of this distribution by the *law of private ownership* of means of production." Kautsky, as is well known, gave another definition—that class is determined by communality of interests derived from commonality of "sources of income" and *the struggle for distribution* of the product. Without any commentary, there is to us a clear difference between the views of the evolutionary (anti-Marxist) Kautsky and Marx's revolutionary dialectic.

If we understand class struggle as the struggle for a role in production, for the distribution of the means of production or against the *law of private property* (and such is the class interest of the revolutionary proletariat!), then the class nature of this *basic law*—of what Marx terms the "pivot" (axis) of the whole system and, therefore, of all bourgeois law—needs no further proof.

But not all communists see it so. In his (what to call it?) review of my book, for example, Professor Reisner exults:

> Comrade Stuchka himself objects to the second part of his own definition (i.e., its *class* nature) . . . [This, of course, is irony!] and rather fully and convincingly. He gives us a mass of examples of the revolutionary *significance of law* created by the oppressed *against the interests of the ruling class*, etc. [Reisner, 1922: p. 179]

There is a list of the struggle in Rome of debtors against usurers, of peasants against landlords in Germany (peasant war), in France (revolution), of workers against labor legislation, etc. But did Cato succeed in having all the debts abolished? Did factory legislation defeat the right of private ownership of the means of production for the capitalist class? Did the peasants win the war against the nobility in Germany? And in France, where they won, did the class rule of the feudal lords continue over peasant land? Essentially, law is determined (or secured) by the means of the state of the ruling class. Without this protection it is not law. So as not to look long for a refutation of Reisner's arguments, I adduce only one citation from a book which has accidentally fallen into my hands. In Professor Reisner's *Fundamentals of the Soviet Constitution*,[2] we read: "If you deprive a private owner of the protection of the state, and abolish the police, etc. *which support his authority, then this law of property disappears*" (1920). Who should be believed: Reisner of 1920 or Reisner of 1923, Reisner of the period of "war communism," or Reisner of the period of "NEP"? For the lawyer a later provision repeals the earlier ones. Does this mean a retreat?

We could mention other, less open opponents of the class theory of law who are adopting this view rather than *retreating from it*. Moreover, we occasionally meet the recognition of the class nature of law in bourgeois publications. See, for instance, *Law and Life*, by Professor Trainin, "for each class—its own law." This is a great victory. Until it recognizes its defeat, the bourgeoisie cannot achieve a class perspective on law. On the contrary, it is condemned to hypocrisy and duplicity.

IV.

The bourgeois revolution declared the natural law of the philosophers to be the positive law of man the citizen. Instead of God's law, it set up the law of all mankind. In reality this law was also class law. The *Declaration of the Rights of*

Man and the Citizen was woven into the bourgeois code (*Code civile*). This was not of course conscious deception, at least, not until class struggle with the proletariat opened its eyes to the real nature of its power; for "only in the name of the general rights of the whole society can a particular class seize power." "The tragedy of the bourgeoisie," if one may use this expression, is that it declared its revolution to be for all mankind, its authority for all people, and its law universally democratic. But it did not realize that it represented only *a class, an insignificant minority*. This is why from the outset hypocrisy, duplicity, and contradiction are the objective and inherent characteristics of its law, despite its intent. This deception occurs consciously, gradually, and in proportion to the growth of class struggle with the majority of the people, the class of the working people.

In *The Revolutionary Role of Law and the State*, I therefore showed how even the best and most honest representatives of the bourgeois science of law had entered a blind alley. They could not arrive at a scientific understanding of law because they could not recognize the class nature of law. To begin with, this was because they did not recognize class struggle. Later it was because, recognizing the class nature of law, they *recognized the revolutionary proletarian legality as overthrowing the law* of the bourgeoisie and establishing the law of the working class.

Proletarian law is another matter. The proletariat struggles for its class interest in the knowledge that its victory, as the victory of the huge majority, means the victory of all mankind. Its goal is the elimination of all classes and the establishment of a classless society. This is the source of its daring in the proclamation of law as a *class category*.

The whole history of bourgeois legal ideology clearly confirms this conclusion. At one time bourgeois society contrasted *theology* with *ideology*. With the first emergence of capitalism appeared a new philosophy, the philosophy of law, so-called natural law. It began in thirteenth-century Italy, leaped to Holland at the beginning of the seventeenth century, then to England in the seventeenth century, France in the eighteenth century and, finally, Germany at the start of the nineteenth century. Is not such a chess-piece movement of a new ideology strange? Is it accidental that this journey, both in place and in time, corresponds to the movement of the development of the beginnings of capitalism? No, it is more than natural, it is necessary. For this new philosophy, this new law and idea is only a mature program of a new class, of the capitalist class, of the bourgeoisie.

The great French Revolution turned this philosophy into reality. It introduced a new "proper," or positive, natural law in the *Declaration of the Rights of Man and Citizen* and then in the civil law, ending natural law, with the exception of its echoes in German prerevolutionary philosophy.

The ideology of natural law is replaced by two schools: *the historical school* on the one hand, and various *psychological schools* on the other. There is nothing hard to understand here. The historical school is the basic theory of counterrevolution or antirevolution. Against *revolution* in the name of history, in the name of *evolution* of the national spirit! Such was the natural slogan of counter-revolutions everywhere, and of the historical school in particular. It contributed greatly to science because it represented the interests of a class, whether of a victorious one or of one about to be destroyed. But it represented it *honestly and openly*.

But with what did the bourgeoisie replace its theory of natural law? It had not and could not have had another source for the new theory other than the ideology of the individual, the psychology of the normal citizen. The psychological school is the class school of society based upon the principles of individualism and private property.

V.

If the class perspective is recognized, I said we could be reconciled to the formula of "a system of norms" instead of, or rather as a supplement to "a system of relations." In reality, we are not inclined to such a compromise, and will remain uncompromising to the end. But our perspective by no means excludes statute, i.e., norms. On the contrary, we speak about the legislative monopoly of state authority (in all its totality). But not every statute creates law—is realized in the system of relations—and not every relation is reflected in statute. However, every relation is recognized by law and is protected as such. This is one complaint. Moreover, in our opinion the system of relations is a material, *objective* element, i.e., law in the objective sense. The legal form, statute, in general is just a subjective element for a norm. As is well known, bourgeois scholarship terms law in the objective sense a norm, and law in the subjective sense the legal relations regulated by it. This is our dispute. We are at *opposite poles* on this question.

Both sides can undoubtedly observe real law in each other's position—law regulating social relations, i.e., combined in a single system, in a single order. This basic law is what the bourgeoisie terms civil law. This is the *purpose* of law in general, for which the remainder—"the whole legal superstructure"—is a means. This is despite the fact that for bourgeois society it could seem the opposite.

We also say that the system of relations is objective, that the system of norms is subjective, the ideational element of law. The question of primacy here lies between the material and the ideal, between existence and consciousness. Of course, on this question we are for the *primacy of the material side*. Following Marx, we understand social relations to be the mutual relations of people in the process of production and exchange. Because of the importance of this question, we must deal with it in somewhat more detail, risking becoming even more boring. But the material side can ultimately win only on the basis of a thorough clarification of the exceptional nature of legal relations and of their extraordinary complexity.

VI.

As is well known, in the preface to his "Critique" Marx terms *property relations* merely a *legal expression for relations of production*. This passage is explained by the upstart German Social Democratic Professor Cunow thus: "Production relations and property relations are, according to Marx, not parallel, but entirely different relations, although from the legal perspective *production* relations are simultaneously also property relations." But here Marx speaks of legal forms as a superstructure on an economic base, i.e., the same relations of production. How should this be understood?

This phenomenon is explained by the dual (or triple) quality of every relation: it is the *concrete form* of a social relation, of a social phenomenon, and it is also an *abstract* form of a social relation, a *legal* form of social relation. Cunow, for instance, speaks of "the social (societal) legal order," and also of "state-codified law." From this derives the unintentional popularity of Stammler's phrase that an economic relation is content, and law is its form. Or, as we say "every economic relation has its legal covering." No, we face *two forms* of the same relation. They do not coincide or, at least, do not always coincide.

The concrete forms of the property relation fully coincide with production relations, and *vice versa*. The revisionist Cunow concludes from Marx's definition that the legal order is a purely mechanical adaptation between social structure and a given mode of production. This has little in common with Marxism. Suppose a class came to power that was previously exploited and then actually abolished the given system of property. Obviously, with a real change in property relations the relations of production would also change. We find this notion of dual forms in Marx's *Capital*:

> In order that these objects may enter into relation with each other as commodities, their guardians must place themselves in relation to one another, as persons whose will resides in those objects, and must behave in such a way that each does not appropriate the commodity of the other, and part with his own, except by means of an act done by mutual consent. They must, therefore, mutually recognize in each other the rights of private proprietors. *This juridical relation, which thus expresses itself in a contract, whether such contract be part of a developed legal system or not, is a relation between two wills, and is but the reflex of the real economic relation between the two.* [Emphasis P.S.] It is this economic relation that determines the subject matter comprised in each such juridical act.[3] The persons exist for one another merely as representatives of, and, therefore, as owners of, commodities. In the course of our investigation we shall find, in general, that the characters who appear on the economic stage are but the personifications of the economic relations that exist between them. [Marx 1867: 1:84]

To this let us add Marx's depiction of the contract between worker and capitalist as a *formally* exercised and formal "realization" (*formalle Vermittelung*) of a relation of "capital." First, Marx's notion is clarified by his characterization of production relations as of property, i.e., as the *law* of property. For Marx, the relation of exchange was also a contract in legal language. And a legal relation, in its turn a contract, was also a formal (but fully concrete) realization of relations of capital. However, at this very point Marx contrasted this concrete form with its abstract form, the *statute*. This abstract, statutory form may be quite far from the concrete form.

Besides these two forms, there is a third form; using Petrazhitskii's fashionable phrase, it is the *intuitive form*. This is the psychological experience which, with respect to a given social relation, occurs within a person, his evaluation of this relation from the point of view of justice, internal legal consciousness, etc.

With class society, these three *forms* of realization of a social relation roughly *coincide*. They move apart only gradually, and a constant interaction occurs between them. Life (in the form of concrete social forms) is reflected in the *creation* of separate individuals, or of a whole class (the third form or ideology of law) and through its consciousness exerts influence on an abstract form (in the form of a statute) which, in its turn, regulates or tries to regulate the first form. This last feature is characteristic of legal phenomena.

But, in the present case where can one find the objective element, the material aspect of law—in the social relation itself (the first form), or in consciousness (ideology), or finally, in the "fusion" of the social relation and ideology (the first and third forms) in the statute (the second form)? I suggest that there cannot be two opinions. There is only one answer: in the first form, i.e., in the social relation itself as a part of the whole system, of the whole structure of such relations. Assume that a known phenomenon is reflected in a whole row of mirrors (direct, curved, lengthening mirrors, etc.). Would we define this phenomenon by the middle of these reflections and not by the phenomenon itself?

There are times when people exist *without the second form* (i.e., without statutes), such as the initial judicial decisions of the feudal lord or the first decisions of the people's court of the proletarian dictatorship. In both cases, there is an almost total absence of statute, although in the latter instance the old laws still existed in the minds of judges and the people.

VII.

According to Marx, a concrete legal relation is also an economic relation, i.e., a relation of production (or exchange). This means that all conclusions that *every economic relation* "has its own legal *cover*" (such expressions are found in the best Marxist families) are based on a lack of understanding. But it is a greater misunderstanding to conclude, from the above citation from Marx's *Capital*, that

"Marx contrasts to this content (the economic relation) the legal *form* which from his perspective is a relation of will, etc." Nothing of the kind! There is no contrast here, for only in abstract analysis are commodities (themselves) exchanged for commodities (things for things). Actually, even this *economic* relation is a relation between people, and every relation between people is a relation of will. In one case it is evaluated from the economic side, from the perspective of the material needs of individual people; in the other case, from the legal side, i.e., from the perspective of the general legal system. But the contrast is really there for Marx in the words, "*whether or not it* (contract) *is expressed legally*," i.e., does it satisfy a statutory form (an abstract form) or not? Comrade Berman, from whom this citation is taken, transfers this second contrast to the first. It corresponds with the view, unconsciously adopted from the antirevolutionary revisionists, that "the center of gravity of legal regulation *lies in the protection*, the defense of *already existing social relations.*" He knows only "the failure of law (in the present case—statute) to keep pace with life," and not the "revolutionary role" of both law and statute in moments of victory of a new class. This is explained by the author's unbridled economism and his deviation from the class concept of law, i.e., from the true evaluation of the significance of the class struggle in law.

But not *every* relation of will between persons is a legal relation, only that relation which enters into the protected system of relations. A forbidden contract may be concluded, but it *is not a legal* relation, it is *not law*, perhaps it may even be a crime. At the same time it may also be an economic relation. We are therefore speaking *of an entire system* or structure of social relations.

VIII.

As is well known, the majority of legal theorists see the origin or source of law in someone's *will*. The bearer of this will, and its nature, have changed profoundly with time: God, a supreme being, an absolute idea, the popular will (the spirit of the people), contract will (*contrat social*), collective will, individual will. This is what the camp of our enemies is like! What unites them? They are united in that they seek the source of law in the minds of people in the form of outside, suggested, inborn ideas, simply in the form of all that is termed ideology.

Even Marxists and communists are among them; the latter through obvious misunderstanding. Among us people love "to discover America," but not where the real America is. The criticism of the old will theories is now superfluous, but to clarify the question of will is timely if only to open the eyes of those who, in the tone of their revolutionary thought are with us, but who through ignorance drag at the tail of the "volitionalists." But the adherents of the theory of will are sometimes laughable. From Marx's citation above, about which I already spoke at length to confirm our view that the legal relation is a relation of will, they conclude:

The legal form from his (Marx's) point of view is a relation of will between people in society taking on the nature either of a direct subordination of individual will (or as we now express it, *individual conduct*) of the ruling class of society, or of free agreement between two or more individual wills, the nature of one general act of will (of contract) protected by *social* authority from violations.[4]

The deceased Marx has often been the object of such additions for which he provided no basis. This addition, so to speak, inevitably rejects the *class* perspective, replacing it with the *social* perspective. Others have also cited this passage and all because of this alluring, misunderstood "act of will."

It is interesting that, juxtaposed in the same *Zapiski* is the article of another adherent of the will theory, Comrade Veger (V.I.V.) who joyfully speaks of the state (as will), making law, "of will as the *moving force* of every social process, including *production relations*," "of will as the *starting point* of class struggle," etc. And he is against the class theory of law. But what does he have in *common with his* neighbor in the journal, Comrade Berman? Only the same journal. I consider him, despite his sharp resistance to the class theory of law, to be our future ally. Instead of searching for "economic fetishism" in my work, due to some clear misunderstanding, he should look under his own eyes. There is taught unbridled economism and legal socialism, and the replacement of revolution with *evolution*:

> Now there is no doubt that the traditional division of forms of ownership of the means of production *into two classes opposed to one another* and absolutely different—*individual and collective property*—will not stand up under any sort of criticism. . . . *Collective and individual property are only opposite poles of development . . . legal institutions, etc.*[5]

We must dwell a little on this beautiful stranger, about which all speak: the concept of will.

> There is an hypothesis adopted by almost all in psychology, and to which in all times, obviously unconsciously, the common sense of mankind has come. This is the hypothesis *of will* as the *cause of our actions*. It is recognized that between the process of association and action there also occurs the *action of will as a particular independent mental ability*. The association of ideas provides only motives, and will selects any of them. . . . For physiological psychology, there is no *need to allow such* an additional and *entirely hypothetical* factor of *mental life*. . . . Physiological psychology explains all mental processes regardless of this hypothesis.[6]

I do not, of course, propose to exclude from use the deeply rooted word "will," but I propose not to be distracted by such an hypothesis, even in the *metaphorical sense*. We have the concept of consciousness as defined by life (by the interest of the class, for instance). It seems to me that for our purposes this is enough. But class will? Is it not merely the "resultant will" of members of the class? Or is it the *collective* will of the class? What are such fictions for? Abstract (e.g., mathematical) formulas are not applicable for social phenomena. We specifically state that class consciousness is reflected in the etiology not of the totality of members of the class, but of the *vanguard* of the class. This idea was formulated more pointedly by Marx in a letter to Engels:

> I explain briefly and clearly: we did not obtain our mandate from the representatives of the proletarian parties; not from any other than we ourselves, but *this mandate is confirmed by the unheard of hatred* directed at us by all the factions and parties of the old world.

If will is only an hypothesis—and one that is essentially superfluous—then we must naturally divide this concept, and that which is around it, into its component parts (sensation, representation, association of ideas, acts), and then the notion will be much clearer. We simply move from will to psychology, and then to ideology.

IX.

The science of psychology rendered great services to the bourgeoisie as a class. It rendered these services according to its own successes, not in the form of physiological psychology—that serious doctrine which is still in the first stage of development and which must become the singular science of psychology—but in the form of all sorts of speculative and autonomous psychologies, right up to quack salon conversation on various themes on the worlds of senses and beyond the senses.[7] It has come to the aid of political economy, sociology and, likewise, the science of law. Here it operates either as individual pyschology (the well-known Robinson Crusoe, the psychology of the normal Philistine), or as contract psychology (bilateral psychological experiences *invented* by the jurist Petrazhitskii), or as the profoundly reactionary school of mass psychology (cf., for instance, Sigel). It began with Robinson Crusoe on a desert island. Now it has taken a more abstract form: "Law is those norms according to which *people would act if* they were led *only by legal motivation*" (Magaziner): i.e., in some airless "society-less" space. Depending on the group from which Robinson Crusoe is taken—from rentiers, or financiers, or industrialists, or land capitalists—the typical theory of law is also obtained. This is most apparent in criminal, but also in civil law and the law of the state. *"Sic volo, sic jubeo."* (What I want, that I will order). Or, "don't get in my way," etc. Individual ideology also relates to the same psychology. This psychology is more modernized in Petrazhitskii who, not finding two-sided psychological experiences in science, simply invented them. What is this other than a psychological abstraction of bourgeois contract? And of course it is no accident that it was developed by a Constitutional Democrat. All this pleiad of bourgeois leaders, raised on the study of Marxism, such as Struve, Petrazhitskii, Novgorodtsev, etc., so truly, in their own way, have understood the theory of economism (they call it Marxism), that our simpleminded say after them: "The viewpoint of Petrazhitskii (or the name of one of the others) leaves nothing to be desired." And when they beckon sweetly, like Petrazhitskii, "between historical materialism and my teaching there is no such lack of correspondence and mutual exclusion, on the contrary, etc.," then Marxists take this bait. "We have not sufficiently valued the *psychological* factor," says Reisner, one of Petrazhitskii's followers, and adds for softening: "as a *reflection* of the economic factor." The latter thought is not very clear, not even speaking of objections to the "theory of factors" long discarded by Marxism. And after this they explain law psychologically, as "an inner experience."

We must briefly pause on the theory of "mass psychology," which has created a fiction of a mass soul, of the soul of the crowd. Without denying either the suggestibility or the general mutual relation of members of a mass or crowd, we of course deny such a fiction as "the spirit of the crowd." In a meeting where there are, say, an equal number of capitalists and conscious proletarians, every propaganda speech will form at least two souls. And is this not like bankruptcy, if we read in one of the representatives of this school:

> There must, then, be some degree of similarity of mental constitution, of interest and sentiment, among the persons who form a crowd, a certain degree of mental homogeneity of the group. And the higher the degree of this mental homogeneity of any gathering of men, the more readily do they form a psychological crowd. . . . [McDougall 1920: p. 34]

This is like a translation of the theory of class interest or the theory of socialism into bad psychological Esperanto. One cannot construct a firm theory of law on such psychologies.

X.

In a review more flippant than serious, in which Professor Reisner (1923) "barked" (an expression from the old "*Russkaia Pravda*") at me for my work, he tries to show that our definition of law allegedly contradicts Marx and Engels, because "law, regardless, is ideology." In order to speak as a critic, it is first of all necessary to understand the object of criticism. Professor Reisner did not understand or did not want to understand our perspective, because it is the direct opposite of the theory of Petrazhitskii that he defends in other places. Standing on two opposite poles, it is difficult correctly to view the object of criticism.

In his review, Professor Reisner cites Engels, but he did not happen upon these citations that relate to his case. In *Anti-Dühring* Engels speaks of

> the old favorite ideological method, also known as the a priori method, which consists in ascertaining the properties of an object, by logical deduction from the concept of the object, instead of from the object itself. First the concept of the object is fabricated from the object; then the spit is turned round, and the object is measured by its image, the concept. The object is then to conform to the concept, not the concept to the object. . . . And when such an ideologist constructs morality and law from the concept, or the so-called simplest element of "society," instead of from the real social relations of the people round him. . . .

Reisner passes here in silence but, according to the recipe of Bernstein & Co. he then contrasts the "young" Engels with the "*Anti-Dühring*" period of the later Engels. Such a contrast is sadly unsuccessful. In the same letters that Reisner cites (in the book of Comrade Adoratskii), namely in the letter of July 14, 1893, we read:

> Ideology is a process accomplished by the so-called thinker consciously, it is true, but with a false consciousness. The real motive forces impelling him remain unknown to him; otherwise it simply would not be an ideological process. Hence he imagines false or seeming motive forces. Because it is a process of thought he derives its form as well as its content from pure thought, either his own or that of his predecessors. [Engels 1893: p. 496]

Later he speaks of the "semblance of an independent history . . . of systems of law" that "dazzle most people" (ibid.). These words show why the revolution in law occurred last, but that it nevertheless inevitably occurred, after Marxism and the proletarian revolution partially opened our eyes to the "real driving forces." We discarded the lie and the phantoms of our ancestors, and we undertook the study of social relations themselves, and of their system as the content and form of law.

When we closed the old courts and assigned "court talk" (legal pleadings) to the workers, I repeatedly had to remind them that they were dealing with the most ordinary relations of people, accessible to the understanding of all. Their legal consciousness, of course, was still based primarily on the old bourgeois ideology. But simultaneously they were developing a *new legal consciousness*, i.e., *consciousness of their own interest as the victorious class* free from ideology, with more and more true "*consciousness of causal forces.*" The masses defeated ideology more easily than the "salt of the earth" intelligentsia.

But where then is the base, where is the superstructure?

XI.

Marx considers various economic categories as abstract things in *Capital*. In his work, "land," "capital," "commodities," "labor power," etc. in effect are exchanged, are accumulated, provide rent, profit, etc. But Marx also depicts their owners as the personifications of these abstract categories—the landowner, capitalist, commodity owner, worker—who, in the system of capitalist economy (he has only this in mind), enter into mutual relations, i.e., volitional relations which are in one aspect, legal relations. In his long-ago published *The Institutions of Private Law and Their Social Functions* [1904], Renner expresses the notion that Marx developed here for the whole legal system. However, it is not this question that interests us here, but rather the explanation that, as we already have seen, is given to the phrase from the "Critique," namely, that a legal relation (for instance, property) is merely a legal expression of a relation of production (and, we add, of exchange). This is civil law in the broadest sense (in our terminology, both private and also public-economic law) as the *basic law*. It would be interesting to study how the "legal" teachers and contemporaries of Marx looked upon this law. Gumplowicz, for instance, directly singles out private law as basic legal relations. In the introduction to the "Critique," Marx contrasts the *forms* of protection, its defenses (justice, police, etc.) to this basic law.

The comparison of base and superstructure pleased Marx as a *figurative expression*, and it was not he who invented it (see his *Theory of Surplus Value*). He and Engels did not use this image very consistently. In the "Critique" Marx speaks of the economic structure of society (the totality of production relations) as a real basis from which the legal and political superstructure arises, etc. He later explains this "immense superstructure" as legal, political, religious, etc., in short, the ideological forms of *"consciousness and struggle between people."* In the *18th Brumaire* Marx writes: *"Upon the different forms of property*, upon the social conditions of existence, rises an *entire superstructure* of distinct and peculiarly formed sentiments, illusions, modes of thought, and views of life" [Marx 1869: p. 421].

In his *Theories of Surplus Value* we find the phrase, "contradictions in material production make necessary *a superstructure of layers of ideologies"* [Marx, 1862: p. 384]. In *"Anti-Dühring"* Engels speaks of "studies of life . . . conditions of human life, social relationships, forms of law and government. . ." [Engels 1878: pp. 108-9). In any case, it is hard to imagine that Marx and Engels envisioned a Philistine architectural image of a multistory house where first, second, etc. real floors are built on a solid "foundation."[8] It seems to me that Marx had in mind a figurative expression of his philosophical notion of being and consciousness. No more and no less. But economic relations (abstractions), and legal relations as their concrete legal expressions (*as concrete systems of social relations of people*), relate to the base; their abstract form (statute, ideology, etc.)

relates to the superstructure.

However, the root of our disagreements consists not of this, but of the question of the class nature of law, and the derivative question of the primacy of the material element over the ideal. We struggle for the materialist concept of law, but not only for the concept—also for its realization.

Notes

1. None of my opponents presented his own concept or understanding against my concept as a whole. Their criticism was limited to individual words and phrases. This is the least fruitful and so the least useful form of opposition.

2. That Professor Reisner in 1920 was not merely seeking his own world view is apparent from his modest words as follows: "If you allow me in this respect to render some glory to myself, which may be somewhat impolite, then I would nevertheless say that the only theorist of the state in Europe, if not in the whole world, who even before any revolution developed the science of the state as a Marxist, to the *greatest consternation of his listeners*, was—*your humble servant*" [Reisner 1920: p. 88].

3. This exact correspondence is because commodity exchange is the characteristic feature of the given system of social relations.

4. Ia. Berman, *Zapiski Kom. Univ. Sverdlova* [Transactions of Sverdlov Communist University] I, p. 29.

5. *Zapiski*, p. 38. Comrade Berman salvages his protective coloring: an extremely philosophical and therefore unpopular language.

6. Prof. Tsigen, *Fiziologicheskaia psikhologiia* [Physiological Psychology], p. 236.

7. The difficulty in distinguishing between science and simple salon talk can be shown by a small example. The *well-known* Viennese Professor Sigmund Freud boasts that he invented the concept "libido," i.e., considered as a quantitative value the energy of all the impulses relating to that which could be signified by the word "love." To this he assigns love for a woman (sexual) and for parents, and for those close, and for art, and very likely homosexual relations, etc. In what way is this not a typical bourgeois scholar? And where should one search in the organism for the center of this all-embracing impulse?

8. See Reisner, *Osnovy sovetskoi konstitutsii* [Fundamentals of the Soviet Constitution] (Moscow: 1920).

6. In Defense of the Revolutionary Marxist Concept of Class Law

I had neither reason nor desire to write a reply to Comrade M. Reisner's review of my little book, *The Revolutionary Role of Law and the State*, the review that was published in *Vestnik sotsialisticheskoi akademii*, no. 1. The reader must assess the book for himself. But I cannot leave without responding to the partly covert attack on our class concept of law. "Covert" in the sense that in a review of a book, which was the first to be devoted to the question of the *class* nature of law, nothing is said about that aspect, while the purpose of the reviewer is crystal clear: *to discredit our* class concept of law and surreptitiously to replace it with the well-known Kadet psychological theory of Petrazhitskii. In my book, I cited Petrazhitskii's sweet words enticing Marxists and Darwinists into his embraces, and I added: "There are some Marxists who have taken this bait and have tried to reconcile the irreconcilable, etc." One of them, of course, was Reisner. The tone of his review shows that he did not give up his infatuation even after 1917. In the future, I emphasize repeatedly, the area of law is the main and *the last refuge* for all ideological survivals and idealistic directions. Ideological theories in political economy, sociology, and law are, so to speak, the last armored cars moving against the materialist conception of these problems.

The reviewer tore from my book only individual propositions or excerpts from them—and these were distorted and misunderstood—so I will repeat our revolutionary Marxist concept of law. Proceeding from the revolutionary understanding of class—to which I had to devote one chapter—I denoted the concept of *class interest* not as the sum of individual or minor interests, but as an "element placing an imprint on the totality of the struggle of a given class," and as "the focus in which the whole life interest of a given class is reflected." I showed that Marx understood class interest (in the revolutionary sense) in bourgeois society as private ownership of the means of production, their relation to which is the

"V zashchitu revoliutsionno-marksistskogo poniatiia klassovogo prava," *Vestnik sotsialisticheskoi akademii*, 3 (1923), 159–69.

decisive element of very existence for any given class.

Under these conditions, and with such a view of class and class interest, I based my definition of law on that developed by the Collegium of the People's Commissariat of Justice (the author of the draft, as Comrade Reisner knows, is indicated in the footnote on p. 113 of my book):

> Law is a *system* (or *order*) of social relations corresponding to the *interests of the ruling class and* (therefore) *protected by its organized force* (i.e., of this class)
> . . .

I then added:

> A formulation of the concept of law more perfect in point of style is, of course, possible but *by and large I* consider this formula perfectly applicable even now since it comprises the chief *indicia* incorporated in the concept of law *of evey sort* in general . . . it renounces the *purely formal view of law* and sees in law a changing social phenomenon *rather than an eternal* category . . . *it rests on the viewpoint of the class struggle and class contradictions.* [Stuchka 1921: p. 20]

In refutation of this *class* concept of law Reisner writes:

> Against the second part of his definition [i.e., its *class* nature.—P.S.] . . . Comrade Stuchka himself *objects* [how ironical!—P.S.] and quite extensively and persuasively. He gives us numerous examples of the revolutionary significance *of law created by the oppressed against the interests of the ruling class,* etc. [Reisner 1923: p. 179]

There follows a succession of ancient struggles between debtors and usurers, peasants and landlords in Germany (the peasant wars), in France (the revolution), of workers on behalf of labor legislation, etc. With these citations, Comrade Reisner demonstrates only that he cannot master the class concept of law. Did factory legislation really destroy the capitalist class's *law of private ownership* of the means of production? Did the peasants win the war against the nobility in Germany? And in France, where they did win—did the rule of the class of feudal lords over peasant land not continue to exist? Ultimately, law is determined *by the defense or support, on the part of the state, of the ruling class and without this protection it is not law*! So as not to search long for disproofs of Reisner's conclusion, I offer only one quote from a book that recently came to me by accident. The book is Reisner's *Fundamentals of the Soviet Constitution,* and in it we read: "*If the private owner is deprived of state protection,* and if the police, which support his power, are abolished, then *this law of private property collapses*"[1] [Reisner 1920: p. 19]. After this, it now sounds strange when this professor proclaims: "As we already saw above, from the examples of the law on hand contrary to the interests of the ruling class, *indications of protection* by that class [i.e. its state!—P.S.] *are by no means present*" [Reisner, 1920: p. 19]. If one excludes the *transitional* period of dual power, when laws may be enforced in parallel relating to *interests* of two different classes, then this is not an improvement on the views of 1920; it is simply *nonsense*. The same must be said about Comrade Reisner's attempts to reduce *the state power* of the ruling class to *simple* "*ideology*" or the always possible compulsion of authority to replace ideology simply with an "*appeal to justice*," etc. Sadly, after five years of revolution in the area of law, when even bourgeois professors (e.g., Professor Trainin) recognize the class nature of law, we still have to disagree about this theme with a professor who is a Communist!

I could end here. But the materialist and idealist, and also the sociological and technical, concepts of law are closely tied to the question of the class concept of law. It is hard to find a recent book or article on this subject without a discussion comparing the "*social* legal order" with "*state-codified* law" (Cunow), and "*official* law, fixed in *statutes*" with "*real* law, functioning in life" (Durdenevskii), etc.[2] The contrast between *concrete, actually existing law*, and the form of law or formal law, is not foreign to Marx. In the preface to his *Critique*, Marx stresses that "*property relations of ownership* are but a *legal* (i.e., in law) expression for production relations" [Marx 1859: pp. 503–4].

In the "Introduction" to the *Critique*, Marx distinguishes property from the forms of protecting this property (courts, police, etc.[3]) and points out "the really difficult question . . . (is) how *relations of production* develop unevenly as *legal relations* [Marx 1858: p. 109], i.e., how material relations and their formal realization (e.g., in statute) are distinguished from one another, etc.

Another conception of the class concept of law is that law is a "system (or order) of social norms," protecting a given system of social relations, corresponding to the interests of the ruling class and therefore protected by the organized power of the ruling class. At first glance, this does not appear to conflict with our definition, and this is certainly a big step forward. But it is insufficient. If bourgeois scholarship and practice calls law a totality or system of norms in the *usual* sense, and the relations which are the content of law merely law in the subjective sense, this is not accidental. Of course, it is also no accident that we, on the contrary, consider a *system of concrete relations* to be an *objective* element, and not their formal expression, which in our eyes is the subjective element in law. We saw that Marx talks of the possibility of "an unequal course of development" of one and the other. This is why, in our opinion, the class concept of law also gives priority to the system of social relations.

Reisner completely misunderstands our definition when he says that I equate social relations in general with law. I specifically speak "*of the system* (or of the order, which here is approximately one and the same) of social relationships," and not of any system, but "*of the system, which is safeguarded* (protected, fixed, or as you wish) *by the organized force of the dominant class*" [Stuchka 1921:

p. 20], i.e., in usual [circumstances] by the state. What is the basis of this guarding, this protection (cf. "sret" in the Declaration of the Rights of Man and Citizen)? In fact, it satisfies the minimum requirement *not to contradict the interest of this class* (i.e., for example—its relationship to private ownership of the means of production). But how do we conceive of this protection? I speak in detail about this in my book: through law, the court, etc., and in general by compulsion and persuasion on the part of the organization of the class.

Comrade Reisner writes that he cannot understand the word "system" here. So sorry! But to clarify, I added the words "or order." Comrade Reisner is probably not hearing this phrase for the first time, if only in the compound word "legal order." We borrowed this concept from Marx and Engels.[4] In feudal society, for instance, individual capitalist relations of production occur very early, but they still do not enter into the system of feudal social relations, of the feudal legal order. These factual relations of people were social, societal, but were not legal. They became legal relations only when they entered into the legal system (quantity transformed into quality) and only from the perspective of this legal order.

What does the word "system" mean in fact? Is it the disordered heap of diverse relations in which people engage with one another for all sorts of reasons? No, above all we speak only of the system of social relations as understood by Marx, namely, as social relations in the process of production and exchange. And *system* by itself means uniting *in a single whole*. Marx sometimes made comparisons with an organism. Order assumes *certain norms, unconsciously* or *consciously* established. Finally, *class interest* and interference with the realization of this interest by the *organized* power of the class points directly to the conscious element in this system of order. I introduced a special section on the relationship between law and statute. Obviously, Comrade Reisner agrees with it because after reading it, he joyfully asks: "Why did you build this fence? Of course, *not just a Marxist*, but *even* any somewhat *positively* thinking *jurist* would fully subscribe to these positions" [Reisner, 1922: p. 177]. I do not share this last joy, and the best proof of it is Comrade Reisner's view. The "fence" demarcating us from bourgeois jurists, I "built" so as to make law a subject of scientific research. Until now, it was technology, politics, and art on the one hand, and ideology and metaphysics on the other. For us there still remained jurisprudence, as technique (e.g., legislative), policy (e.g., administrative and legislative), art (e.g., justice as the application of law). But the place of metaphysics, or of ideology, is taken up by *science, the sociological study of law, the theory of law, as part of Marxist sociology*. It is possible to discover a certain regularity in the development of the system of social relations. For the ideologue, law has until now remained something "unusually variegated and contradictory."

We also speak of a system of "social relations." The word "relations" or "mutual relations," if one speaks of people, always presupposes the well-known *volitional interrelation* of people, and not only their physical contacts. For example, take Marx's well known statement:

> In order that these objects may enter into relation with each other as commodities, their guardians must place themselves in relation to one another, as persons whose will resides in those objects. . . . They must, therefore, mutually recognize in each other the rights of private proprietors. This juridical relation, which thus expresses itself in a contract, whether such contract be part of a developed legal system or not, is a relation between two wills, and is but the reflex of the real economic relation between the two. It is this economic relation that determines the subject-matter comprised in each such juridical act. [Marx 1867: 1:84]

Entering into mutual relations with one another (in the process of production and exchange), people consciously or unconsciously each time conform their actions with the extant legal order or rise against it. I do not say "with the statute" because a statute is both narrower and wider than law (not all events are provided for by statute and not all statutes are effective). When we repealed all the statutes of the old government, we nevertheless protected *a certain system, a certain order of social relations*, which had not found its expression in law. When we promulgated a civil code under NEP, we wrote in its first article: "Civil law rights [i.e., rights of economic inequality.—P.S.] *are protected by statute*." Comrade Reisner says that even here the proletarian dictatorship recognizes as law that which contradicts its class interest. To this we answer: "No, its class interest is the revolution. This code is a concession to the interests of the revolution and the revolutionary class." And moreover, we read in the same Article 1: "with the exception of those instances when they [civil law rights] *are exercised in contradiction with their social and economic purpose*." In deciphering this rather unclear formulation, we read that *proletarian authority will not tolerate a radical contradiction of its class interest*. It thus clearly stresses its class position on law.

However, metaphorically, we have been speaking the whole time in different languages. Reisner himself does not give his own definition of law; he merely affirms on each page: "law, no matter what, remains ideology." Trying to show the contradiction between myself and Marx and Engels, on the question of the significance of ideology, he quotes—not without errors—two or three entire pages of out-of-context excerpts from my work in support of the full agreement of my words with those of our teachers. If Reisner here put forward his own, i.e., psychological theory of law, then the matter would become much clearer.

I showed in my book that in "The Legal or Classical World View of the Bourgeoisie," Engels sees that this world view was victorious over the *religious world view* that was in power before it. In place of the *legal or bourgeois world view*, I put forth the communist world view. . . . When Engels spoke of *law as ideology* he was contrasting this latter word to *teleology*: here "idea" took the place of "God." In my book, I often repeat what a role history, tradition, and ideology have played in law up to now. But here and now we must take the position of true historical materialism. In *Anti-Dühring* Engels speaks of the "old beloved" ideological or, as it is still called, the a priori method of learning the qualities of a thing not from the thing itself but, on the contrary, developing it from the concept of the thing. First, the concept of the thing is derived from the thing; then, reciprocally, the item is *evaluated* by its reflection, i.e., by the concept. Such an ideologue constructs *morality and law not from real social relations* in which people live but *from ideas* (concepts), etc. Such was Engels' understanding of the significance of ideology in *Anti-Dühring*. But the revisionists (and after them, obviously, Comrade Reisner) contrast the later Engels to the Engels of *Anti-Dühring*. Alas!—such a contrast will not stand up to criticism.

> Ideology is a product accomplished by the so-called thinker consciously, it is true, but with a false consciousness. The real motive forces impelling him remain unknown to him; otherwise it simply would not be an ideological process. Hence he imagines false or seeming motive forces. Because it is a process of thought he derives its form as well as its content from pure thought, either his own or that of his predecessors. [Engels 1893: p. 496].

This is how Friedrich Engels explained the concept of ideology in a letter to Mehring (I cite from a book by Comrade Adoratskii). He speaks further there about the "semblance of an independent history . . . of systems of law . . . that dazzles most people" [Engels 1893: p. 496]. We must ask, at a time when Marxist theory and a great revolution have at least partly opened our eyes to "the real causal forces," must we still deal with the concept of law as exclusively ideology, i.e., as formal law (initially as statute) or the abstract notion of law upon which the philosophy of law worked and which, ultimately, led to every bourgeois theory even including Petrazhitskii's? No, such a method would contradict Marx and Engels, and therefore we have discarded it.

In his youth, Marx took a course in contemporary science of law and, of course, he used the terminology of the leading representatives of the science of law of the time, e.g., *Volkswillen* (will of the people) in the area of law, phrases from the organic school about problems of state and society, etc. [5] Today we would have used, of course, the terminology of the most advanced representatives of modern science—for instance, the sociological school, which truly tries to approach law from a scientific and not purely *technical* ("statutory interpreters'") or metaphysical ("philosophers'") perspective. But as I have already shown, Marx did not stop here. He then provided the material for a truly Marxist definition of the scientific concept of law. It remains for us to finish this work. In my preface I wrote: "I would be happy if my work served *as an incentive for more fundamental work in this direction*." I can state that this incentive is felt, that comrades responding to this call have now been found. If Comrade Reisner again tries to reply to me with Petrazhitskii's conception, he will fully deserve this answer: down with this Kadet doctrine!

Marx points out that, in his conception *all law* is based on economic inequality, for even economic equality in the bourgeois world is in fact inequality. . . . How does Comrade Reisner conceive of law in *primitive* communism?[6] Did inequality exist there? Why speak of communism in such a case? With inequality appeared the first rudiments of the class state and the first rudiments of law. . . . But to confuse every "custom" (i.e., that which usually is done) and "habit" (that which has turned into something familiar) *with law*, as with a concept connected with inequality, is obviously wrong. When Engels spoke of "*Mutterrecht*," he hardly understood law in the same sense as Marx's concept "bourgeois law." One should not confuse concepts. Comrade Reisner feared that I was comparing these primitive customs with "technical rules of conduct in the economy" [Reisner 1922: p. 180]. He asks ironically if this means "rules of better poultry raising?" I am unacquainted both with poultry raising and with its perfected rules. But I am inclined to think that these primitive personal customs and habits were even simpler than the rules of elementary poultry raising and that they did not share the characteristics of law. On the contrary, they could exist later, contrary to law or despite law, depending upon whether they either contradicted the interest defended by the ruling class or were simply "legally irrelevant" for them, i.e., *indifferent* from the point of view of law. Another matter is judicial precedents or, as Comrade Reisner likes to call them, the same "*customs of the ruling* class." These were the first laws, the initial law—of inequality.

It is necessary to distinguish the class interest of the ruling class, i.e., *law*, from the class *interest of the former or future* ruling class already or still *not law*. The first laws and customs or judicial precedents of the ruling class appeared in the princely period of Russia. There then existed a number of customs not recognized as law, just as we do not recognize very durable customs (e.g., those of black marketeers) of the capitalist class as law if they are not included in our codes. We do not regard these customs as law and often even consider them to be criminal; nevertheless, they frequently remain unpunished.

Comrade Reisner, as a true student of Petrazhitskii, sees perhaps the basic phenomenon of his intuitive law in customs—in so-called customary law. For us this is a secondary question. It is important to establish once and for all that law is a class concept. On this, in general, the communists among us are agreed, at least for the period of class society. Comrade Reisner stands alone, by himself. And it will be hard for him to come to this general point of view until he gives up his "evil genius"—Petrazhitskii. None of us denies the significance of psychology for Marxism and for jurisprudence, but the *psychological conception of law* may be termed the legal theory of the bourgeoisie on the same basis as Comrade Bukharin cleverly termed the psychological theory of the economists, terming it the rentier theory. Here the word psychology is equated with ideology in Engels' sense (see above); but this additional confusion in this area is nothing other than the duplicity and hypocrisy inherent in bourgeois society in general and in its law in particular.

The burden was on me to introduce in my small book the class perspective for the first time in the theory of law. I tried to reveal the class bias of every school— of natural or philosophical law as the class program of the bourgeoisie. Similarly, I showed that the science of law could not become scientific if and because it was not based on and *could not be based* on a class viewpoint. *I posed these questions*, and the correct posing of the question, even with an incorrect answer, was worth those sheets of paper (which were, incidentally, very difficult to obtain at the end of 1921!) which the RSFSR spent on this book. I will be very happy if someone makes significant improvements in our definition. But for this purpose the old ideological and psychological tales of an "educated cat" from the seashore will hardly do.

Notes

1. Comrade Reisner accuses me of equating—yes, of equating—law with private property. But Marx himself cited Linguet's famous words: "The spirit of the laws is property." And this is the basic law.

2. I take authors that I have come upon entirely by chance.

3. Marx and Engels use a metaphorical contrast between "base" and "superstructure." It is only a figurative expression in their work. In Marx we find the phrase that "contradictions in material production make necessary *the superstructure of ideological strata*" [Marx 1862: p. 384]. Engels speaks in *Anti-Dühring* of the study of the conditions of life of people, *of social relations, of the legal and state forms together with their ideological superstructure*, philosophy, religion, art. But the Marxist Reisner understands this metaphor in the concrete architectural sense, in the form of a grandiose *multistory* house (see the course of lectures on the Constitution cited above). I objected to such an understanding for jurists in my book.

4. "In a modern state, law must not only correspond to the general economic condition and be its expression, but must also be an internally coherent expression which does not, owing to inner contradictions, reduce itself to nought" [Engels 1890, p. 492]. Engels here repeats for law what Marx (p. 93) said of social relations in *The Poverty of Philosophy*: The production relations in every society form a whole [Marx 1848: p. 166]. I have this citation and it could explain to Comrade Reisner the concept of the system.

5. My pointing this out is called "unmasking *heretical* Marxism in Marx" by my reviewer. At the same time he defends even Comrade Pokrovsky who, with his well-based suspicion of jurists, has accidentally borrowed from them the word "artificial" for the definition of statutory norms. The reader can judge for himself my attitude toward Comrade Pokrovsky's deep understanding of Marxism from the book itself; he does not need Reisner's defense. Let Comrade Reisner continue to divide social norms into natural and artificial norms, i.e., mental experiences.

6. Reisner even writes: "In primitive communism *there is no developed private property*" [Reisner 1923: p. 180].

7. Lenin and the Revolutionary Decree

In the spring of 1917 the Bolshevik party's Central Committee authorized a group of responsible Bolsheviks to establish a legal company for obtaining a printing plant for the central newspaper *Pravda*. As proof of his identity, Lenin presented to the notary the only *legal* document that had by some miracle been preserved: a certificate of the Council of Lawyers of the district of the Leningrad Judicial Chamber of 1892 describing him as a lawyer's assistant. At the time, I did not know that Lenin was a lawyer, and I was somewhat surprised reading this certificate. I had noticed little juristic about Vladimir Ilich up to that time! Right up to, and even after, the October Revolution he did not look very kindly upon jurisprudence and lawyers. In this respect he had much in common with Marx. In fact, there was so little of the lawyer in him that even later—though careful and masterful at editing decrees, and enjoying a phenomenal memory—he displayed neither memory nor understanding of purely "legal" matters. In summer 1918, having seen the book by Comrade Goikhbarg which came out (at that time) about our civil law, Lenin therefore leafed through it with great interest as a Soviet novelty. At once he proposed publishing it in Germany, *in German*, for propagandistic purposes—he joyfully noted that we even have a *decree on divorce*. I answered, "Vladimir Ilich, don't you remember that you yourself edited the decree on divorce at the session and then signed it?" It must be said that Vladimir Ilich always in fact carefully read that which he signed. "I sign quite a few decrees," noted Vladimir Ilich with his usual smile, "Am I supposed to remember all of them?"[1] It should be noted that he then took as lively an interest in the draft of the decree on divorce as in the one on the emancipation of women. I often reported to him that I was receiving five or six written or telegraphic inquiries daily on the outcome of this project.

But it would be a great mistake to think that Vladimir Ilich was generally indifferent toward *revolutionary decrees and laws*. Indeed, I would rather say

---

"Lenin i revoliutsionny dekret," *Revoliutsiia prava*, Sbornik I, 1925, pp. 33–39.

that he had (at the first period of our power) an *excessive belief* in decree; he castigated severely every condescending attitude to decrees of the new authority with his favorite saying (in the first epoch of Soviet power) about our not knowing how to think in a governmental manner. I am afraid that even in his last period Vladimir Ilich did not read very joyfully, if it appeared in front of him, the advice that a judge "does not have *the right* to apply the existing norm (of the revolutionary) decree" but must preferably be guided by "*the general bases* of Soviet legislation" or the "general *policy* of the Workers' and Peasants' government." He probably would have made his usual gesture, stroking the back of his head. Vladimir Ilich was an enthusiastic supporter of our draft decree (No. 1) on the Court. Essentially, the decree had only two provisions: (1) eliminate the old court and (2) repeal all the old laws. At the time, while some comrades were doubtful, or even directly negative about the draft, the People's Commissariat of Justice was appraised by Vladimir Ilich as the "most revolutionary People's Commissariat," and this was largely because of that draft. But even he was obviously disturbed by one objection: that we did not have enough new laws for the People's Court from the workers. As is well known, we introduced the formulation (see the original draft in the materials of the People's Commissariat of Justice, II, p. 104):

> [L]ocal workers' and peasants' revolutionary courts are approved, guided in their decisions and sentences not by the written laws of overthrown governments, but by the *decrees* of the Council of People's Commissars, revolutionary conscience, and revolutionary legal consciousness.

In order to speed and facilitate the passage of the decree, Vladimir Ilich agreed to release it solely through the Council of People's Commissars rather than the Central Executive Committee where, although it would have been adopted, it would probably have met fervent opposition from the "coalition parties" of Left Socialist Revolutionaries and partly from the "Internationalists." The draft was passed in the Council of People's Commissars, because Comrade Lunacharskii turned from a skeptic into its enthusiastic defender in the name of revolutionary legal consciousness, thereby confirming that this concept came to us from Petrazhitskii (see his article in *Pravda*).

Vladimir Ilich disliked a phrase with no concrete content. He was attracted neither by "revolutionary conscience" nor "revolutionary legal consciousness." But when other comrades were trying to soften the words in the decree on "the burning of old laws," Vladimir Ilich brilliantly found a revolutionary and fully concrete solution:[2] he proposed to add to the article a note that all laws are recognized as repealed that contradict the decrees of the new government and also the programs—minimum of the victorious parties, the Social Democrats and Socialist Revolutionaries. This note was included in the decree, and caused a misunderstanding even among the "Marxist Internationalists" who were then semi-friendly to us. Only recently an anonymous article was published here; it was written by Engels and Kautsky in *Neue Zeit* of 1887, which then was unknown to us and probably also to Lenin. In this article we read the same thought:

> This is not to say, of course, that socialists will fail to present certain legalistic demands. An active socialist party is inconceivable without such demands, or any political party at all, in fact. The demands emerging from the common interests of a class can only be realized when that class gains political power and can give its demands universal validity in the form of legislation. Every struggling class must therefore formulate its demands as legalistic demands within a program. [Engels and Kautsky 1887: p. 219]

If we are correctly to understand Lenin's attitude to the revolutionary decree, we must therefore recall his attitude to the Party program. It is well known that Lenin saw the program both as agitational and organizational material to attract, unite, and organize the masses, and as the program of the *future* government— every serious political party must be ready at the necessary moment to seize power. "Dispute tactics, but let's have clear slogans." "Clear answers that do not allow two interpretations, answers to concrete questions about our political conduct." I know of no politician who, before seizing power, placed stronger emphasis on the concrete formulation of the program than Lenin. But he viewed the program from the position of the revolutionary dialectic. The outmoded parts of the program lost their significance for him; mercilessly and sincerely he discarded them. He formulated this position boldly in his article on the new Party program in the fall of 1917:

> We do not know if our victory will come tomorrow or a little later (I personally am inclined to think that it will be tomorrow). . . .

> We do not know and cannot know anything of this. No one is in a position to know. It is therefore ridiculous to discard the minimum program, which is indispensable while we still live within the framework of bourgeois society, while we have not yet destroyed that framework, not yet realized the basic prerequisites for a transition to socialism, not yet smashed the enemy (the bourgeoisie), and even if we have smashed them we have not yet annihilated them. All this will come, and perhaps much sooner than many people think (I personally think that it will begin tomorrow), but it has not yet come.

> Take the minimum program in the political sphere. This program is limited to the bourgeois republic. We add that we do not confine ourselves to its limits, we start immediately upon a struggle for a higher type of republic, a Soviet Republic. This we must do. With unshakable courage and determination we must advance

toward the new republic and in this way we shall reach our goal, of that I am sure. But the minimum program should under no circumstances be discarded, for, first of all, there is as yet no Soviet Republic; second, "attempts at restoration" are not out of the question, and they will first have to be experienced and vanquished; third, during the transition from the old to the new there may be temporary "combined types" (as *Rabochii Put'* correctly pointed out a day or two ago)—for instance, a Soviet Republic together with a Constituent Assembly. Let us first get over all that—then it will be time to discard the minimum program. [Lenin, 1917a: pp. 171-72]

Indeed, even on March 8, 1918, Lenin warns:

not in any way (to) reject the use of bourgeois parliamentarianism. It is a utopia to think we shall not be thrown back. . . . We say that if ever we are thrown back, while not rejecting—the use of bourgeois parliamentarism—if hostile class forces drive us to that old position—we shall aim at what has been gained by experience, at Soviet power. [Lenin 1918a: p. 137]

Here is a model of the revolutionary dialectic, a model that our revolutionary jurists should utilize for decree, statute, and code. Lenin himself—perhaps without his noticing—consistently brought this dialectic to life with respect to the decree. He insisted strictly on the program of his Party, and he demanded respect and execution with respect to his revolutionary decree. He proclaimed "the first task of every party of the future is to convince *the majority of the people* that *its program* [emphasis P.S.] and tactics, are correct" [Lenin 1918: p. 241]—and, having taken power he set the same task for the revolutionary decree and revolutionary soviet administration. When the "left" opposition of the party ridiculed his decree on railroads, Lenin answered seriously: "*Give us your draft of the decree*, for you are citizens of the Soviet Republic, members of soviet institutions. Try to give us your draft of the decree." In other words, the ruling Party speaks in the language not of declarations, but of decrees: "The recent *decrees* on the measures taken by the Soviet government show us that this is the path for the proletarian dictatorship . . ." [Lenin 1918e: p. 432]. "If there will be a fight on the question of the distribution of bread among the hungry, then we will go to that struggle with *bold decree*," but in the decree rates must be set so that ninety percent of the peasants will be with us. This means that the decree must convince the masses. And when a constitution was approved which gave only "what had been won and written down," then Lenin declared directly: "Now that the Constitution has been endorsed and is being put into effect, an *easier period* [emphasis P.S.] in our state affairs is beginning" [Lenin 1918b: p. 37].

When we were determining our *political plans and publishing our decrees* [emphasis P.S.] . . . it was clear to us we were coming up against the most decisive and fundamental issue of the whole revolution, the most decisive and fundamental issue, the issue of power—whether power would remain in the hands of the workers; whether they could gain the support of all the poor peasants. . . . [Lenin 1918d: p. 27]

You can see the role that Lenin allots everywhere to decree.

But Lenin demanded both unconditional respect to this language of decrees by the agencies of power, and also the broad popularization of published decrees among the masses. In *Decree on the Exact Observance of Laws*, initiated by Lenin at the Sixth All-Russian Extraordinary Congress of Soviets, we read:

> During a year of revolutionary struggle the working class of Russia has developed the fundamentals of the laws of the RSFSR, the *exact observance* of which is *necessary* for the further development and strengthening of the authority of the workers and peasants of Russia. On the other hand, the unceasing attempts at counterrevolutionary plots and war . . . make in certain instances inevitable the taking of extreme measures not foreseen in the legislation in force or deviating from this legislation. On this basis the All-Russia Extraordinary Sixth Congress has decreed: (1) *to call all citizens* of the Republic, *all agencies and all officials* of Soviet authority to the *strictest observance of the laws* of the RSFSR promulgated and to be promulgated by central authority. [S"ezdy, 1959: p. 93]

On the other hand, all can still remember how Lenin struggled for broad accessibility of promulgated decrees for the masses. From the constitution he demanded specificity—for instance, listing the items of jurisdiction of the Congress of Soviets and the All-Russia Central Executive Committee (in Art. 49), and he enacted a decree to the effect that the Constitution must be prominently displayed in all Soviet institutions, and that the study of it be introduced in all schools and educational institutions of the Republic. Nadezhda Konstantinovna Krupskaia introduced a draft in the Council of People's Commissars on the popularization of decrees and their distribution in the countryside. From Lenin's keen interest in this particular project, all knew clearly that his thought was working steadily in the same direction. He not only demanded strict fulfillment of decrees, but himself believed in his own decrees and their *persuasiveness*.

Perhaps he sometimes became too involved with a decree. For example, when the Left Socialist Revolutionaries, having taken over the administration of the People's Commissariat of Justice, delegated the compilation of the criminal code to their "learned" member of the board, Shreider, even Lenin teased us Bolsheviks that the Social Revolutionary specialists were apparently accomplishing something. And it became necessary to select the especially absurd articles from this excuse for a code (the draft of which, at the time of the withdrawal of the Socialist Revolutionaries from the People's Commisssariat, had already even been printed for distribution to the members of the All-Russia Central Executive

Committee) to convince Lenin of the total unsuitability of the draft. This draft was a reworking of the old Tsarist Code, and *in places even* aggravated the position, for example, of the workers.

The first period of so-called War Communism ended, and the period of the New Economic Policy, with its codes, arrived. Lenin firmly repudiated those decrees unconnected with the new policy, and signed the new codes. It is most interesting to read how he now characterizes the decrees of the first period.

> At one time we needed declarations, statements, manifestos, and decrees. We have had enough of them. At one time we needed them to show the people how and what we wanted to build, what new and hitherto unseen things we were striving for. But can we go on showing the people what we want to build? No. Even an ordinary laborer will begin to sneer at us and say: "What use is it to keep on showing us what you want to build? Show us that you can build. If you can't build, we're not with you, and you can go to hell!" And he will be right. (October 17, 1921) [Lenin 1921: p. 73]

About political laws remaining in force, Lenin said in the same passage:

> Soviet laws are very good laws, because they give everyone an opportunity to combat bureaucracy and red tape, an opportunity the workers and peasants in any capitalist state do not have. But does anybody take advantage of this? Hardly anybody! Not only the peasants, but an enormous percentage of the Communists do not know how to utilize Soviet laws to combat red tape and bureaucracy, or such a truly Russian phenomenon as bribery. What hinders the fight against this? Our laws? Our propaganda? On the contrary! We have any number of laws! Why then have we achieved no success in this struggle? Because it cannot be waged by propaganda alone. It can be done if the masses of the people help. [Lenin 1921: p. 75]

In his speech (of March 27, 1922) at the Eleventh Congress of the Party Lenin said:

> Passing laws, passing better decrees, etc., is not now the main object of our attention. There was a time when the passing of decrees was a form of propaganda. People used to laugh at us and say that the Bolsheviks do not realize that their decrees are not being carried out; the entire whiteguard press was full of jeers on that score. But at that period this passing of decrees was quite justified. We Bolsheviks had just taken power, and we said to the peasant, to the worker: "Here is a decree; this is how we would like to have the state administered. Try it!" From the very outset we gave the ordinary workers and peasants an idea of our policy in the form of decrees. The result was the enormous confidence we enjoyed and now enjoy among the masses of the people. This was an essential

period at the beginning of the revolution; without it we should not have risen on the crest of the revolutionary wave; we should have wallowed in its trough. Without it we should not have won the confidence of all the workers and peasants who wanted to build their lives on new lines. But this period passed, and we refuse to understand this. [Lenin 1922c: pp. 303–4]

The new codes have another nature. In the All-Russia Central Executive Committee, in the report on the adopted codes, Lenin stated: " . . . here we have tried to maintain the dividing line between what can satisfy the ordinary citizen's legitimate needs in present-day economic conditions, and what is abuse of the NEP—the things that are legal in all other countries, but which we do not want to legalize" [Lenin 1922: p. 393]. "But," adds Lenin:

> [W]e shall leave ourselves a perfectly free hand in this matter. If everyday experience reveals abuses which we have not foreseen, we shall forthwith introduce the necessary amendments. As far as this is concerned, you are all well aware, of course, that, unfortunately, no other country can as yet vie with us in the speed with which we legislate. [Lenin 1922: p. 393]

But how can Lenin's views on decree, law, and legality be reconciled with his own definition of dictatorship as authority unrestricted by any laws? Most of all, this means that the dictatorship of the working class *is not limited by the laws of another class*. It casts them off at once. For itself it issues laws—obligatory programs—but even there, in *exceptional* cases, *extraordinary measures* are allowed in the struggle with the counterrevolution. It is well known that with the start of the new period, Lenin wanted to transfer the center of gravity from the Cheka to the Procuracy. From Lenin's notes published by Comrade Kurskii in the preamble to the minutes of the Congress of Workers of Soviet Justice of 1924, it is apparent what significance he gave to the conduct of his new legality. Here he obliged the Procuracy to "ensure the establishment of a really uniform understanding of legality in the whole republic, regardless of any local differences or of any conflicting local influences."

As examples, I quoted here some short citations, refraining from personal reminiscences as an inappropriate source for evaluation. My purpose was to show Lenin's flexible yet firm approach to legality in the present period. For him this derived from his preparatory work for the Party, which he in his thoughts was already preparing for the future role of the ruling party, of the dictatorship of the proletariat in union with the peasantry, but under the hegemony of the working class. The program is decree, the Party is authority. This was then the perspective of his thought.

I think that this short note will help to clarify what is at first incomprehensible—Lenin's hostility to the lawyer in general while at the same time as a lawyer using all the legal methods of the given period for the defense of the oppressed, whether these methods be from Parliament or even from the Tsarist court (see the article by Comrade Pashukanis). The whole matter consists of the dialectic or, more accurately, of Lenin's revolutionary dialectic—the direct opposite of that formal logic which holds in its tongs the entire legal world of bourgeois society and its vestiges.

Notes

1. Recall that later Lenin also said (March 30, 1920) [Lenin 1920] "I cannot remember even one tenth of the decrees that we are carrying out."

2. Later, Lenin proudly declared: "Let them shout that we, without reforming the old court, immediately scrapped it. By that we cleared the way for a real people's court and not so much by the force of repressive measures as by massive example, the authority of the working people, without formalities; we transformed the court from an instrument of exploitation into an instrument of education on the firm foundation of socialist society. There is no doubt whatever that we cannot attain such a society at once" [Lenin 1918c: p. 464].

8. Bourgeois Law

This concept has several meanings. On the one hand, it is what is now called civil law (*bürgerliches Recht*) in general or, more accurately, it is a division of *the law of obligations* as embracing so-called civil commerce (the contractual exchange of the products of labor) on the basis of the right of private ownership to the means of production (the contractual exchange of commodities). Bourgeois law is also understood in a broader sense as the totality of all legal relations and norms in contrast to Soviet law on the one hand, and feudal or natural-economy law on the other. As is well known, in the "Critique of the Gotha Program," Marx noted that bourgeois law is the "application of a like scale to different people who in fact are not identical, not equal to one another" [Marx, 1875, p. 18], and that it *continues even into the first phase of communism*. Other than those of bourgeois law there are no other norms. We see that life, in our revolution, has somewhat departed from Marx's latter view, because under the extreme length of the transitional period, there has naturally been formed a special *Soviet* law for the transitional period. This obviously contains elements of bourgeois law, but in essence it introduces profound changes in principle into all social relations, including law. It would be most interesting to follow from the Marxist perspective the genesis (the course of development) of the bourgeois revolution in the area of law in the sense of a system of concrete relations. Regrettably, we still have no such work, and no such work on legal ideology. To do these studies at this time is beyond our capabilities. Like every revolution, the bourgeois revolution started with destruction. "From the external side it seemed that liberalism only *destroyed*: it destroyed the superseded feudal and municipal economies and did not create a new one, but *it cleared the way* for truly national economic forms" (Bucher).

In the course of five months (in 1789) France was dotted with the ruins of the old organization and the attempts at the new. All the principles of the new regime

---

"Burzhuaznoe pravo," *Entsiklopediia gosudarstva i prava* [Encyclopedia of State and Law] (Moscow, 3 vols., 1925–27, 1:296–99.

were proclaimed. By the force of things *destruction went faster* than organization, and *disorganization (désordre) embraced the masses.* [Laferriere]

But of what did the newly proclaimed principles consist? We find them in *The
Declaration of Rights.* "The right of ownership is a right belonging to *every*
citizen, *at his discretion* to use and dispose of his *property,* his incomes and the
fruits of his labor and his industry" (1793). This formula contains in brief Marx's
view of the basis of the whole bourgeois revolution:

> The perfected political state is by its nature the species-life of man in opposi-
> tion to his material life. All the presuppositions of this egoistic life continue to
> exist in civil society outside the sphere of the state, but as proper to civil society.
> When the political state has achieved its true completion, man leads a double life,
> a heavenly one and an earthly one. . . . He has a life both in the political
> community, where he is valued as a communal being, and in civil society where
> he is active as a private individual. . . . [Marx 1843, pp. 93–96]

What do these words mean in legal language? First, there is a gulf between state
organization and the organization of production and exchange, i.e., between
public (state) and private law. Second, there is an atomization of civil society by
the assignment in the civil code of the main emphasis on the human personality in
the abstract-legal sense, where an attempt is made to declare everything economic
as irrelevant and legally indifferent.

This dualism, which consistently moves through the whole life of bourgeois
society, is very clear in bourgeois law. Under this law anyone may deal at his own
discretion with his own property, subject only to the condition that he owns it.
Suppose he owns no property? Well, then he owns "labor" (manpower) and may
also at his discretion use its fruits. What does this mean? This is deciphered in the
Declaration of Rights of the third year of the revolution with the words "his
personality (that of a man) is inalienable property," but "every man may rent out
his time (we know from Marx that in capitalist society time is the measure or
weight of the commodity—manpower) and his services."

The apex of this universal bourgeois dualism is the division even of his world
view: "to materialism in production—the base; and to idealism in consciousness—the superstructure. We would characterize this as "*objectified hypocrisy.*"
In fact, the bourgeoisie, as the third estate, abolished the estate order in order to
replace the estate division with a purely class division of mankind. In its revolution the bourgeoisie thought it was the liberator of *all mankind*; however, it
liberated only an insignificant minority while [creating] enslavement of a new
type with respect to the overwhelming majority. At first, this hypocrisy was
unconscious, but the bourgeoisie continues to speak in the name of "liberty,
equality, and fraternity," or "democracy," when it has become clearly class
conscious so that now it has become consciously hypocritical. It *is unable not to*

continue this hypocrisy. This is why the hypocritical law and hypocritical legality about which it had dreamed, and which it created with such enthusiasm, has been finally turned into a fetish *ruling over the bourgeoisie itself.* This is repeated in production, where equipment, the machine, the product of the hand of man, *rules* over man.

In general, one can create a brief distinguishing outline of the condition of classes: in feudal society, the role of any class itself and of the groups belonging to it is provided for by *law.* This class is an estate, and means of production *may belong* only to persons of a certain class; in *bourgeois society* both membership in a class and the right of ownership of means of production are a private affair of each person *(Privatsache)*, a question of fact. Finally, the *victory of the proletariat* declares a monopoly of *ownership of the workers and peasants state* (in time, of all society) of the means of production, *with exceptions* specially allowed (e.g., the use of small-scale production, under the laws of the New Economic Policy, etc.).

This means that bourgeois law, as the class law of the period of the flourishing of capitalism, is like every law in that it supports and protects the basic interest of the class, here the capitalist class, changing, of course, in proportion to change in capitalism itself. Of what does this basic interest consist?

In the age of predominance of *mercantile* capital, this is the *exchange interest.* The law of obligations, the law of exchange of commodities, places over things the ''idea of equivalence,'' of formal equality over the ''idea of domination.'' Mercantile capital changes into industrial capital, undermining agricultural and domestic (craft) production, and leads to the industrial separation of the city from the countryside. Money economy also replaces ''feudal property and subordinates it to the conditions of capitalist production.'' (Marx). The Great French Revolution placed this capitalist property at the basis of its *Declaration of Rights.* ''The bourgeois law of capitalist property is identical to estate law—in terms of the means of production, and commodities in general, with everything simultaneously being declared a commodity.'' After the monopoly right to land of the nobility, ''the mobilization of land ownership'' turns *land into the most movable commodity,* as, for instance, in France. After this all of the law of obligations from the law of exchange of commodities is turned into a simple abstraction— ''the form of transfer (or title) of property.'' This means that bourgeois law—in the narrow sense of the word—is the law of obligations and the law of commodity exchange.

Since mercantile capital strives for centralization and unification, for identical conditions of exchange in general, it reflects the same striving in law. The law of commercial paper is everywhere the same, entails statutes common for all states and with the maximum unification on the international scale. After this comes civil law in general, where unity on the general European scale is based on the reception of Roman law. This means a *unity of statute,* of legal norm.

But the unity of the norm here means only the unity of form. The dualist bourgeois law does not recognize real subordination to norms. This real subordination to norms is related to the first phase of capitalism, to free agreement under the conditions of free competition, and in the monopoly phase of capitalism to the one-sided and individual dictation of these norms (for instance, of prices), rejecting freedom of contract, but preserving only economically compelled mass "adhesion," i.e., subordination to an offer.

Any bourgeois code (q.v.) confirms this characteristic, of course, allowing for the particular features of capitalist development in different countries.

9. Jurisprudence

The division of labor. . . manifests itself also in the ruling class as the division of mental and material labor, so that inside this class one part appears as the thinkers of the class (its active, conceptive ideologists, who make the perfecting of the illusion of the class about itself their chief source of livelihood), while the others' attitude to these ideas and illusions is more passive and receptive, because they are in reality the active members of this class and have less time to make up illusions and ideas about themselves. [Marx and Engels 1845, pp. 47–48]

The ruling-class thinkers of primitive society were priests. The clergy. In bourgeois society this role is occupied by lawyers, scholars of jurisprudence.

[I]n the seventeenth century the new world view made its debut—the world view that was to become the classical one for the bourgeoisie, namely, the juridical world view.

This was the secularization of theology. Human justice replaced divine law, or God's justice; the state assumed the role of the church. Economic and social circumstances, formerly sanctioned by the church and thus believed to have been established by the church and its dogma, were now regulated by the state and held to be based on equity. [Engels and Kautsky 1887, p. 204]

Engels depicted remarkably well in 1887 the role of lawyers and juridical specialists in bourgeois society. Today, statistical data on the composition of any parliament confirm this characterization. For example, in France 300 of 745 deputies were lawyers in 1908. This special estate of jurists literally *develops law* for the bourgeoisie, understandable only to the jurists. Afterward, this estate of jurists becomes an intermediary between law (more accurately "the

---

"Pravovedenie," *Entsiklopediia gosudarstva i prava* [Encyclopedia of State and Law] (Moscow, 3 vols., 1925–27), 3:431–39.

code of laws'') and other mortals.

In ancient Rome jurists play such an important role in the life of the state, and their jurisprudence was called ''the knowledge of the affairs of God and man, the science of law and justice.'' In bourgeois society this science is presented in universities as a special preparation for state administration. But bourgeois legal science limps along on all four feet. Its serious representatives express doubt— ''can it be a science at all?'' The well-known Windscheid cleverly and accurately called it ''a handmaiden, but with the crown of a monarch on its head.'' It could not be scientific until it adopted the class perspective (even if of the ruling class). However, it could not do this. To introduce the class (revolutionary) perspective into the science of law it would have ''justified'' the proletarian revolution, and would have declared it to be legal and proper. Only when the proletarian revolution is victorious does the bourgeoisie also adopt a ''revolutionary'' (i.e., for us— counterrevolutionary) perspective. Only then do they begin to speak openly of their class law.

I will not linger on Roman jurisprudence, even though it had interesting stages of development, from priests of the church turned into priests of the secular, i.e., the first special estate of jurists. In the twelfth century, Roman law, by reception, became the law in force for all of feudal Europe. The Roman civil priests, the ''doctors of law,'' were also resurrected, bringing their class law in the interests of the ruling classes to the point that the revolutionary peasants (of the peasant wars of the sixteenth century) termed them fleecers and bandits, and pursued them with sticks. As a new part of the propertied class, the bourgeoisie was gradually growing in the new society; with the bourgeoisie, as a parallel ruling class of the cities, its theory of law was also created. Interestingly, this begins with a complete break between the theory and practice of positive law and the philosophy of law. Natural law as a philosophy—the theoretical program of the rising class—is entirely in the hands of non-jurists. It shares interesting leaps forward with emergent capitalism: from Italy (Thomas Aquinas—thirteenth century) to Holland (Hugo Grotius—sixteenth century), England (Hobbes, Locke), and France (Rousseau) where, with the victory of the bourgeois revolution, *a union of theory and practice* was achieved: the ''philosophy'' of natural law was turned into the ''declaration'' of the positive ''rights of man and citizen.'' Natural law (q.v.) disappears. But the duality continues to exist in positive law itself, in its hypocrisy. Certain echoes of natural law still are transferred into the philosophy of the backward revolution in Germany—in the dualist Kant and the dialectic idealist-monist Hegel. In the atmosphere of revolution, for a time Hegel interests some of the bourgeois intelligentsia. ''But this cleavage (between the intelligentsia and the remaining part of the class—P.S.) in the case of a practical collision, in which the class itself is endangered, automatically comes to nothing'' [Marx and Engels 1845, p. 48]. It was necessary for the proletariat to arise, for Marx's revolutionary conclusions drawn from Hegel's dialectic for the revolutionism of this Hegelian intelligentsia to disappear. Natural law, and its school of jurisprudence was buried forever. The place of the revolutionary school of natural law is occupied by the counterrevolutionary *historical school* (q.v.)—Hugo, Savigny, Puchta—"trying to legalize the meanness of today by the meanness of yesterday" (Marx). To them, law consists of a statement of the "national will" and in its slow development. This school introduced a valuable contribution of legal material into the science of law: popular customs, historical materials, etc. It paved the way for a scientific approach to law. The historical school supplied both our Slavophiles and other bourgeois nationalists with its scientific baggage.

Freed from the romanticism of the historical school and its "national spirit," the bourgeoisie turned to its own self. The "normal Philistine" who ruled in its political economy was transplanted also to law in the form of various *psychological* schools, among which should also be counted the so-called sociological school. This latter declared sociology to be the science *of man* as a member of society, i.e., of the same "normal Philistine." The psychology of the normal bourgeois, his ideology or will, makes law. Membership in one or another stratum of the bourgeoisie gives certain shades of emphasis to all these theories, mainly the petty bourgeoisie, for the purely bourgeois jurists discard the *science* of law entirely and prefer its *technique* (legislative and law application).

Frightened by the ghosts of its own revolution already turned into a counter-revolution, bourgeois law produced the most trivial of all the legal philosophers—Jeremy Bentham (1748–1832). All these alchemists of law searching for the magic formula for their justice were inspired by Bentham. Marx called him "the genius of bourgeois stupidity." His "higher principle for human life is the utilitarian principle," i.e., "the striving toward pleasure and the avoidance of pain." "The greatest *possible* sum of happiness for the greatest *possible* number of people." "The interest of the individual is at the same time also the social interest," etc. Bentham left an endless number of books. He enjoyed a certain popularity among us until the very day of the revolution. During the decade before the war, probably only the German Professor Stammler successfully competed with Bentham—Stammler, famous for his deepening and correction of Marx. This was something in the nature of "idealistic materialism" in law.

Before 1905 we had developed our own "natural law" in a Russian form, to the "intuitive law" of the psychologist, Constitutional Democrat, Professor Petrazhitskii. His great talent won him bourgeois popularity both in Russia and beyond its boundaries, because he knew how to find a formula for the bourgeois revolutionary slogan that would pass the censor, "intuitive, i.e., internal legality." When he formulated his idea of law as the "idea of love between people," he, so to speak, exceeded the Viennese psychologist Freud (compare his "libido"), who was popular not merely among us.

In Germany, with the flourishing of the Bismarkian era, a fresh stream arose for the moment—daring thought in the person of Professor Jhering, who proclaimed his *"struggle for law"* and his theory of *"protected interest,"* but not class struggle nor theory of protected *class* interest. Stopping halfway, even Jhering reaches the same blind alley of teleology and volitional theory. Even Muromstev—the daring scholar and follower of Jhering—cannot lead the theory of interest out of this blind alley. Even he, having discarded the volitional approach and teleology, stops before the spectre of class struggle, saving himself in eclectics. He left the circle of legal theorists and went into politics and by no accident, later became a Constitutional Democrat representative in the State Duma.

The first wave of "socialist" legal theory of law arises in the petty bourgeois movement of "juridical socialists," as Engels termed them. The greatest and most interesting representative of this movement was the Viennese Professor Anton Menger. This theory of peaceful, *legal* growth into a new—socialist—society embraces social democracy of the entire world in the area of law. However, Anton Menger is more interesting than his followers, particularly if they are Social Democrats. Menger did not even deny instances of revolutionary development of law (for instance, the reception of Roman law in all Europe, the borrowing of English law of the state, etc.) and, most importantly, he did not hide his bourgeois form of thought.

An interesting criticism of bourgeois law was given by the petty bourgeois anarchist, Professor Gumplowicz, but it did not develop into a special school, and the militant Gumplowicz himself became stuck in the same conciliatory tendencies. The various sociological schools in law also provided nothing interesting. It is true that their approach became interesting, but all of them, Ehrlich and others, stopped in disbelief of lack of understanding before the class nature of law, and were stuck in fruitless economism.

The teaching of the natural law philosophers and the abstract formulas of the revolutionary positive law of the bourgeoisie—its principles of equality, legal freedom of contract, free subject of law, etc.—merely reflected the principle of equivalence in the exchange of commodities as the universal social relation. As society moved from simple commodity production to capitalist exploitation as the leading mode of production, and especially to the stage of monopoly capitalism and imperialism, the contradiction between freedom of contract and freedom of the individual in economic activity was more and more revealed. "The merchant buys only to sell *more dearly*," but the monopoly capitalist is guided not by the principle of freedom and equivalence but by the principle of dictation (at the expense of another class) of the conditions of the distribution of the production of labor, not equalization (*Gleichmacherei*) but superprofit *(Plusmacherei)*. This is why even the bourgeois theory of law, however conservative it was, slowly submitted to economic influences. Especially in France toward the end of the nineteenth and the start of the twentieth centuries, protests were raised against the clearly obsolete theories of the French Revolution. The search began for new principles to reconcile law with economic reality. First, we have the theory of Duguit (q.v.) on social functions. Duguit terms *metaphysical* the theory of free will of the subject of law and freedom of contract; however, he terms both his theory of law and of the state realist, for he derives it from the *fact* of existence of law and the state. The old theory, in the words of Duguit "at a certain time" "of the individualist state" (read: simple commodity exchange) corresponded to fact. Now this is no longer true. The social division of labor (read: the division into classes) creates social interdependence (solidarity). "Man does not have the right to be free." Now freedom consists of an obligation, "to fulfill one's social function," for by virtue of the principle of solidarity "each individual must fulfill some function in society." The existence of classes is a fact that Duguit does not consider it his right to criticize. "The owner has the obligation and also the power"; to this sacred function of the owner corresponds the sacred function of the unpropertied, of the worker. The exploitation of the worker is the right of the capitalist, for this is a fact. Comrade Goikhbarg, the person among us who chose this theory, overlooked its basis in monopoly capitalism, with its striving to establish capitalist planning of the economy, and found in it socialism. Even now, Duguit has great influence on legal theorists, particularly in our country.

Another French group of jurists headed by Saleilles, Geny, and others, can be put in the same category of legal theorists of the period of monopoly capitalism with their theory of adhesion to a contract compulsorily dictated by the other side. They are less known here than Duguit, who, despite the close kinship of these theories, polemicizes with them.

Finally, to the same period of monopoly capitalism corresponds also the theory headed in the opposite direction, *not toward a reconciliation with economics but toward a full break with it.* This theory denies that economic or social relations have any significance for law. This is a school and schools (for here there are as many schools as authors) *of normativists* (cf. Normativism). Their task is to *purge* law of all *nonlegal* (historical, social, legal policy) admixtures, to turn it into a science of "pure paragraphs" (of articles of the law). This must be a "pure science of law;" it must limit itself to a "purely normative approach" to the area of the *obligatory*, discarding all life and all *purpose* (Kelsen). This in a certain sense is a legal "law by the article" (or paragraph) Robinson Crusoe adventure. Among other authors this theory is turned into pure legal mathematics. All this, brought to an extreme, to an absurd belief in *law*, in law in which we must be interested only in the technique of form and not in the content, goal, or base.

A second wave of social-law reconciliation began with the revolutionary era of 1918. The mixture of the theory of social functions, the attempt at state war "socialism" of the West and the conscious social deception—such are the illusions that at the start of the world revolution began to "envelop as illusions" of the current moment for the capitalist class. In Germany we find a number of people (the most important of them—Hedemann) who cloaked in socialist khaki all the exploiting military-economic measures of imperialist Germany. These are the old songs of the socialist jurists, from which now, with the onset of and in proportion to the advance of the fascist period, all of them try to separate themselves under various noble and ignoble pretexts. It is most likely that they will find a way to their direct opposite, to the pure normativists. It is no accident that a real cry is now being raised *about the growing popularity of Kelsen*. It is possible that Kelsen will become the Bentham of the twentieth century.

Legal theory was first turned into a science by the 1917 October Revolution. First life, then theory. All the laws of the old regime were burned in the literal sense of the word. Life posed the question of the eternal nature and eternal life of law and it definitely was decided *negatively*. The *idea of class law* was raised and strengthened. A new science of class law appeared. This was a true *Bolsheviza-tion* of law, but about this, see "Soviet Law." It still remains to say a few words on the "Bolshevization" of bourgeois law in the reactionary sense. The bourgeoisie began to learn from the "Bolsheviks." This must particularly be noted in the person of the leaders of the Italian Fascists (Mussolini and others) who copied not only the methods of state administration but also criminal law, etc. But, of course, this mimicry became a caricature in the absence of the power of the working people. A government of an insignificant minority cannot simply adopt the methods of a huge majority of the working people. Its failure both theoretically and practically is unavoidable. Even in the theory of bourgeois legal scholars an emphasis on the class nature of bourgeois law can be found. However, this assumes the form of cynical honesty by a small handful of the counterrevolutionary minority. All these tendencies first appear in politics and in the theory of the state, but from the state to law is just one step.

We also established the class perspective on law and thereby gave law an independent place among the sciences. But Soviet law is just being developed by life; we still lag behind life. In the field of theory, we have been unable to free ourselves from the fetters of law and the law of the bourgeoisie. Our attempts to create communist legal universities, our own Soviet law schools in state universities depend upon lecturers and teachers in the majority noncommunist, or persons who at least have not freed themselves from the bourgeois legal outlook. Positive results are not yet apparent although, of course, youth itself knows how to develop its world view as the young bourgeoisie did in its time, developing its new understanding of law under the teachers of an outmoded world.

In the Section of the Theory of Law and the State of the Communist Academy, in the Institute of Soviet Law, in the latter's and its journal, a small nucleus of communists are at work. Finally, a large army of practical jurists is distributed throughout the whole department administering justice, but they are too occupied with practical work and self-preparation. When all these forces are connected with the new law—as a real science of law and a Soviet class law—then a force will be formed that can bravely go into battle with the old bourgeois (legal) viewpoint in the area of law. The Section of Law and the State of the Communist Academy declares:

First, we combine the *revolutionary-dialectic* method both in scientific and in practical work in law method in direct contradiction to metaphysical, formal-dogmatic method and finally at best, the historical-evolutionary method of bourgeois jurisprudence. Second, this means *a class approach* to the study of state and law, because we consider that these phenomena are rooted in the material conditions of social life and develop in the process of class struggle. Finally, *as materialists*, in the study of state and law we proceed from material social relations to draw therefrom an understanding of the ideas and concepts of the people in their interrelationships.

10. The State

"Political literature provides a multitude of different definitions of the state but none that is generally accepted" (Korkunov). This is the conclusion of almost all the theorists of the bourgeois science of the state. Given the fact that in these disputes there are disagreements about the *internal nature* of the state, and about its *foundation and ultimate goal*, and that there is no agreement about the *external formulation* and statement of the definitive basic concept, a conclusion can only be drawn "about the depth of the existing disagreement" (Gierke). Others go still further and state directly that the "basic and most general concepts of this science, perhaps, *will always be outside the area of our full understanding*" (Lehning). For the Frenchman P. Leroy-Beaulieu "the view of contemporaries on the state, its nature, and role seems exceedingly confused"; "their thoughts on these questions are lost in a fog." But after this, these critics give new definitions no less confused and foggy. At the same time as the state seems to be something most concrete (recall the words of Louis XIV: *"L'Etat c'est moi"*) to some, and somewhat concrete, but endowed with supernatural force ("the all-powerful state") to others (e.g., Petrazhitskii), it is "merely a particular abstraction unseen by anyone, which people thought up and called the state and to which they demand obedience, while in reality it is a "simple mental experience."

Why are all the theories of the state so different? The non-Marxist Franz Oppenheimer has cleverly answered:

> Because they all are *class theories*, which are needed not for the discovery of truth, but as weapons in the struggle of material interests . . . and this is why we, from the concept of the state, can understand the nature of theories of the state, but never from theories of the state, the nature of the state. [Oppenheimer 1919, pp. 7–8]

"Gosudarstvo," *Entsiklopediia gosudarstva i prava* [Encyclopedia of State and Law] (Moscow, 3 vols., 1925–27), 1:655.

But Oppenheimer, as a typical representative of the ideologues of the capitalist bourgeoisie, did not stray far from his colleagues. He, too, did not decide to embrace the class perspective bravely and openly. For him, of course, the semi-anarchist intellectual Gumplowicz was higher and nearer [to the question at hand] than Marx's revolutionary dialectic theory. The absurd dualism, contrasting political and economic "means" was closer to him than Marx's monism.

Marx's and Engels's *revolutionary-class perspective* on the state was at the heart of revolutionary Marxism. In the *Manifesto of the Communist Party* the conquest of political (state) power was defined as a *means*—the only means—*for liberation* (i.e., economic liberation) of the *workers*. Leninism formulated this thought more concretely (q.v.) under conditions of the worldwide revolution, and it implemented it in one of the great powers. The revolutionary-class perspective on the state fulfilled a militant role in the class struggle, and for the first time enabled a scientific definition, scientific criticism, and scientific understanding of the nature, origin, goal, and role of the state. We Marxists, defining the state in Marx's and Engels's words, say that *the state is a weapon in the hands of the ruling class for holding the oppressed classes in subordination.* In a society where power is in the hands of a minority class of exploiters (and before the [Paris] Commune and the power of the Soviets, the world knew no other state), the purpose of power is the exploitation of the oppressed masses. "The executive of the modern state is but a committee for managing the common affairs of the whole bourgeoisie" [Marx and Engels 1847–1848, pp. 110–11]. In the period of the proletarian dictatorship, this goal consists of the final suppression of the bourgeoisie, in aiding the achieving of a victorious end to all class struggle right up to the full elimination of social classes, to the foundation of classless socialist society, after which the state itself finally withers away.

The origin of the state

The question of the origin of the state in Marxist literature causes no disputes, and so I think I will deal with it here only briefly. Lenin's major work *State and Revolution* acquaints us with it and, of course, the basic work on this question is Engels's *The Origin of the Family, Private Property, and the State.* It was Engels who first considered this question from a Marxist perspective. He showed how the family, clan, etc. were formed and how the appearance of private property broke the economic equality of people. As long as the labor of man was so unproductive that it barely sufficed for the support of the life of the working person, there were no surpluses and reserves and, accordingly, there could be no exploitation of man by man. Once a product above the most necessary means of existence appeared, reserves were formed, and so appeared private property and the division of the clan into economically unequal people.

Engels writes:

The state is by no means a force binding society from outside. The state is the product of society at a certain stage of development; the state is a recognition that this society was lost in an insoluble contradiction with itself, was split into implacable opposites, which it was incapable of escaping. And so that these opposites, *classes* with contradictory economic interests, did not devour themselves and society in fruitless struggle. A force standing so to speak above society became necessary, a force which could moderate the conflict, and hold it within the bounds of order. And this force deriving from society but placing itself above it, more and more alienating itself from it, is the state. [Engels 1884, pp. 326–27]

Engels writes on ancient Athens:

In the meantime, however, the state had quietly developed. . . . First, it created a public power which was no longer simply identical with the armed people in its totality; secondly, it for the first time divided the people for public purposes, not according to kinship groups, but territorially, according to common domicile! [Engels 1884, p. 280]

This means, according to Engels, (1) "The state assumes *a particular social authority* separated from the whole mass of members constituting it" "with special armed guards" at its disposal, (2) "at the basis of the *new state structure*" were placed (a) *territorial division* and (b) "*property differences.*"

The origin of the state is explained here only in the most general terms; in fact, the possibilities were quite varied. In places, because its economic life within the clan became complex, the clan was compelled to transform itself into a state; in other cases, this transition was the result of internal and external wars between tribes or among tribes on the one hand, and the already emerging state, on the other. But even when the clans united in tribal clan-groups, so to speak, voluntarily turned to a state structure, the decisive role was always played by armed force on the one hand, and spiritual force (the caste of priests and religion, the church in general) on the other.

The class nature of every state

Engels said:

[S]ince the state arose from the need to restrain class conflicts, but at the same time it was born at the height of the conflict of these classes, therefore, as a general rule, it is *the state of the most powerful socioeconomic class*, which, as a consequence of this power becomes *also politically dominant* and, thus, obtains new means to hold the oppressed class in subordination and to exploit it. Thus, the ancient state was primarily the state of slaveowners for the subordination of slaves; thus, the feudal state was the agency of the nobility for the subordination and restraining of serfs and dependent peasants, and the modern representative state plays the role of a weapon of exploitation of hired labor by capital. In the majority of historical states, the rights granted to citizens are proportional to their property status. Thereby, it is openly recognized that the state is an organization of the *propertied* class for its protection from the propertyless class. [Engels 1884, p. 328]

Lenin provides the first scientific basis for the proletarian type of state, and defines it as having a goal not *of exploitation, but of struggle against* exploitation, defense of the *propertyless* classes from the propertied, the state as the proletariat organized into the ruling class "for the subjugation," for the "holding in subordination" of the class of former oppressors, i.e., the bourgeoisie (see "Leninism"). This is the state of the huge majority of the working people against the minority of the exploiters.

It would be erroneous to imagine, as some theorists do, that the original state was exclusively the result of external influence. Possibly, in the depths of the clan or tribe itself, the requisites gradually grew in quantity for a change to a new order qualitatively different from the clan. Aside from *such* a dialectical leap, other leaps are also possible through wars, both internal (uprising, civil war), and external (conquests). It is both possible and plausible that there were certain formations of the transitional period from the classless clan or tribe to the class state. Such transitional states may be considered the so-called patriarchal state as a transitional formation to the slaveowning state, i.e., the original democracy, limited kingdom, or the republic of "free citizens" of ancient times, as equally in the Roman Empire it was possible to recognize a transitional state to a new regrouping of society in the form of the feudal state and "rural district states." Such transitional stages of the state of a transitional era are necessary, and they exist during every supplantation in power of one class by another.

The revolutionary class perspective is reflected mainly in the view of social classes. Marx's understanding of class reduces to the fact that class is a category of persons connected by communality of interests which (i.e., category of persons) determines their role in production, and the distribution of the elements or means of production. And since this distribution of the means of production takes the form of private ownership of the means of production in class society, this ownership also defines the membership of classes and their struggle. The distribution of the means of production also determines the distribution of the product of labor. Class struggle, corresponding to this, is struggle for a role in production, for a new distribution of means of production, for or against private ownership of the means of production. But since the right of private ownership, like every other right, is based upon the authority of the class state, then class struggle is also political struggle, i.e., *struggle* for *state power* for one's own class or for the *overthrow of the power of the ruling class.*

Classes in power change, and at the same time the rule, task, and goal of the state also naturally change. But so long as the oppressing classes succeeded one another in power, all of them had *something in common*: ensuring freedom of exploitation by a means corresponding to the state of productive forces of the given era and given society.

"The *old society* was based on the principle: *rob or be robbed; work for others or make others work for you; be a slaveowner or a slave*." [Lenin 1920a, p. 293] (emphasis P.S.). Marx stated his revolutionary view on the transition *to a new society* in his letter to Weydemeyer:

> As far as I am concerned, I cannot claim credit for discovering the existence of classes in modern society, nor for the discovery of their struggle with one another. Bourgeois historians long before me identified the historical development of this struggle of classes, and bourgeois economists, the economic anatomy of classes. What I did that was new was to prove the following: (1) that the existence of classes is connected only with certain *historical* struggles peculiar to the development of production, (2) that class struggle *inevitably leads to the dictatorship of the proletariat*, (3) that this dictatorship itself constitutes merely a *transition to the elimination of all classes and to a classless society*. [Marx 1852, p. 528]

The goal and tasks of the state

Speaking of the goal of the state, we use this word not in the sense of a goal consciously given to it by someone, or of goals internally set for it (innate goals), such as the realization of an "absolute" or "moral" idea, an idea of "solidarity" or general "well-being," etc., etc., but in the sense of the concrete aspect that historically explains the meaning of its existence. Of course all theories are essentially nonsense if they prove that the goal of the state consists in the protection of the interests, not *the power of the propertied*, but of the subjugated, oppressed, i.e., of the "subjects," that the institution of mastery-slavery exists in the interests not of the masters but of the slaves. Equally insubstantial are theories of an *average* interest of current or all contemporary and future "members of the state."

As a creation of a class the state has purely class tasks: the protection of the basic interests of the given, i.e., ruling, class. Only to the extent that this class represents the interests of the development of a whole society at a given time does the state also have more general goals and tasks. We saw that Marx and Engels defined the state first of all as a weapon, an organization that protects a *propertied* class from a *propertyless* class, as a weapon of class *exploiters* for the *subjugation* of the *expropriated* class or classes. In the period of *proletarian revolution* *Leninism* puts forth another, more general Marxist definition of the state: it is a weapon of the victorious ruling class to *hold the vanquished class in subordina-tion*; only in *this sense* is it an oppressed class, not for purposes of exploitation as, for instance, exists after the victory of the proletariat, but *for the elimination* of exploitation of man by man, i.e., of *classes in general*, and for the creation of a classless society, of socialism.

These tasks also change in proportion to the transfer of state power from the hands of one class to another. For the class of *feudal* nobles this was power protecting feudal private property, the power to take tribute (land rent) consistent-ly in various forms. For the *capitalist* class the purpose of the bourgeois state is to *ensure the freedom of private ownership* to means of production, to extract *profit*, and to acquire surplus value. Depending upon the stage of development of capitalism (mercantile, industrial, period of free competition, and then monop-oly-imperialist, bank, finance capitalism), the role and tasks of the state also change to a certain degree, which can be noted also in the theories of the state. But the essence of all these states of exploiting classes is to *ensure the freedom of exploitation* of man by man. The proletariat struggles against private ownership of the means of production and to eliminate this with classes in general. It only needs a temporary state to achieve this goal. As this goal is achieved the very concept of the proletariat disappears, and so too does state. But also this *state-dictatorship* (q.v.), as a weapon in the hands of the proletariat, has certain nuances depending upon the course of the class struggle: the struggle for the suppression of the landowners and the bourgeoisie, the struggle against their return and revitalization, and the struggle for the transformation by the proletar-iat of the working peasantry ino a single class of employees (see Peasantry).

The types of state and their history

According to Engels, three characteristics distinguish the state from the clan. These are authority, territory, and property, i.e., class division of the population. The first role in the history of its creation was played by authority, at first, *as a fact*, and only later, as an idea, an ideology, and finally, as a theory. State authority arose earlier than it recognized itself as such. Just as the religious world view was consistently replaced by the legal, and the latter by the proletarian class, so there was a succession of theories of the state: religious, legal and finally, class. The second characteristic of every theory of the state is its national character. Every theorist begins with his own state: the ancient Greeks from the city (*polis*, hence politics), Rome, from its *civitas* (union of free "citizens" of its city), the feudal from its "patrimony" (patrimonial theories), etc. Bourgeois science subjects all these definitions to criticism, is disillusioned with all of them, and returns to the theory of the "state as a simple fact" (see Duguit).[1] Only the class theory of the state goes further in its criticism. It criticizes both the theory of the state and the state itself; not only in word, but in deed does it develop the historical state.

The primitive state

The direct successor of the *clan* is the so-called *patriarchal* state. This is the first type of state that can properly be called the precursor of the true class state in view of its weakly expressed class division of people. After it, or perhaps, instead of it, is the so-called *primitive democracy* of free citizen slaveowners with a huge number of exploited slaves. This primitive democracy of slaveowners is complicated by the parallel division of free persons into classes of exploited and exploiters (conquerors, for example). We see a prominent example of this in Rome where—in the competition between *two types of labor*, that of "free" people and that of slaves—slavery is economically victorious. This decides the fate of the state.

The difference between these two societies and these two states is rather significant. In the first, the state power of the patriarch mainly protects *production* and external security and only incidentally the *external exchange of products*, because *the economic conditions are* still *inadequate* for *internal exchange*. In the second, authority protects not only *production*, on the basis of slave labor, but also *internal exchange* between free citizens, or rather families and households. In the first case, state power is interested in the "subjects" only as producers; in the second case, this power was involved *with the producers* in the process of production *and the consumers* in the process of exchange. In the first case, we face the typical form of *master and slave*; *in the second*, along with that form is also a provision for civil commerce, for equilibrium, *equality on the basis of an equivalent*, of that which the French call *commerce juridique*. In the second, there is a new phenomenon: the constant division *of the city from the countryside*, of the location of authority and free commodity exchange from the place of residence of the mass of oppressed landholders—at first the latter are slaves, then serfs.

The patrimonial and feudal state

This is state in which state authority exercises power over the whole land and its populace. The patrimony belongs to the possessor; this is his authority, but in what does his authority consist? The old Russian word *volodeti* (to possess) originally meant "to gather tribute" (see Comrade M. Pokrovsky, *History of Russia*) from those under his authority or "tribute payers" (the literal meaning of the Russian word for "subjects"). Here, simple linguistics gives us the clue. The combination of a *whole class* of such owners also constitutes an essentially feudal state, a particular type of union (federation) of patrimonial and vassal states, the head of which takes on himself all the habits of his vassals (his "court," his guard, etc.) and finally, authority *over them*. Authority is explicit domination over subjects without any admixtures. But the bosom of the feudal order contains a new social division between *city and countryside*. This division has a new meaning: a division into two types of production, peasant landholding and city industry (at first, handicrafts), to agricultural countryside and industrial city (cities of another type existed from ancient times).

The division of labor leads to the formation and rapid economic growth of a *new class*, of capitalists. From maritime trade they become rich and strong and soon become equally powerful with the class-estate of feudal nobles in the form of a nucleus of a third city-estate. Naturally, state authority therefore changes.

This is the period about which Engels wrote:

> By way of exception, however, periods occur in which the warring classes balance each other so nearly that the state power, as ostensible mediator, acquires, for the moment, a certain degree of independence of both. Such was the absolute monarchy of the seventeenth and eighteenth centuries, which held the balance between the nobility and the class of burghers; such was the Bonapartism of the First, and still more of the Second French Empire . . . and Bismarck in Germany. [Engels 1884, p. 328]

Absolutism

(q.v.) This is a state form in transition to the bourgeois state. This absolutism-autocracy was a different type of organization. The whole apparatus previously consisted of the noble estate hierarchy, not as an estate that elected the king, but as a service estate selected by the king. On the other hand, in economic policy "all its measures are almost in every detail *a copy* of the economic policy of the *cities* of the middle ages." It is the economic system of this transitional period.

Police state

One form of absolute monarchy is considered to be the police state. In general, the tasks of governing the state of the middle ages were unknown. The state provided security only in the narrow sense of the word (internal and external). Economic and "cultural" matters were the tasks for the church, the commune, and the workshop. That which was later understood by the word "police," as *tasks of administration*, arose first in the cities. Gradually, the state takes over these functions from the city through broad intervention in the economic activity and even the private life of the population. In this period it takes on the name police state. Its origin relates to the period of mercantilism; it existed during the sixteenth, seventeenth, and eighteenth centuries. Its methods consist of borrowing the new methods of administration in the cities and the unlimited broadening of these functions. Under the name of "police welfare," this area of intervention embraces both the private economic sphere (handicraft, manufacture, trade) and cultural and home life (school, morality, struggle with luxury, extravagance, etc.). "The people, like a sick child, must be shown what it should eat and drink." These words of Frederick the Great of Prussia clearly characterize the police state as the typical form for Prussia. In essence, it was simply *unorganized* interference by the state in social relations by individual measures or individual orders ("ordinances"), and not by *general* statutes (legality) and a broad legal order. The police state is characterized not by the particular power of state authority, but by its comparative weakness. The state achieved its "omnipotence" and authority only with the victory of the bourgeois revolution. Later, in the so-called "legal order" of democracy even the police functions had their expression in special law, in so-called "police law," divided into the area of police of "security" and police of "welfare." This law partly corresponds with so-called administrative law which both squeezes it out and replaces mercantilism, whose slogan was the creation of a state economy closed to the outside world. Its characteristic feature is the extraordinarily broad interference of the state in the economic sphere.

This was historically the first type of state capitalism. The authority of the feudal estate was transformed into the bearer of the new economic system. The mere conquest of this authority by the bourgeoisie was insufficient.

State and revolution

The transitional stage between a state of two different classes must be a *revolution*. Lenin argues that the transitional stage between the two, the state as the agency of domination of the class of the capitalists and the state as the agency of rule of the proletariat, is the revolution. But this is a general rule. The *peaceful, voluntary transfer* by one class to another of its *power* does not happen in history. The young Marx and Engels formulated this notion thus:

> [A]n earlier interest, the peculiar form of intercourse of which has already been ousted by that belonging to a later interest, remains for a long time afterwards in possession of a traditional power in the illusory community (State, law), which has won an existence independent of the individuals; a power which in the last resort can only be broken by a revolution. [Marx and Engels 1845, p. 70]

In our country, sadly, data only exist on the transition from the feudal state to the bourgeois, and from the bourgeois to the Soviet order. Peasant war, these peasant revolutions, as a consequence of their defeat, everywhere led via counter-revolution to the strengthening of the feudal state.

There is a basic difference between earlier revolutions and the proletarian revolution. For the first time an exploited class (the proletariat) is victorious with the peasantry as another exploited class, although of a different type. Therefore, in all earlier revolutions: the class in power *changes*, the class in essence *changes*, but the *continuity of power* remains. Lenin insists that the proletarian revolution consists in the overthrow of the bourgeoisie and in the destruction, the ruin, of its state machine" [Lenin 1917, p. 419].

Despite the mutual proximity of the concepts of state and revolution, Lenin was the first to entitle a theoretical work on the state, *State and Revolution*. How do we explain this? Bourgeois science dislikes revolution just as the bourgeoisie itself dislikes it. Even if it has occurred, the fiction is created that it did not, as if there was merely a change of persons in power and not of class. From this derive all the theories on the eternity, continuity (*Continuität*) of the state and its authority. Marx wrote that bourgeois revolutions "are short-lived; soon they have attained their zenith, and a long crapulent depression lays hold of society. . . ." [Marx 1869, p. 401].

Bourgeois revolution and the state

The ever-expanding monetary economy, in connection with the commodity exchange that led to an ever more universal means of exchange, destroyed the feudal world view. Like the English revolution of 1649, the French Convent of 1793 was also led by the petty bourgeoisie. Their ideal was equality based on a balanced equivalent. However religious were the English and their revolution, with their analogies from the holy writ, the divine origin of power lost credit even for them. Long before the revolution, the French revolutionaries waged a fierce struggle *against God*. The contract of commodity exchange, transformed into a basic right, had to become the basis also of a new philosophy, an idea not of a concrete but of an abstract social contract (*contract social*). It was therefore possible freely to make contracts, and in civil commerce, a certain *basic contract* was necessary (analogy: law and the basic law—constitution), regardless of whether the contract was for the benefit of the monarch [Hobbes 1642] or Parliament [Locke 1689]. "The state is transformed into an apparatus created for the protection of rights" (cf. the first three declarations of the Great French Revolution of 1789, 1791, and 1793).

Marx showed in *Capital* how in the exchange of equivalents (manpower—money) the right to the product of one's labor was transformed into its direct opposite, into the right to acquire another's unpaid labor, and how equality under free contract was transformed into hired slavery. The same occurred with *political equality*, transformed by the free "social contract" of the Declaration of Rights into its direct *opposite*—into a system of masters and slaves by the class dictatorship of owners of the means of production, having an identical right to the absolute protection of private property and using it (see below the theory of Hauriou). The petty bourgeois theorists of the revolution started with the *consumer*, because only in the sphere of the process of exchange could they find data for the idea of equality. Marx's idea that the ownership of the means of production determines the distribution of products was alien to them.

In Germany and other countries, where the revolution was delayed and 1848 with its quasi-revolution left intact a very large medieval peasantry, the Reich-state found its own theory, alien to all social contract or allowing it only in a form distorted by German philosophy. At first landowning, later Junker-capitalist state power, put its imprint on the territory as on the practice. This was the law of production and not of exchange; its basis was the producer and not the consumer.

Was political democracy necessary for the bourgeoisie whatever happened? Lenin answers this question:

> Generally speaking democracy is only one of the possible (although theoretically for "pure" capitalism also the normal one) forms of the superstructure over capitalism. Both capitalism and imperialism, as the facts show, develop under all political forms, *subordinating all of them to itself*. Therefore, theoretically at the root it is wrong to speak of the "unrealizability" of one of the forms and one of the requirements of democracy.

If we look at the history of the French Revolution (even that of Aulard), for example, then we can see how slowly the bourgeoisie agreed to a bourgeois republic even under the revolutionary pressure of the radical petty bourgeoisie and the workers (the same occurred in 1917 Russia, with the Constitutional Democrats), and the more so given that their economic organization was ready.

> One of the fundamental differences between bourgeois revolution and socialist revolution is that for the bourgeois revolution, which arises out of feudalism, the new economic organizations are gradually created in the womb of the old order, gradually changing all the aspects of feudal society. The bourgeois revolution faced only one task—to sweep away, to cast aside, to destroy all the fetters of the preceding social order. By fulfilling this task every bourgeois revolution fulfills all that is required of it; it accelerates the growth of capitalism. [Lenin 1918a, p. 89]

The bourgeois state or bourgeois ("pure" also) democracy

The transfer of power from the feudal serfholder to the bourgeoisie implies a revolution never encountered in the history of mankind, both in economic relations and in ideology, a revolution of productive forces and a revolution of production relations.

What did the bourgeoisie expect from this new power? The protection of the freedom to exploit private property, liberated from the confinement of feudalism, including also the right to one's own manpower and the noninterference of authority in commerce without the expressed desire of the parties.

Formal political equality in words, so to speak, subordinated the producer to the consumer, at least in the abstract. For the purpose of ensuring this noninterference on the one hand, and, on the other hand, in the form of moderation of this struggle, which preceded the revolution and the result of which was a new form of state agreement, theorists of the revolution tried to devise a system of various *balances* between (1) the separate agencies of power in the so-called system of the separation of powers (into legislative, executive, and judiciary), and (2) authority and the limits on power by citizens or subjects or between individual groups of the population (the former estates, now classes). To the extent that it was a question of the feudal lord, early capitalism (trade) strove to ensure freedom of commodity exchange. The relations of the worker as the seller of manpower were attached by it also to the sphere of commodity exchange. "Everyone may *rent out his time* and his services" (i.e., manpower, which is measured by time) reads the declaration of the third year of the French Revolution.

What basic changes did the revolution effect in the characteristics of the state?

The revolution declared that *territory*, in the name of the same idea of property, was to be the fatherland of the whole nation instead of the private property of the patriarch-monarch.

In North America, at the moment of its founding, the revolutionaries of some states, true to the demands of the Levellers, demanded real nationalization of all land. But their demands failed. In France, the first Declaration of Rights spoke of such ideas, but emphasized that alienation would be allowed *only* for compensation.

This means that nationalization "of all land" was possible only mentally, "as an idea." The borders of the fatherland, until now under the defense of the "fist" of the knight, in the future would be also sacred in idea. The duty of defense of the fatherland! *"Allons, enfants de la patrie!"*

Basic *legislative power* was formally given by the revolution to those who presented the mandate of the voters (how they obtain the mandate is a separate question), and after this the holders of these powers transfer an *authorization* of *executive* power for administration to the representative of the majority, to a cabinet of ministers with the premier at the head, and themselves either engage in chatter, or go home (cf. Mussolini's draft). Herbert Spencer writes of this as a "giant trading enterprise or company with all the qualities of a company organization." Actually, one can make a complete analogy between the development of the state and a company, right up to a stock society.

The composition of the *nation* underwent the greatest changes of all. The estates and corporations were destroyed and dispersed into individuals, and they stopped somewhat only before the family. And then the simple totality, the sum of this dispersed mass was declared a single nation. Its organization, at first, was forbidden in principle.

Sovereignty was declared not in the name of a single state authority, but in the name of the whole nation. In fact, it was usurped by the [ruling] class and transferred to its state authority.

The victorious bourgeoisie, which held the oppressed classes *beneath it*, did not realize into what a *false* role it had fallen. Later it came to understand this role, but continued to conduct the affairs of state consciously and systematically, by means of deception and illusion, as the representative of the whole nation and society, although in fact it represented only part of society and was the most malevolent or greedy opponent (i.e., exploiter) of the huge majority of this nation.

The characteristics of the bourgeois state. Most state theory recognizes the basic characteristics of the state as: (1) territory, (2) authority, with the addition—sovereignty, and (3) population, people, nation. Some call these characteristics the *elements* of the state, but this is clearly meaningless if you make the division of these elements in German: country, people, and ruler (*Herrscher*). They go still further and with these characteristics divide states into various periods: "Under feudalism the essence of the state was seen in territory, under absolutism in its authority, under democracy—in the people," and then view the nineteenth century as a synthesis that combines these three characteristics. Even Engels noted the necessity of these three characteristics: authority, settled nature of the population, meaning territory, a division of people into classes, i.e., in the sense of organization of classes.

People—nation

The basic characteristic of the state must be considered to be the division into classes; where there are no class divisions there is no place for a state. The clan might have common slaves; this still does not turn it into a state. It is therefore necessary to have two or more classes; their combination, or organization, is now called a people or nation. It was not always so. In Rome, *populus* meant merely the totality of privileged *quirites* (citizens); in the middle ages, in the clear, legal expression of class (estate) society, the estates viewed themselves as estates and not as a single people: "We, the people, i.e., the Klimov peasants"; the peasants spoke only of themselves (e.g., in Chekhov). "We the people of the United States" (see their constitution) so only the *bourgeois* nation called itself, as the *totality of classes* in North America and before that in England (1649). Only Marxism introduced into the nation-state the concept of class *organization*. With this qualification the nation-people is, let us say, the basic characteristic of the state even when the term "nation" was still unknown.

Power

We have already spoken of state power. Here we will reflect briefly on the nature of this power. Its basic characteristic is the monopoly of arms. Engels contrasts it, in the very origin of the state, with the prior arming of the whole people. Engels also remained true to this view with respect to later history. "In France," he wrote, "after each revolution, the workers were armed; therefore, for the bourgeois, being at the helm of the state, the first commandment was the disarming of the workers."

Of course, along with coercion, authority also has another means of state influence: persuasion. But when class interest fragments society, verbal persuasion of the oppressed majority by an insignificant minority of oppressors would be hopeless in the long run. Only under the proletarian dictatorship does persuasion of the whole mass of the workers by the *avant garde* and the "bringing of this mass" under its hegemony in the struggle against the minority of former oppressors, have real chances.

Authority must be *sovereign*. It is true that the medieval state still was not recognized as such. In our country, doubts have arisen about the necessity of the concept of sovereignty in general, but practice (diplomacy, the Constitution of . . . the USSR) uses it. If we do not have our own definition of this concept, then it is necessary to use the *bourgeois* definition of it. But we know that for bourgeois science these explanations serve as a means for concealing the true meaning. "Sovereign or supreme authority means authority to which, on the one hand are subordinated, under authority, all persons relating to the given territory, but which, on the other hand, itself, by law (*de jure*) is not subordinate to any other authority." There is no reason to dwell on the fact that what is *de jure* does not always correspond to the *de facto*.

Territory—country

This is primarily an *external condition* of the existence of the state. This concept was included in the characteristics of the state not in the feudal, but in the bourgeois state. Jellinek initially discovered it in Kerber in 1817. "The state as a civil society in specific land boundaries." The feudal state consisted of a multitude of "territories." The number of serfs (as in Russia) was often more important than the exact boundaries of land. Now it has been transformed into the "idea of territory." We read: "the whole country as one man," instead of nation. To it relates also the extra-territoriality of a ship on a voyage, of an embassy in foreign countries, etc. In any event, this concept is closely tied to the concept of nation; with this concept it keeps its significance even in the state transitional to socialism and communism, under the proletarian dictatorship.

The state and ideology

We have already seen the disputes between bourgeois scholars about whether the state is real, or merely an idea, or merely a psychological experience. There is no need to look at bourgeois books, because even in communist publications you will find these thoughts echoed. "The state is only one of the class *ideological* forms" (Reisner). But the state existed before the "idea of the state," just as law existed before the "idea of law," or classes before class consciousness. Marx taught that class exists "in nature" before it is "made a class for itself" (*The Poverty of Philosophy*). And Engels writes about the lag of class consciousness (*Anti-Dühring*):

Furthermore, when by way of exception the inner connection between the social and political forms of existence in any epoch comes to be known, this as a rule occurs only when these forms have already by half outlived themselves and are nearing extinction. [Engels 1878, p. 109]

Engels described the origin of the state. When the growth and development of productive forces led to the division of people into groups by property position; when people went to a non-nomadic life and a special social authority was in place, taking the form of an armed guard against the unarmed mass of the rest of the population—then we could speak of the state. But the division into property groups, "classes" did not at once create a special ideology. The setting of territorial boundaries antedated the "idea of the state boundary" and the armed "detachment with appendages" already existed; but scholars still argue about the "idea of armed authority" and state coercion. With time, of course, both the idea of the state and a whole political ideology appeared. But they appeared as (using Engels' definition) "consciously incorrect," i.e., with an "idea of the false or illusory motive forces," which thereafter also as "tradition" and prejudice have an *effect back* upon the development both of production and in general of social relations (see Legal Ideology). In the historical succession of world thought, one may draw a sharp line signifying, so to speak, the watershed between the old and the new world. Such is the replacement of the religious world outlook by the *legal* or classical bourgeois, noted by Engels, in which the *church and God* are replaced by the *state and its authority*. In the understanding of society, this means a transition from *idealism to materialism*. Earlier dreams of the *return* to primitive communism ("to the lost heaven") are replaced by the striving *forward* to a new communism as the synthesis of the whole previous movement of mankind.

State and party

To the extent that the lawyer is occupied with the science of law, he is indifferent to a party; for him, the question of a party is for sociology or politics. Only the Americans make an exception on this question; otherwise their statement of the state structure of North America would lose real meaning. Party (from "pars"—part) is the political organization of *part* of some class; it is factually impossible to unite an entire class in a party. But parties of a minority cannot do without parts of other classes, because their strength is that, by deception and illusion, they attract members of other classes. But the party of the majority, of the workers that is, can seriously struggle for the involvement of the whole class only after victory.

In essence, this is the organization of part of a class to struggle for state authority and to limit this authority.

Thus, all modern governments are basically party governments, but they recognize themselves as such perhaps only in parliamentary countries under the so-called two-party system. The war led to a system of *coalitions, large*—of representatives of *all* parties, *small*—of representatives of one agreement or another—of a block of a party. The basic role in these coalitions was played by the social-traitor parties. After 1917, attempts appear to form so-called "third parties" from the middle classes. In essence these *third parties* present themselves as *Socialist parties*, becoming after the formation of Communist party organizations largely petty bourgeois (cf. party). Only Soviet authority (cf. Leninism) openly recognizes itself as a class-party government, as a party dictatorship.

The *form* of the state

The state is the form of the organization of classes or of political organization ("Politics is the relation between classes"—Lenin), but the real form is by no means identical to the idea (on the relation of form and content see "Legal ideology"). That ideology follows slowly after facts is clearly apparent in human opinions about the forms of the state. From the time of Aristotle, only somewhat augmented by Polybius, state theory is expressed in the scheme: monarchy—tyranny—aristocracy—oligarchy (government by "the few")—democracy—ochlocracy (government by the "crowd")—again monarchy, etc. "So it was, so it will be." To this scheme Rome added a new division: *monarchy* (later absolute or limited) and *republic* ("nonmonarchy"). Mankind had to make do with such a poor division of forms for millenia. A subsequent division based on the type of the head of state is even further from the class concept than the first—at least in the latter some note is taken of divisions within the nation since it considers a change of forms as a violent upheaval. But what sort of theory can be constructed here other than the old fable of Polybius? "In the course of development every monarchy turns into a tyranny; the tyranny falls and it is replaced by an aristocracy which, turning into an oligarchy, causes general discontent, and is again overthrown and replaced by democracy." And since in the opinion of Polybius, "every democracy is turned into an ochlocracy, the government of the mob, of the crowd, then this government is overthrown and turned again into a monarchy," etc. A shaggy dog story!

For the first time, Marx creates the system: from nonstate (clan) and classless society, the transitional state, for the elimination of the state in general—nonstate and classless society.

> The dialectic is concrete and revolutionary, it distinguishes the "transition" from the dictatorship of one class to the dictatorship of another class from the "transition" from the democratic proletarian state to the non-state ("withering away of the state"). [Lenin]

There is, therefore, a new, basic division of *types* of the state: into the state of the propertied classes and the *Soviet* state (see Leninism).

States can be divided into *simple* states, *complex* states, and unions of states.

Of all the historical forms of unions of states in Europe, only two are preserved today: the union of states (confederation) and the united state (federation). But before there were several of these forms of complex states. Leaving aside temporary contractual agreements, such as alliances ("agreements"), ententes ("consents"), etc., theory, in the person of its luminary, the late Professor Jellinek distinguished:

1. Based *upon international relations of dependence* of one state upon another (protectorate).

2. Suzereign and vassal states, a survival of the feudal order *(Staaten-staat)*.

3. A *monarchial combination of states*:

(a) personal union, an unplanned or accidental union of monarch—this is sometimes called also a minimum union;

(b) a real union—a planned, i.e., based upon agreement, *long-term union* of two or several states having a *common monarch*. After the fall of the Austro-Hungarian union this form also belongs to history.

4. A union of states.

5. A united state.

A union of states is distinguished from a united state if it has a central *sovereign* authority (a *united* state, e.g., the USSR) or not (a union of states), or if the constituent parts of the union enjoy *independent* supreme rights (union of states) or if they depend upon the union's central authority (see *Autonomy*). The World War hypocritically put in first place the characteristic of the right of *self-determination* of individual national parts of states. These theories are all fruitless if they are alien to the class approach and the revolutionary dialectic, or if they are limited to the formal comparison of all the historically known types of state unions. Only introducing the concept of *class sovereignty* (q.v.) *and proletarian hegemony* in the federation of the state of the transitional period along with the true slogan of the right of self-determination can we create a real theory of the complex state (see Federation).

State and church

We shall deal here with this question just briefly, at the level of the historical relationship between church and state. The ancient world propagated the belief that law is an invention and gift from God (the Digests of Roman law), and as ancient as the belief that law is blessed by God. From church teaching that "the state is an evil which has become a necessity as a result of the sinfulness of man in paradise" (i.e., in his natural condition), the first teachers of natural law drew their idea of the natural condition. Augustine constructs the idea of the heavenly kingdom (the state of law—*civitas Dei*) as a contrast to the earthly kingdom. But the centralized Christian church in the person of the pope—owing to its centralization, its rigid hierarchy and its property accumulation—acquired great power by which it subordinated even the state. It had one advantage over the worldly authority of the time: it alone had access to the oppressed classes (slaves, peasants, etc). In turn, the relations of church and state went through three stages: the state subordinated to the church, the state equal to the church, and the church subordinate to the state. When the single church power, with its holy hierarchy, dealt with the fragmented feudal state, its authority was understandable; it dictated laws not only to peoples, but to kings and emperors. Through hard battle the state gained "superiority" and subordinated the church, using it to further the interests of the authority of the ruling class for the oppression of the masses. But the separation of the church from the state (in North America, France) did not mean a rejection of its use as an agency of "persuasion" of the oppressed masses.

The bourgeois state and its apparatus

Marx's writings on the "18th Brumaire" revolution in France clearly characterize the fate of the bourgeois state in general. At first, the revolution perfected *parliamentary* power in order later to *overthrow* it. Having achieved this, the revolution perfected *executive power*, reduced it to its clearest expression, isolated it, set it up against itself as the sole target, then to concentrate all its forces of destruction against it. And then Marx came to his prophetic conclusion about the need for the dictatorship of the proletariat: *"All revolutions perfected this (state) machine instead of smashing it"* [Marx 1852, p. 477].

Of what does a parliamentary government consist? We have already seen that it is merely a *party* government of the bourgeoisie, a *dictatorship* of the bourgeoisie. How is it run? At the head of each "department" there is a responsible member or representative of the party (a minister) for "managing policy." But does he manage? By no means! The ministry, i.e., the huge apparatus (in America it is called the "machine" as in a factory) under his "command" is usually a *permanent*, politically irresponsible apparatus that conducts all the administrative work. In MacDonald's "workers" government in England we saw how helpless this responsible leader was. About our bureaucracy, Lenin wrote:

> [T]he state is in our hands; but has it operated the New Economic Policy in the way we wanted in this past year? No! . . . But we refuse to admit that it did not operate in the way we wanted. How did it operate? The machine refused to obey the hand that guided it. It was like a car that was going not in the direction the driver desired, but in the direction someone else desired; as if it were being driven by some mysterious, lawless hand. [Lenin 1922c, p. 279]

In the *18th Brumaire* Marx provides the classic statement of the development of this apparatus in France:

> This executive power with its enormous bureaucratic and military organization, with its ingenious state machinery, embracing wide strata, with a host of

officials numbering half a million, besides an army of another half million, this appalling parasitic body, which enmeshes the body of French society like a net and chokes all its pores, sprang up in the days of the absolute monarchy, with the decay of the feudal system, which it helped to hasten. The seignorial privileges of the landowners and towns became transformed into so many attributes of the state power, the feudal dignitaries into paid officials and the motley pattern of conflicting medieval plenary powers into the regulated plan of a state authority whose work is divided and centralized as in a factory. The first French Revolution, with its task of breaking all separate local, territorial, urban, and provincial powers in order to create the civil unity of the nation, was bound to develop what the absolute monarchy had begun: centralization, but at the same time the extent, the attributes, and the agents of governmental power. Napoleon perfected this state machinery. The Legitimist monarchy and the July monarchy added nothing but a greater division of labor, growing in the same measure as the division of labor within bourgeois society created new groups of interests, and therefore, new material for state administration. Every common interest was straightaway severed from society, counterposed to it as a higher, general interest. The parties that contended in turn for domination regarded the possession of this huge state edifice as the principal spoils of the victor.

But under the absolute monarchy, during the first Revolution, under Napoleon, bureaucracy was only the means of preparing the class rule of the bourgeoisie. Under the Restoration, under Louis Philippe, under the parliamentary republic, it was the instrument of the ruling class, however much it strove for power of its own. [Marx 1869, pp. 477–78]

Later, in the days of the Commune, Marx wrote to Kugelman:

If you look at the last chapter of my Eighteenth Brumaire, you will find that I declare that the next attempt of the French Revolution will be no longer, as before, to transfer the bureaucratic military machine from one hand to another, but to smash it, and this is the preliminary condition for every real people's revolution on the Continent. And this is what our heroic Party comrades in Paris are attempting. [Marx 1871, 420]

The proletarian revolution and the state

We will not deal at length here with the proletarian revolution; the whole *Encyclopedia* has the goal of deepening its explanation. With respect to the state, the task of this revolution is "not simply to possess a greedy state machine and to put it in motion for its own goals," but to "*destroy it.*"

The essence of Marx's theory of the state has been mastered only by those who realize that the dictatorship of a single class is necessary not only for every class

society in general, not only for the proletariat which has overthrown the bourgeoisie, but also for the entire historical period which separates capitalism from
"classless society," from communism. Bourgeois states are most varied in form,
but their essence is the same: all these states, whatever their form, in the final
analysis are inevitably the dictatorship of the bourgeoisie. The transition from
capitalism to communism is certainly bound to yield a tremendous abundance
and variety of political forms, but the essence will inevitably be the same: the
dictatorship of the proletariat. [Lenin 1917, p. 413]

What changes must this revolution make in the nature of the state? For now it
does not destroy the concepts of *territory—fatherland*. Before the victory of the
revolution Marx's words in the *Communist Manifesto* remained in force: "for the
worker there is no fatherland," now with victory, the working class has its
"socialist fatherland," which it must protect *from its class enemies* (Art. 19 of
the Constitution of July 10, 1918). Only the uniting of the whole world in a *single*
Union of Soviet Socialist Republics will make this concept unnecessary. Not
sooner.

The second characteristic of a state, the *nation*, does not disappear, but its
significance changes. First, the slogan of equality of all nations is contrasted to
the bourgeois slogan of the *unity* of the nation, i.e., the oppression by the ruling
nation of the state of all the others. But how should the equality of nations be
understood here? As *the right to self-determination*, i.e., separation. Second, the
proletarian state is a state of the working people (workers, workers and peasants)
in which the classes themselves have undergone great changes.

> It was not difficult to get rid of the tsar—that required only a few days. It was
> not very difficult to drive out the landowners—that was done in a few months.
> Nor was it very difficult to drive out the capitalists. But it is incomparably more
> difficult to abolish classes: we still have the division into workers and peas-
> ants. . . . Hence the task of the proletarian struggle is not quite completed after
> we have overthrown the tsar and driven out the landowners and capitalists; to
> accomplish that is the task of the system we call the dictatorship of the proletar-
> iat.
>
> The class struggle is continuing; it has merely changed its forms. [Lenin
> 1920a, pp. 292-93]

"For the first time in history there exists a state where there are only two
classes, *only the proletariat and the peasantry*." "Along with them there are
whole *groups of remnants* and survivals of capitalism. The struggle between these
two classes has the goal of "eliminating the difference between worker and
peasant, *to make all employees*." Only then will socialism arise, *a classless
society where there is no place for the state*.

State authority exists in the proletarian state as well, but this is authority of a new type, a dictatorship (q.v.) of the proletariat or of the proletariat and the poorest peasantry. The first example of such authority was the Commune; its developed and lasting form is Soviet authority (see "Dictatorship," "Com__ mune," "Leninism"). Lenin has written that the Soviet-type of state has been won by us; it is a step forward for all mankind. The struggle of this dictatorship is *extremely long*.

> Abolishing the bureaucracy at once, everywhere and completely, is out of the question. It is a utopia. But to smash the old bureaucratic machine at once and to begin immediately to construct a new one that will make possible the gradual abolition of all bureaucracy—this is not a utopia, it is the experience of the Commune, the direct and immediate task of the revolutionary proletariat. [Lenin 1917, p. 425]

State and law

The question of the relation of state to law and law to the state is a dual one: (1) the role of the state in the formation and support of the legal order (see "Law"), and (2) the role of law in the structure of the state itself. We will deal only with the latter here. Bourgeois democracy calls itself a *Rechtsstaat*—a state creating law and at the same time bound by law. Simply speaking "equating the concepts of the *legal* and the *constitutional* state is a general feature of the modern German doctrine of the law of the state (W. Geisen). And the crown of the constitutional regime is parliamentarianism" (q.v.). The essence of this theory is the problem of how can law, passed and repealed by the state, become obligatory for the state itself. In the understanding of general bourgeois legal theory, this is equivalent to the posing of the question "about the law of state authority obligatory for the very state authority which issued it." In the theory of the normativists (see below) this is solved by declaring the *identity* of state and law.

The history of the theory of the state has not yet been written, if one does not consider a simple list and statement of various theories in a bourgeois publication, at best by an evolutionary method. Such a history requires a class approach, and the application of a revolutionary-dialectic method. Of the histories available to us, the best is still Professor Gumplowicz's book. There is no doubt that the history and analysis of the various theories of the state from the perspective of revolutionary Marxism would yield very interesting results. At the same time it should be said that this is a most difficult task which, if done superficially, would cause more harm than good.

The theories of the ancients, such as the Greeks, were limited to the coming together of the state with the clan, family, "household" (*oikos*) and unions of households (*synoikia*), i.e., a village-city. The city (*polis*) served as the starting point for the creation of the word politics (*politeia*) and for Aristotle's phrase about man as a political (i.e., city) animal. The Greeks unwillingly transferred their concept of the *polis* (city) state to the barbarian states. The Roman society of the privileged *quirites* (*civitas* from *civis*—citizen) played approximately the same role in legal theory. To the word *civitas* (state) was added another name—*populus* (people, now nation) consisting of the same *quirites* in contrast to the *plebs* (see "Roman law") and then after the victory of the *plebs*—*respublica* (literally "common thing"), at first designating property of "all the people," later the name of the state with elected magistrates. All ancient theories moved among these strata and concepts. The Middle Ages either repeated the Greek theories (in a Byzantine light) or were limited to religious explanations of the state authority of the church and the feudal lords. God "delegated" his authority to the prince, king, lord, etc. (from which there was the principality, the kingdom as a state). These theories survive only in religious (Catholic) universities. However, they threaten to arise anew with the renegade bourgeois intelligentsia, with its world view reverting to first cause without a glance at God. The bourgeoisie was born in the struggle *against God*, against religion. For it "human justice replaced divine law, or God's justice; the state assumed the role of the church" [Engels 1884, p. 204]. Kelsen adduces an interesting parallel between these two ideologies, the religious and legal theories, showing how all sorts of analogies were moved from the religious world view into the science of the state. From this originated various organic theories equating the state with man—a living organism (Hobbes' *Leviathan*, etc.). The whole English revolution occurred under the sign of clerical analogies. Thus, people at first made a concept of God in their own image and likeness in order later to transfer this concept of God-church to their own union.

English bourgeois law is older in years than others. Significantly, it provided the forms of bourgeois democracy for the whole world, not as ideology but as fact. Moreover, it is often misinterpreted (see Marx's letter to Lassalle), and more often misunderstood (cf. the well-known researcher of English self-government, Gneist). As the result of a bitter civil war, this state nevertheless had no written constitution, which to this day is the combination of real class forces. As becomes a state ruling in the *world market*, its parliament, or rather its lower house, is built on the principle of equality taken from the world of consumers, commodity exchange. Every civil freedom of England derives from this. The authority of the former feudal lords, now forming the lords of the upper house, and of the chief lord (lord-baron), the king—these are outlived decorations from the far past. In fact, neither the consumer nor the feudal lord *rules*, but *industrial and merchant capital* and its party government. Naturally, in such conditions the theory of the state is also distinguished by extreme abstraction and fogginess.

The English theory of the state (to the extent that it provides a theory and not merely a history) is entirely legal. Those grandiose problems that its great economists once posed have had no effect upon the theory of the state in England. The most daring book in this area imparts a smell of the musty past; those great upheavals experienced by England in 1649[2] and in 1840 (Chartists) find almost no theoretical expression. "At the present day students of the constitution wish neither to criticise, nor to venerate, but to understand . . . [a professor's] duty is neither to attack nor to defend the constitution but simply to explain its laws" [Dicey 1889, pp. 3–4]. For the liberal, the dogma of the all-powerful nature of parliament is still sacred, for the conservative, the dogma of the *supremacy of the king*,[3] at the time when both parliament and still earlier the king were turned into a more or less empty form and "the real rulers of society"—as John Chipman Gray cleverly states—"remain undiscoverable." The conservative lawyer Caries, it is true, explains that the "degree of participation in the electoral system *must* be determined (it was indeed so determined in England) by the *material* influence of the various social *classes*." The same is repeated in different words by Dicey: "A sign of a healthy society is that social classes are *in agreement, the rich guide the poor, and the poor trust the rich*" (ibid.). But these words do not enter their theory; they are included in brackets.

At the same time in England—as in ancient Rome—the earlier fierce battles of class struggle were expressed in "basic laws," i.e., in the written agreements of the English constitution. In general, all that is written in the constitution is the result of a real struggle, and all that exists under the name of unwritten law depends today on the real relation of class forces. Finally, as I said above, today those remain as monuments and organizations of two warring classes, the House of Lords and the House of Commons.[4]

Of course, even to England the war had to bring more frankness. Prewar England, perhaps, could still be imagined in Dicey's form: "Two features have at all times since the Norman Conquest characterized the political institutions of England: First . . . the omnipotence or undisputed supremacy throughout the whole country of the central government. Second . . . is the rule or supremacy of law" [Dicey 1889, p. 171]. "This rule of law in essence means the right of courts to punish for an illegal act by whomsoever it was committed" (ibid.). After these phrases the author could look at the order of the "constitutional" heartland with Olympian contempt! However, behind this form was hidden the unlimited rule of parties—i.e., of classes—through an all-powerful prime minister, ministers, and his cabinet[5] or, rather, an irresponsible, unchangeable bureaucracy, the apparatus of this cabinet, with its class traditions. But this fact does not exist for the legal theory of the state. Classes and parties in general do not exist for this theory, and the class composition of Parliament is entirely a matter of indifference. What is the class nature of the court and in general of the whole state apparatus? England guarantees law and equality *only for the bourgeois*, but one must learn of this from other sources, for instance from newspapers and stock exchange meetings.

Opposition to the English theory has recently emerged. But this goes no further than syndicalism, no further than the well-known industrial democracy (with "equal rights" of the enterprise and the worker!), as a supplement to political parliamentarianism. Take Laski, for example, a representative of the group of young scholars. He rather soberly recognizes that in England "the opinion of the State, at least in its legislative expression, will largely *reproduce the opinion of those who hold the keys of economic power*" [Laski 1919, p. 81]. His thoughts are sometimes hard to understand, and are intelligible only when one remembers that he proceeds from the state *as an organization of consumers*, for otherwise there is no place for equality. As Laski writes, "(The state) deals with men in the capacity that is *common to them all*. It regards them as the users of certain goods" [ibid. p. 83]. So long as questions are decided by the *majority* of consumers—"so long as political power is separated from economic (i.e., from industry)" [ibid. p. 91]—the decision ("jury") of the nation will always be mixed up. But he sees the reuniting of political and economic power in the introduction of a special industrial Parliament,[6] obviously on the model of the German councils of workers and employers. The author is not daring enough to proclaim the superiority of the authority of the producer over the political power of the consumer, but proposes merely the parallel creation of *two new Houses of Parliament of producers*, leaving to the old Parliament the role of the body for the consumer or, as he expresses it, the "political" role. It may be said that the author has written the theory of the "workers'" government of MacDonald before the actual appearance of this government.

The American theorist is strikingly frank, a frankness uncustomary in Europe. There is no reason, of course, to hide the fact that the country that has defeated the whole world "on the technical front," is actually *governed by money*. The late president, Professor Woodrow Wilson wrote:

> Neither did I give [in the first edition] sufficient weight . . . to the powers of the Secretary of the Treasury . . . he has exercised not political but business power. He has helped the markets *as a banker* would. . . . The *country* feels *safer* when an *experienced banker*, like Mr. Gage, is at the head of the Treasury, than when an *experienced politician* is in charge of it. [Wilson 1900, pp. vii-viii]

Until its liberation, North America was an English colony. According to the original plan, the United States Constitution was supposed to be a statement of the English state structure, without a king, with a federal Senate instead of the House of Lords, and with a certain preponderance of authority for the first house. In fact, the House of Representatives, as the result of its almost comically huge staff (its division into 47 autonomous committees), to a certain degree defers to the relatively less numerous Senate (about 100 members). The president, as the executive authority, especially since the times of conquering colonies (the Philippines, etc.), has formally ever more influence. Actually, the fate of the country is decided by the convention and the caucus of the ruling party, particularly the fraction of this party in Congress (this is the joint name of both houses). The two parties exchanging power have lost their original class character, and now both are equally capitalist and represent simply the interest of one financial group or another. This means the full decomposition of parties, in which place act monopoly capitalism, the "financial leaders," and their "machine."

Wilson notes the peculiar characteristic of the guarantees of American democracy given by Adams:

> Is there . . . a constitution upon record more complicated with balances than ours? In the first place, eighteen states and some territories are balanced against the national government. . . . In the second place, the House of Representatives is balanced against the Senate, the Senate against the House. In the third place, the executive authority is, in some degree, balanced against the legislative. In the fourth place, the judicial power is balanced against the House, the Senate, the executive power, and the state governments. In the fifth place, the Senate is balanced against the President in all appointments to office, and in all treaties. . . . In the sixth place, the people hold in their hands the balance against their own representatives, by biennial . . . elections. In the seventh place, the legislatures of the several states are balanced against the Senate by sextennial elections. In the eighth place, the electors are balanced against the people in the choice of the President. [Wilson 1900, pp. 12–13]

Such a complex balance of powers, in Adams' opinion, is America's own invention. Wilson here adds the most important type of balance: between the states and the central government.

But Wilson shows how the government centralizes, how the individual states lose power, how the federal court, by the text of the Constitution standing as if above Congress, is subordinated to the same party system (i.e., by increasing the number of members of the "unchangeable" court). The basic official authority is the majority of a special executive committee of Congress of three representatives of the party in power and the president as the distributor of all the executive apparatus. As a result of all the balances in the most complete bourgeois democracy, in which by law all the governors, judges, prosecutors, etc. are *elected* and even *recalled* by the people, the sole essence of democracy—a free field for the development of the class struggle—has almost completely been eliminated and there remains only one perspective although perhaps not an imminent one—the revolutionary perspective. Even Wilson describes with envy the "flexibility" of the English state structure compared with the American. The state apparatus is the machine of the United States; this is the *mechanization* of the European bureaucratic apparatus.

The German theory of the state is based upon the definition of the state as a society divided into "*Herrschaft und Beherrschte*," masters and slaves (literally "masters" or "rulers," and "ruled" or "directed"). In this presentation the state is a single personality, the subject of state law, provided in its unity with its rights of rule in relationship to the multitude of subjects (*Beherrschte*). This theory, first developed in the 1860s by Albrecht and Herber, is adopted by all the luminaries of German science including Laband and Jellinek (the father). It was adequate for the pre-war *Junker*-capitalist regime. "The legal personality of the state consists of the fact that the state has *independent* (its own) rights of rule for the purpose of conducting its tasks and duties and its own will for rule. . . ." And the essence of rule consists of the right of "*free persons* (or their combinations) to order actions, inaction, or services and to *compel* them to *execute* the order" (Laband). "The existence of *relations* of rule for the state is so necessary that without *relations of rule a state is inconceivable.* The state has authority in order to rule. To rule means to have the ability to obligate unconditionally (*auferlegen*) . . . other wills to carry out its will; to conduct its will contrary to other wills. The authority unconditionally to conduct its will contrary to other wills belongs *only* to the state" (Jellinek, 172). This means the generally recognized *monopoly* of rule! For *Laband*, this is fully real authority. For Jellinek, this personality of the state is not concrete; it is a purely *abstract concept of personality* as the bearer of the single power of will (*Willensmacht*), and this single power of will is presented as the totality of the *will of all* the "ruled." But if one has in mind that the liberal Jellinek always places "the consciousness of monarchs (*Fürsten*) and nations" on the same level, then it is clear toward what sort of *total will*, this single will as the resulting will, (q.v.) will lean. Against Jellinek's theory, some of the Germans themselves (cf. Lenin) object that the state is "*a fully real legal or volitional relation* between the *Herrscher* (in the sense of the monarch) and the subjects." It must be remembered that revolutionary natural law derived from the social contract of the French and English does not lie at the basis of this will theory for these subjects; the German philosophic understanding of the basis of natural law is in the form of "*duty*" and "*powers*" corresponding to it. "In all rights there are hidden obligations (duty)," etc.

The basic feature of the German theory of state law, as the *will of the ruler*, fully corresponds to the structure of the German empire. Just as under the emperor or union of monarchs, under a president and union of presidents, real power is the "producers," the *union of the agrarian and the industrialist*. This is why during the war it was relatively easy to move temporarily from free commerce of free commodity owners to state monopoly and prohibitive prices. Who holds the decisive element of state authority? "The Kaiser" or now his temporary surrogate—the president, but of course with the qualification "Und der König absolute, wenn er unsern Willen tut."

Let the king (the Prussian king was also the Kaiser) be an absolute monarch, but let him conduct *our* (i.e., class) will." They gave royal honors to the deceased president (Social Democrat Ebert) because he truly fulfilled their will. There was one exception: autonomous Bavaria, which pledged allegiance only to *its own* king and his temporary deputy. But the state apparatus? "In every modern state, the authority for the conduct of administration is in the hands of the bureaucracy; *the development of bureaucratisation* is a definite *indicator of the degree of modernization* of a given state." [Weber 1961, pp. 249–53].

And citizens? German theory knows only ruler and subjects. Admittedly, it is based upon law and the theory of the separation of powers or functions, "but at times of crisis one of the powers always has the plenitude [of authority] innately characteristic of the state, and provided with it, decides the dispute. (All dreamed up theories of equality lost before the crude legal reality revealed in such conflicts.) The theory of balance . . . has not proved itself." But what guarantees of rights remain in such a case? "Political guarantees lie in the real relations of power of the organized factors in the state; these are "the greatest *social* forces: social boundaries, religion, law, morality," and legal guarantees—legality (execution of the law), but with the qualification: "legality and illegality *depend upon social forces*" (Jellinek).

We see that here all the class elements are carefully covered with various abstract formulas. Because Germany is a "united state" *(Bundesstaat)*, therefore, of course the type of the German *bund* (union) is the "only healthy and normal form of state combination." "Individual union states have their supreme rights only due to the tolerance of the empire and by force of its will." "The union has the right without the consent of union states unilaterally to amend the constitution, i.e., it may deprive individual union states (only all in equal amount) of their rights of supremacy" (Laband). This is the theory of the European bourgeois-*Junker* (landowner) dictatorship at the stage of capitalist imperialism.

A peculiar variation of the German theory in its abstract legal part is contributed by the *Austrian normativists*—Kelsen, etc. How, in fact, can anything be found in common in this prewar jumble of constitutional phrase (Vienna) and the heart of despotism (its Slavic provinces), between legal freedom and economic slavery, if not in the abstract legal *norm—in the article of the law*. Everything else (social, economic) in the concept of the state is discarded as supra-legal (supra-juridical, meta-juridical—a new word, in the form of "metaphysical"). The state is declared to be *identical with law*, i.e., with the norm; law and the state are merely two sides of the same phenomenon. "For the jurist the state exists only to the extent that it is turned into statute, not as a social power, nor as an historical formation, only as a subject and object of new statutes." This abstract state cannot deal with living people, but only with their actions. "Someone in gray," some abstraction *must act* (in one way or another). This is the norm. . . . The totality of such "duties" is the legal order, on the one hand, the state order, on the other. "The idea of duty was the basis of the German "revolutionary" philosophy of law for "subjects." The German theory of rule put at its basis the opposite pole of duty, namely, the *authority of power*. There resulted a theory of rule but based on *general will (Wille)*, and since in German *Wille-Wolen* means *desire*, this then is power of the will.

For Austria, Kelsen sees in the state sees only an abstract democratic obligation *(das Soll)* of human actions. But why must the Austrian working masses be subordinated to exploitation? Because they are powerless before the Entente bourgeoisie? No, *by virtue of the principle of duty*. Kelsen enjoys notoriety among us, popularity, thanks to his criticism (based on Kautsky) of Soviet authority. He uses, they say, Marxism for his theory of the state. It is characteristic that the theoretical star of the German Social Democrats on legal questions, Professor Radbruch (the former Social Democratic Minister of Justice) as recognized by Kelsen himself, came closest to him.

The theory of pure bourgeois dictatorship in open form is found in the French author Professor Maurice Hauriou (*Principes de droit public*).[7] Like every original theory of the state, Hauriou's theory has a purely national character; this is the theory of the Third French Republic. However, I add the qualification that the author gives us the French theory of the prewar and prerevolutionary period (the book was written in 1910) and, of course, he had before him neither a strong industrial proletariat nor a powerful proletarian party. Instead, there was a full-scale bourgeois reaction of the kind that exists now.

The essence of his teaching: The meaning of the existence of the state order (regime) consists in "protection," the "guarding" (*proteger*) of civil life; "its apparatus is constructed to maintain civil order." Of what does this civil life consist? In the realization (*faire-valoir*) of property obtained and family life (*commercium* and *connubium*). However, the family here plays a role only as the nucleus of property, a means to obtain the transfer of property; on the sentimental side of the family the author speaks with full contempt. Civil commerce is defined as the dreams of the French bourgeoisie in general and also of its theorist. This for him is the source of the "supremacy" (*suprématie*) of *civil law*.

The author places *individualism*—the "achievement of the Great French Revolution"—at the basis of the world view. However, this individualism is not abstract, but fully concrete; the individualism of a man with a property qualification, a bourgeois, with *property* from which it is possible to extract income. "A true blessing is rent from land or monetary capital." The author starts with a polemic against the German public law theory of rule which he dates from Herber (1865) and sees consistently in Laband, Jellinek, and other luminaries of the German science of *public law*. For Hauriou, legal personality and its power of will (*Wilensmacht*) are not the starting point, but only the final point of research. Its basis is material life and accordingly, civil law (legal *commerce*—its commerce *juridique*). "Legal commerce is the totality of legal forms born (*engendres*) by *economic commerce*." This sounds almost "Marxist," but Hauriou at once gives his own petty bourgeois coloring to every French bourgeois legal theory: and for him the center of gravity is in the organization of the satisfaction of human needs, *in exchange*.

Hauriou is a great eclectic. His system of law is based upon an endless system of balances. The (German) sole theory of the system of rule is for him, simply the mystical omnipotence of authority. "It is insufficient to divide people into rulers and ruled; it is necessary to establish *equality* between them."

How can this equality be established? Up to now there exist classes condemned to work; previously, this position was confirmed in law, now potentially all may participate in "civil life," but *de facto*, they are condemned to a working life and as workers are outside so-called civil life. The whole totality of all potentially free people must organize "like passengers on a steamship" and "a reciprocal counterpoise *in the nation* for the march ahead." The juridical personification of such a national organization is the state. The order of the state should be understood as the discipline necessary for this march. For a march to where? This goal is extremely unclear for Hauriou. Although he also speaks of the "era of progress," he himself sharply criticizes the "idea of solidarity" and similar artificial ideas of Duguit and others. For him the idea that the social function of capital and capitalism is sometimes peacefully converted into socialism is simply laughable. The state, for him, it is true, is a historical product at a certain stage of development of individualism. But his system of balances is created for the *preservation* of order in which there will *eternally* be those in power (rulers), i.e., in a democracy, the select (*élite*), a conscious minority of leaders [ruling over] the exploited mass (the ruled).

He shows how the state is separated (*séparation*) from the individual, ruling over him; how the military power is separated from the civil and how the civil power thereafter subordinates the military; how the church is separated from the state and how later the state subordinates the apparatus of the church. He shows how the nation is separated from authority in the form of political decentralization, and is itself subordinated to authority. He shows how state institutions were formed and the state apparatuses obtained their current development with division of functions. For him, society itself is nothing other than a combination of two elements: political institutions and juridical commerce. As the result of the play of balance (this is the work of political leaders) the outcome is contemporary bourgeois state authority to which everything is subordinated and which "leads" the "organized" *nation*. It is true that one threat exists for the state (the author expresses himself more cautiously: "discontent")—it is actually a "regime of classes" and does not guarantee a "*real balance*." However, having considered the data on the class organization of the proletariat (merely syndicalist), he is reassured; the socialist party disturbs him as little as parliament which as the *proxy* of the people in contrast to the general staffs, is for him simply one of the *agencies of administration.* His basic "equilibristics" (*équilibre*, balance) reduces to balance first between the principles of political and economic power, and second between centralization and decentralization. We saw above how for him *centralized political* power in fact *subordinated everything else.* The word "clever mechanism" is the best characteristic for the system uncovered by Hauriou. He has a special French coloring, but at the same time Hauriou draws the democratic content, in general, in the most bourgeois form.

The "Italian" type of state is, now, *fascist* in theory, and Mussolini in practice. As is well known, Mussolini loves to call himself a revolutionary. To a certain degree he is right: he has brought a whole revolution to the bourgeois state, and he took power by force, though without direct bloodshed. Only in Italy—where the Communists almost had power, where communism was smashed because of the tardiness of the leaders on the one hand and their direct betrayal on the other, where all the liberal-democratic theories lost all faith—could such an overtly Fascist party remain in power for long. In a speech to the parliament which Mussolini called on his having come to power, he openly stated: "I myself called Parliament, but when I saw that 33 speakers introduced 33 different approaches to the order of the day, I said to myself perhaps it is not worth abolishing this Parliament but the whole country will thank me for a compulsory rest from Parliamentary activity."

While we see that Hauriou based his open theory of the dictatorship of the bourgeoisie on the citizen consumer, and deals with the syndicalist producer only casually, the theory of fascism is orientated to the *producer*. "For his *fatherland* there are no exploited and exploiters; there are *only citizen producers*; all of them starting from the capitalist right down to the unskilled worker, from the director to the janitor of the factory, in the fascist hierarchy they are all recognized as a useful element of *production and the grandeur of society.*" From this, the principle may be deduced by which "in the organization of fascist associations (corporations) there are included in equal measure, both *landlords* and *peasants*, both *factory owners* and *hired workers.*" For now this theory remains only a theory. Attempts of the current general secretary of the Fascist associations, Rossiono, to involve landowners and factory owners, have not had success. Mussolini is a "nationalist and patriot of the *classless fatherland*," such is his theory of people and territory. His state authority is the *party apparatus*, constructed *abstractly*, not on a class basis but on the basis of the atomized individual. Do you not find here the theory of the bourgeois state brought to the extreme? Hauriou lacks a theory of the party; in France there are the same "33 parties," cliques, as in Italy. Of course, a party without support in class interest is condemned to perish if it does not put forth deceptive, attractive slogans—illusions. On this last method, *conducted with all the means of modern technology*, is based the force of the government, the party, and its "machines" in North America. Mussolini also has these approaches; he lacks only the technology and the means of the land of the dollar.

The perishing of the state

If we read in bourgeois literature of the fall of the state, then this means either the "annexation" of one independent state or the liberation of one previously joined through such annexation, i.e., a real or imaginary self-determination of the constituent parts of the fallen state. In the revolutionary literature on the fall, death, "withering away" of the state we speak in another sense, in the sense of the transition to a stateless, classless society. The anarchists also (see Anarchists) have a negative attitude toward the state and demand its immediate destruction. We do not differ with the anarchists *about the elimination of the state as a goal.* We affirm that for the achievement of this goal, it is necessary to make temporary use of the arms, means, and methods of state power *against* the exploiters, since for the elimination of classes there is necessary a temporary dictatorship of the oppressed class. Marx selects the sharpest and clearest statement of the questions against the anarchists: *overthrowing the yoke of the capitalists, must the workers "lay down their arms" or use them against the capitalists* so as to destroy their resistance? But the systematic use of arms by one class against another—what is this if not a "transitional form of the state"? [Lenin 1917, p. 463].

So revolutionary Marxism, Leninism (q.v.) reached the same theoretical conclusions to which October 25, 1917 had led: about Soviet authority, the dictatorship (q.v.) of the proletariat, and the state of the transitional period. The bourgeois state *does not "wither away"* according to Engels, but *"is eliminated"* by the proletariat *in the revolution. "The proletarian state or semi-state withers away after this revolution."*

Notes

1. I mention Duguit here as a well-known theorist who created a whole school. The theory of social functions was introduced almost simultaneously by the Austrian theorist of imperialism, the social democrat Marxist Renner (Karner), who was close to legal socialism.

2. Only 1688 is called the "Glorious" Revolution. Political simpletons are frightened by the "Long Parliament" (cf. Dicey).

3. Both views are formally correct, for this omnipotence is expressed in the mystic formula "of the King in Parliament" meaning that this single power consists of a trinity, the King, the House of Lords (higher), and the House of Commons (lower).

4. Formerly, the king and the upper and lower houses were called "the three estates of the realm."

5. A noted commentator on the English constitution, Lowell, recently formulated this position: "The Ministry legislates with the consent of Parliament."

6. " . . . provision must be made for some central authority not less representative of production as a whole than the state would represent consumption. There is postulated therein two bodies similar in character to a national legislature" [Laski 1919, p. 88].

7. This work will appear in Russian translation in a publication of the Communist Academy.

11. Revolutionary Legality

Under the Tsarist regime, the Constitutional Democratic journal *Law* appeared in Leningrad on the eve of our bourgeois revolution. Its "revolutionary" slogan was legality—legality under the Tsarist (Duma) laws. It continued to appear under the same slogan even after the February Revolution. This was not surprising because the February 1917, Revolution did not repeal the Tsarist laws in general. In 1922, its successor journal *Law and Life* appeared in Moscow under the same slogan "law"—without clarifying whose law. Moreover, we had already proclaimed the slogan legality in 1920, but to this we added revolutionary legality. Some of our revolutionary comrades were offended by the word law, while in bourgeois circles and among jurists close to them they laughed at the impermissible, or at least obsolete combination of the words "legality" and "revolutionary." What in fact do we mean by "legality," and especially "revolutionary" legality?

The developed bourgeois state calls itself a *Rechtsstaat*; its basic meaning is the self-limitation which "state authority imposes upon itself." Legality, equally obligatory both for a private individual and for the state authority as a whole and its individual agencies in particular—this is the basic slogan of the *Rechtsstaat* theorists. We are well aware how much hypocrisy is hidden in every bourgeois law, where political equality conceals economic inequality, where a class nature hides behind a general democratic phrase. Law by itself is *nothing other* than *an organized means of state administration*. This quality distinguishes the modern state from the preceding state from the period of the law of the fist, from feudal law and from more obsolete forms. In these preceding state forms, administration usually consisted of isolated, more or less accidental and unsystematic measures. Law constituted merely an exception. Law and legality, by themselves are *merely a form* whose content depends on which class is in power, and which

"Zakonnost' revoliutsionnaia," *Entsiklopediia gosudarstva i prava* [Encyclopedia of State and Law] (Moscow, 3 vols., 1925–27), 1:1150–55.

class protects power and administers this state.

Naturally, the proletarian revolution—the first revolution to be confronted by as developed a legal system as the bourgeois—*had to destroy* not only the bourgeois class state authority but also its *class law and statutes*. When Voltaire proposed the burning of the old laws and the writing of new, better ones, he was confronted by a relatively small number of such laws. The proletarian revolution has had to deal with *an entire system*, with piles of laws and with legality rooted by tens and hundreds of years in the consciousness of the masses. As a result, it carried out the necessary revolutionary work of destruction.

Only our malevolent critical opponents could call us anarchists who deny all law and all legality. In fact, the first steps of the victorious proletariat are characterized by its *excessive belief in law*. In fact, the revolution, which was carried out with unheard of organization, could not give up the most perfected (i.e., the most organized) means of action by state authority. However, our critics have not forgiven the revolution our destruction of legality and the toppling of bourgeois law.

It was clear to us that from the time of the October Revolution all laws of former governments should in principle be considered repealed. The *Decree No. 1 on the Court* formulated this: "The courts shall be guided in their decisions and sentences by the laws of the overthrown governments only to the extent that these laws have not been repealed by the revolution, and that they do not contradict revolutionary conscience and revolutionary legal consciousness." Our formulation was cautious because we knew how steadily even burned laws live on in the memory and consciousness of people. But the decree unambiguously stated the notion that *all laws were repealed*, with the exception only, etc. However, because the jurists who became people's judges nevertheless buttressed their decisions and sentences with citations from the old Code, Article 22 of the *Decree on the Court* of November 25, 1918, included a categorical demand: "*Citations* in sentences and decisions *to the laws of overthrown governments* are forbidden." The end of old legality!

Since new laws, covering the whole area of law still did not exist, there could not therefore, yet be a new type of legality. In addition, we were living in an intensified revolutionary atmosphere. At this time the revolutionary initiative of localities and individuals both at the center and in the provinces was most energetically expressed in various "self-help," disorganized actions. This was the period when the turning point of the Civil War forced us to resort to some extraordinary measures, and to some extent *extraordinary measures* were proclaimed *as the general rule*. Conditions on the external front made it impossible for the justice agency to draft all-encompassing codes for the intensely revolutionary epoch until the beginning of the retreat [i.e., the New Economic Policy].

This [policy] retreat became possible and necessary with the ending of the external front. However, an economic retreat, in the absence of codes, was also a legal retreat, because it actually relegalized part of the former system of relations. The bourgeoisie eagerly assumed that this retreat was turning into a panic, a return to the "old legality" without looking back. Then we counterpoised revolutionary legality to it. We formulated in written laws the limits of our retreat. All that was not put in those codes during our retreat, the revolution and its victories remain in force. The interpretation of these laws must be restrictive rather than liberal. What does this mean? This means that everything that existed in the area of law before the 1917 October Revolution has sunk into eternity, and that which was reinstated is a concession limited by the boundaries of law and not subject to broadening without a special law.

This is why we call our law revolutionary. Our law must be enforced strictly, but it must look forward in the direction of the revolution, not backward toward counterrevolution. We have now officially proclaimed this principle in the introductory law for the Civil Code. Here lies another danger. One comrade cleverly formulated it with the words: "we are enforcing law, but not legality," i.e., we have come to believe too much in the letter of the law. But there is another extreme: once again a condescending attitude toward revolutionary law.

Viewing law as a "system of social relations, a form of organization of production and exchange," we introduce into our definition of law the class interest and the protection of its workers' and peasants' state authority. We do not *discard law*: we define precisely its role and proper place.

In 1918, in my piece in the October volume, I have proposed the division of our codes into two parts: "*fundamental principles*, obligatory for enforcement, and *technical instructions and guides* in which *only the most general provisions are obligatory*. Whether these are *rules on court procedure* or on Soviet land tenure, gardening, or beekeeping, the *obligatory nature everywhere will be equally qualified*." Regrettably, we have not gone the route indicated. Instead, we have mixed general principles and technical rules in one code, *declaring them equally obligatory*. Hidden here is the root, the danger of the contradiction between revolutionary law and revolutionary legality.

But in addition to this objective quality, revolutionary legality also has a subjective peculiarity. The judge and in general the representative of workers' and peasants' authority represents the interest of the working class as a whole. Our voluntary retreat to the New Economic Policy was in the interests of the workers' and peasants' revolution, because it also coincides with the class interest of the victorious working class and its revolutionary legal consciousness. Thus, class justice converges with old legality which simultaneously is also revolutionary.

Recently, particularly in connection with the turning point in our policy with respect to the countryside, the question of the practice of revolutionary legality has been raised most sharply. Lenin's published letter of May 20, 1922, about legality is at the base of our practical work. Lenin draws here a strict boundary between the province of legality and the domain of expediency. The procurator pursues legality and his right and duty therein is to "pursue the establishment of truly *uniform understanding* of legality in the whole republic notwithstanding differences in local conditions and in spite of all local influences'' [Lenin 1922a, p. 364]. ''Law must be uniform, and the root evil of our social life and of our lack of culture is our pandering to the ancient Russian view and semi-savage habit of mind, which wishes to preserve Kaluga law as distinct Kazan law'' [*ibid.*] [''from Kaluga to Kazan'' is a Russian expression meaning ''from one end of Russia to the other''—Eds.]. But the Procuracy alone cannot eliminate illegality; its right is merely *''to take the matter before the court . . .''* [*ibid.*]. The court itself ''has the right to say that although there has been a definite infringement of the law in a given case, nevertheless, certain circumstances, with which local people are closely familiar, and which come to light in the local court, compel the court to mitigate the penalty to which the culprit is liable, or even acquit him. Unless we strictly adhere to this most elementary condition for maintaining the uniformity of the law for the whole Federation, it will be utterly impossible to protect the law, or to develop any kind of culture'' [ibid., pp. 364–65].

Lenin distinguishes between the role of the procurator and the role of the Workers' and Peasants' Inspectorate which ''judges not only from the viewpoint of the law, but also from the viewpoint of expediency'' [ibid., p. 365]. It is true that the recent Article 4-1 of the Criminal Procedure Code grants the court and the procuracy the right to quash unimportant cases for inexpediency, but this is an exceptional right not subject to extended interpretation.

Our law also distinguishes between the observance of legality from the perspective of law in general and the supervision of legality *from the point of view of the All-Union Constitution*: the latter right is exercised through the Supreme Court (q.v.) of the Union and the procurator attached to it.

12. Law

"The question of the nature of law is one of the most difficult and until now unsolved problems. Up to the present time a number of essentially different theories have contended with each other for exclusive authority as the general theory of law." This was the conclusion of bourgeois prerevolutionary science (see the *Great Soviet Encyclopedia* article "Law") even after the concept of law, and the class struggle over this "law," had existed for thousands of years.

However, the proletarian revolution did not for a moment hesitate before any difficulties; it first had to solve the problem of law, by critically evaluating it from the point of view of revolutionary class struggle. This task was not easy. Not so long ago the notion of contrasting the class state of the transitional period to the class state of the bourgeoisie still appeared with mindless daring. Lenin's work on *State and Revolution* and the October Revolution almost simultaneously solved this problem, and the problem of the state as well for which the bourgeois legal science was helpless as before law.

Before the 1917 revolution, those Marxists who had the courage to speak of the class justice of the bourgeoisie, timidly contrasted to it the unbiased, classless, or extra-class ("socialist," in the terminology of the program of the German Social Democrats) court of democracy. The October Revolution boldly wrote the Decree on the "class People's Court of the proletariat." This idea has grown much stronger after nine years of revolution. The area of law still remains. Revolutionary sacrilege against sacred, universal law was committed for the first time in 1917-1918, first in fact and later in theory. The first official Soviet definition of the concept of law was provided by the People's Commissariat of Justice of the RSFSR in 1919 (*Sobranie uzakonenii* [Collection of Legislation], No. 66, item 490) in the guiding principles for criminal law: "law is the system (or order) of social relations corresponding to the interests of the ruling class and protected by

---

"Pravo," *Entsiklopediia gosudarstva i prava* [Encyclopedia of State and Law] (Moscow, 3 vols., 1925-27), 3:415-30.

its organized force (i.e., by the class state).'' On the basis of this definition, theoretical work on law from a revolutionary Marxist perspective began. The question is now much clearer, and the dispute is limited to whether law should be termed this ''system or order'' as a ''form of organization'' of social relations on the other hand, or the ''system of norms or statutes'' which ''establishes, regulates and protects this order of social relations'' on the other, as a considerable number of Communists propose. The revolutionary-Marxist conception of law, in the overwhelming majority of authors, has assimilated the *class* viewpoint on law in the current sense.

The origin of law

Of course, we reject the eternal existence of law as an eternal unchanging idea of law, whether this idea be of divine origin or inborn, or derived from some immanent, internal, inalienable goals. For us, everything is changeable. Accordingly, law as a concept of a social nature is changeable and changes with social relations. But where is the the formation of law? In order to find it, let us turn to the philological origin of the word ''law.'' Already the late Lafargue shows how in many languages the words meaning law also mean the concept ''direct,'' straight line: *ortos* (Greek), *rectum* (Latin), *derecho* (Spanish), right (English), *droit* (French). We can also add the Russian word *pravda* [*pravda* means truth in modern Russian but it was used as the name of the old Russian code of laws—Eds.] which is typically contrasted with *krivda* [*krivda* means falsehood, but is from the Slavic root for ''crooked''—Eds.]. Clearly, this combination in one word of the concepts of ''straight'' and ''law'' is not accidental. It relates to the initial *measurement of land* indicated by Lafargue. A straight line of a boundary was the first sign of law, of truth. Thus, in the first attempts at commodity exchange, the cubit and the yard—the sacred means of measurement—had to be straight; a *crooked* yard in some languages is considered a sign of untruth, of non-law. What is the conclusion? We conclude that the genesis of the concept of ''law'' is found *no earlier* than the time of the first *private* ownership of land and the period of regular commodity exchange. In Rome the original law on alienating a thing actually refers to the time when only the law of alienation of so-called *res mancipi* was known. In essence, this consisted of land and stock (including livestock and slaves).

Division of the tribe or group into individual households, villages, settlements, etc. was a direct consequence of technical revolution, obviously of the ''invention'' of the use of plows. But this original private ownership of land (still far from the later type of ownership) was not necessarily connected with the birth of state and law. As long as there was enough land, there was nothing to put in strict boundaries. Boundaries, i.e., *straight*, ''legal'' border lines were required only with the birth of a certain property accumulation and, thereafter, of inequality. Then this ''truth'' was sanctioned by the authorities: boundaries or boundary markers were declared sacred, and were "blessed" by the authorities. But from whom was this "truth" defended: from beasts or from natural phenomena? No, it protected the results or the area of the application of the labor of people (the owners) from other people. This regulated and limited social relations in the process of labor.

Thus, instead of diverse unearthly ideas of law, the starting point is the essentially down-to-earth idea of land law. The first concept of "truth" as "legal" (also direct) *delimitation* of private property in land has an essentially practical, even substantive significance. Everything within the limits of such a "Russian" (or Roman or German) "truth" is the property of the family, household, or individual. From this began the development of both the law of private property and law *in general*, in the first category of so-called law in the subjective sense. From this the concept of subjective law is transferred to the area of so-called public law or of the state, of this class organization of rule. So-called public subjective law is understood in the same civil law sense, from "the law of property" to election law, to the inviolability of the person and the home.

Land law is the basic law, for under the form of the law of ownership or possession it takes on the nature of relations of rule of slavery as the basis of every division of society into classes and, accordingly, of every class law, etc.

This origin of law is contradicted by the theory that law originates in commodity exchange. This theory is presented by Comrade E. Pashukanis in his very interesting work *The General Theory of Law and Marxism*. Pashukanis proceeds from the concept of commodity fetishism and—this is his contribution—he shows how this commodity fetishism inevitably creates a fetishism of law:

> Capitalist society is above all a society of commodity owners. This means that in the process of production the social relationships of people assume an objectified form in the products of labour and are related to each other as values. Commodities are objects whose concrete multiplicity of useful qualities becomes merely a simple physical covering of the abstract quality of value, which appears as the ability to be exchanged for other commodities in a definite ratio. This quality appears as something inherent in the objects themselves, by force of a type of natural law which acts behind people's backs entirely independent of their will.

> But if a commodity acquires value independently of the will of the subject producing it, then the realization of value in the process of exchange assumes a conscious volitional act on the part of the owner of the commodity. . . . Thus, in the process of production, the social relationships of people realized in the products of labour and assuming the form of an elemental law, require for their realization a particular relationship of people as managers of products, and subjects whose will rules objects. Therefore, simultaneously with the product of labour assuming the quality of a commodity and becoming the bearer of value,

man assumes the quality of a legal subject and becomes the bearer of a legal right. A person whose will is declared decisive is the subject of a legal right. . . . Thus, contractual relations arise from commodity exchange. However, once it has arisen, the idea of contract strives to assume a universal nature. [Pashukanis 1924, pp. 75–76]

The author categorically concludes: "the development of law as a system was caused *not by the needs of authority but by those of commodity exchange.*" But Marx affirms exactly the opposite when he speaks of the *"revolution in relations of property* from which as *its basis,* came the change in the mode of production," and to the effect that *"the distribution of the means of production (i.e., of the relations of authority) predetermine also the distribution of the product."* We know from Roman history that the first form of alienation, in law, related in fact not to commodities but to land and stock (*res mancipi*), i.e., to the means of production.

Comrade Pashukanis is correct to the extent that he speaks of *bourgeois law,* but not of law in general as we understand it. If we speak of law as a class concept that dialectically changes with the corresponding relation of forces of social classes, and corresponding to the succession in power of classes, then we must know that bourgeois law is preceded by feudal law. This was distinctly recognized by Marx for whom the unconditional, decisive importance belongs to the principle of authority, namely, authority over people by means of things (from which derives the so-called law of things).

We must conclude that *in time* law as the concept of authority (i.e., the legal right to land, the law of things), arises *earlier* than the concept of the legal right *to a product* (i.e., the law of obligations), which has its basis in labor. In jurisprudence these two types of law are broadly designated as the law of immovable property and the law of movable property. Bourgeois science states that "the law of movable property and the law of immovable property are gradually converging." In other words, gradually, in the course of the development of a commodity economy and of capitalism, especially, two initially different concepts *merge*: law as authority and law as a contract for the exchange of equivalents; or, the law of things and the law of obligations. However, even in bourgeois science the opposite tendency may be noted: "Without seriously violating the interests of one side or the other, it is impossible to subordinate movable and immovable property to one and the same norms," so we read in the explanations to the draft of the Swiss Civil Code.

However, these authors cannot conceive that this is a case of the merger of two class laws, property—feudal and obligations—primarily bourgeois. Moreover, the law of obligations in the stage of monopoly capitalism returns anew to the basis of "rule" over people by means of things (through the medium of norms) and not by "free" agreement.

The work of Comrade Pashukanis made a great contribution to the theory of law; once and for all the theory of bourgeois law was deprived of its fetishism with the discovery of its real basis. But it remains to coordinate it with the theory of law as authority. While feudal law is presented to us in the form of direct (primarily) authority, authority in bourgeois law is "indirect," i.e., it occurs through the mediation of a system of abstract legal formulas, norms of the free legal subject, etc. The interesting story of the transformation of feudal law into bourgeois, the subsumption within the formulas of equivalent commodity exchange of all other social relations, including land ownership and purely personal relations, has not yet been written. Further, it must be noted that having discovered the real nature of bourgeois legal ideology of the first period, the second period of capitalism remains to be studied. The latter period moves away from pure commodity exchange and again turns to the open authority-slavery of monopoly capitalism (q.v.) and imperialism (q.v.). This is discussed briefly in the article "Jurisprudence."

In any case, the origin of law from land is firmly and clearly established by revolutionary Marxist theory.

Law and class

I have said that for us all law is class law. But law existed in preclass society and it will not exist in classless society. In class society no ruling class can do without law. The state was formed to hold the subjugated class in oppression. Law is the direct organizational form of this subjugation, and is broadly the organization of the exploitation of the subjugated class. *Class interest* has special significance for the concept of law, for the protection of which both law and the state exist. This means, of course, neither the separate interest of individual members of the class which often contradicts the interests of other members of the same class, nor the whole as the simple sum of the interests. It means *its basic interest—the interest of the class as a whole*—which may at a given moment be forced to or voluntarily arrive at certain compromises or concessions.

> The separate individuals form a class only insofar as they have to carry on a common battle against another class; otherwise they are on hostile terms with each other as competitors. On the other hand, the class in its turn achieves an independent existence over against the individuals, so that the latter find their conditions of existence predestined, and hence have their position in life and their personal development assigned to them by their class, become subsumed under it. [Marx and Engels 1845, p. 65]

The victorious proletariat eliminates the exploitation of man by man in general. However, this is a protracted class struggle; during this transitional period a state of a special type—a proletarian dictatorship—is necessary for the final suppression of the oppressors, and likewise a special Soviet Law. "Written"

Soviet Law (q.v.) is preceded by *proletarian legal consciousness* (q.v.) as *the victorious class, consciousness of its class interest.*

Law and the state

The close bond between them is obvious. It follows from our definition of the concept of law that there can be no law if there is no state. But in developed social relations it is sometimes difficult to distinguish between stages of the movement, for example, between tribal and state organization, between the initial class society and classless society, etc. Most likely, law and the state arose simultaneously. All the more so because in this period production relations and relationships of domination—the concrete system of relations and the abstract system of relations—coincided most closely. The role of the state consisted of the protecting, guarding, and, initially, in conducting the given organization of social relations by law and its application through all of its apparatuses. In the *Manifesto* Marx wrote that the aim of gaining political power was to reorganize society'' (i.e., social relations). Of course, bourgeois right in regard to the distribution of *consumer* goods inevitably presupposes the existence of the bourgeois state, for right is nothing without an apparatus capable of enforcing the observance of the standards of right'' [Lenin 1917, p. 471].

Fixed law and law in motion

Law, like every social relation, can be considered either fixed or in motion. The first method, the dogmatic, is a distinctive characteristic of bourgeois science. "Having attained supreme authority," the victorious bourgeoisie proclaims its state and its law as perfected, eternal and sacred. It objectifies these relations either in an idea or a concept, or in the positive law as a norm of conduct. Then, by deduction from the former, or by explication of the latter, these "objective," abstract relations are applied to concrete life in relationship to which part of this society permits (although the steps may be imperceptible) progress or development as the "internal development of the idea of law." This is what is called the *conservative* element of law.

The class theory of law can only be revolutionary. It considers law in motion, i.e., the revolutionary dialectic—in the process of class struggle. It sees in law not eternal categories but changing relations. But this law plays a revolutionary role as the law of the ascending class, as the form of social reorganization. Law is revolutionary even in the moment of restoration, only this time it is *counterrevolutionary* because, as Marx said, in counterrevolution there is, nevertheless, revolution.

Considering the question of law *in a revolutionary-dialectic manner*, we conclude that the laws of movement or development of social relations in general apply to it. We reject the view that denies in general the possibility of discovery of such laws of development. Bulgakov, for example, is incorrect to state that "Marx considered it possible to measure and transform the future by the past and the present, but *each era brings new facts and new forces of historical development*—the creativity of history does not shrink." As revolutionary dialecticians, we follow Marx: it is true that each era brings new facts and new forces; therefore, "each historical period, i.e., each period of economic development, also has its special economic laws of motion." We therefore distinguish between *feudal, bourgeois, and Soviet* law. But, we say, all forms of class law have also their general laws of motion or development, especially at the transitional moments from one period to another. When a new class is victorious—particularly if both struggling classes stand at opposite poles (for instance, nobles-peasants, capitalists-workers)—the nature of law changes sharply. But all law *has in common that it protects the interests of the victorious class, etc*. Even communists err on this point—both those who consider it impossible to find a general definition of the concept of all class law and those who, having studied only bourgeois law, proclaim their conclusions as *general for all class law*. This is put forth very sharply in the comparison between bourgeois and proletarian law, because history knows no leap so immense as the transfer of power from the capitalist class to the class of hired workers (see Bourgeois Law and Soviet Law).

Base and superstructure

This question appears very clearly in the problem of law and the state. In essence, here, the question is reduced to the question of life and consciousness. Ignoring the problem that the superstructure is sometimes understood more materialistically (*cf.* Comrade Bukharin), it is most important for us to emphasize that the comparison between law and economics, and base and superstructure, is in any event *a metaphorical expression* that should not be understood literally. For instance, Lenin shows that after the triumph of Soviet power, the proletariat can place the missing foundation under its new superstructure—the New Economic Policy and the "cultural revolution." All this essentially relates to the problem of dialectical or economic materialism (q.v.). Here I say only this, that law, as the concrete "organization form of production relations," coincides with the production relations themselves and is completely inseparable from life; however, legal norms (statutes and legal ideology) are obviously superstructure.

Of course, we do not need to show the predominance of the base (production relations in dependence upon production forces) over the superstructure. The reciprocal effect of consciousness upon life is equally indisputable. If in law we see consciousness and organized influence upon society, and if revolutionary law is nothing other than a form of social reorganization, then all doubts on this account disappear. The assumption here is the degree to which we are conscious of the laws of social development, for our effectiveness goes only on the lines of this development. Of course, until now law most often actually served as a restraining, conservative, counterrevolutionary element in the hands of the oppressing classes.

Law and statute (norms)

Even among Communists it is very likely that the opinion still prevails that law and statute are more or less the same: that law in the so-called objective sense is actually the totality of norms, the code of laws. In essence, such a helpless attitude toward questions of law is explained by the fact that we have not yet outlived that "legal world view," which, in Engels' words, is the classical world view of the bourgeoisie. In the bourgeois world view, where statute usurps the place of God, law primarily consists of the sanctification, or the fetishization of statute.

There is no other era in history when the thirst for statute so embraced a whole class as it did for the "third estate" in France of the eighteenth century. Its basic slogan was "constitution and laws." The first revolutionary meeting was called a "constitutional" meeting and the second a "legislative" assembly. But the constitution is merely the basic law, the law of laws. What is the cause of bad morals, asks Condorcet? He answers: bad statutes. Combassres, one of the authors of the Napoleonic Code, wrote in 1794 that "the statute is the embryo of new morals." To be outside the law, to declare someone "outside the law" entailed a verdict equal to capital punishment. "I define revolution as the coming of the statute"— this was the conclusion Michelet drew from the entire French Revolution. The word "statute" is made into an abstract symbol of the revolution. Montesquieu called his basic work, *The Spirit of the Laws.* Like "Reason" and a "Higher Being," also "statute" was given a special holiday by the decision of the Legislative Assembly of 1792 on the first Sunday, June 9, with the participation of the authorities and the national guard (*cf.* Leroux, *Statute*).

But the statute of the third estate also found its revolutionary protest. In the first months of 1792, for example, serious disorders arose in the suburbs of Paris over the high cost of bread, and the mayor refused *in the name of statute* to set a ceiling below the price, his reply provoked an uprising. The mayor called out the troops, but they deserted him; he was killed to shouts of "Long live the nation" by the same people who swore allegiance to the nation, statute, and the crown on the basis of the Constitution of 1791. This means that even then protest against the statute arose in the name of something else: bread. The ideologues of the French Revolution, with Montesquieu as their champion, equated statute and reason in the same way that the king was equated with God. In statute they sought brief formulas for conduct. The first draft code included 719 articles (the Code Napolon has 2,000), but it was rejected as too complex. Even earlier a bourgeois writer (Linguet) replied sarcastically to Montesqieu's question "what is the spirit of the laws?": "It is property for the bourgeoisie." This means that the "idea of statute," this "wisdom of the statute," etc. is nothing other than the "idea of protecting the law of private property.''

Marx and Engels wrote in the *German Ideology* that:

> Since the state is the form in which the individuals of a ruling class express their collective interests and in which all civil society of a certain era is concentrated, then it follows from this that all institutions of a social character are created by the state, and come about thanks to this political form. This *explains the illusion* that law is based upon will and moreover upon free will torn from its real basis. *Precisely likewise law in its turn is also reducible to statute.* [Marx and Engels 1845, p. 99]

What is the actual relation between law and statute? If one discards the cases when a statute has ceased to be in effect, or has become ''latent,'' or has disappeared in fact, and if one discards the plethora of relations not covered by statute—then statute is actually the ideological expression of the law of a given era. Often, this is a class compromise or agreement as is indicated by the Latin word *lex*. In statute the power of the ruling class ideologically reflects the form of organization of social relations but supports the collective views of the ruling class or of its leaders (which are one and the same in fact) of their interests. In the *German Ideology* Marx demonstrated how ''*relations* in jurisprudence . . . become concepts,'' or, elsewhere in the same work, that ''a relationship *for philosophers* is an idea''; ''they know only the relationship of 'man''' to himself and thus ''*all real relations* become *for them ideas.*''

The Constitutional Democrat Professor Muromtsev wrote: ''Instead of a totality of norms, law is *a totality of legal relations* (a legal order). The *norms* themselves appear as *an attribute* (appendage) of this order.'' The word ''attribute,'' of course, is insufficient here. Statute is something more; it is the program of the ruling class coercively made obligatory for the whole people with all the measures for its conduct. It represents, to a certain extent, boundary markers, signs of delimitation, set up for social relations, or the policies in the organizational life of these relations. This ''norms of conduct'' definition is not widespread, and already resembles a survival of the past.

Law in the objective sense, law in the subjective sense and law-justice or intuitive law

What is the meaning of this threefold division of law among bourgeois legal scholars? Law in the objective sense is what the jurist calls the totality of all norms in which, in his view the idea of law is *objectified*, and the truth-justice of the legislature (will of the people) is embodied. On the contrary, for him law in the subjective sense represents the legal relations between legal subjects that correspond to these norms. In the whole totality of this view, legal ideology, the idea of law, plays the decisive role. This threefold nature of law exists in bourgeois society, but it has not existed everywhere and always. On the birth of law in general these three different types of one and the same social relation coexisted, Marx pointed out in the introduction to his *Critique*, "relations of production develop unevenly as legal relations" [Marx 1858, p. 109]. But concrete relations ever more diverge from the law (abstract statement of relations) and from ideology (the abstract concept of this relation). In bourgeois society, legal fetishism of the law corresponds to commodity fetishism, and the idea of law (just law—*billiges Recht*) is contrasted with the one and the other. The center of gravity is transferred to *statute* and, *until the victory* of the bourgeois revolution, *to the idea* of law (natural law). The real concrete legal relation is turned upside down; our task is to put it back on its feet. "Realization never can be anything other than realization of life, and the life of people. This is the realization of the process of their living."

From all that has been said, it follows that this division of law is not acceptable for a Communist. What is objective above all is the concrete relation of production or exchange. One can speak of law in the objective sense only in this concrete area of concrete legal relations. On the contrary, in class society statute and the idea of law are subjective. But the very disunity of the concrete and abstract social relation also remains until full victory is obtained and production relations arising from elemental relations reflecting the domination of a thing (e.g., of the machine) over man, are transformed into conscious relations. When the division of mankind into classes is eliminated, then the state and all law will wither away.

Law and morality

The concept of morality, of morals, is much less clear than the concept of law. Is it related to law? Is it closely related, or alien to law? Usually these concepts are contrasted by the characteristic "internal-external." As internal rules of conduct in contrast to external or as norms of regulation of "internal" or "external" relations, you will note a certain curious movement of the words "internal" and "external" relating them first to "use" (internal or external), and then to the result of this use. However, for man, what should be considered internal and what external? Comrade Gurvich points out in *Morality and Law* the interesting fact that law sometimes approaches and sometimes moves away from morality. "Science began with the fundamental opposition of law and morality. . . . However, once law ceased to require criticism from the class affirming its political authority, law began to converge with morality." ("Law is the ethical minimum"). Comrade Gurvich concludes that "in the consciousness of the law-making class, a legal action corresponds, generally, with a moral motive; for it is indeed the law-making class." But when a subordinate class is forced by law to carry out an action that is morally bad, it yields neither to law nor to morality, but to naked force. In this respect, Comrade Gurvich is right. But when he speaks of the very nature of morality and transfers it from anthropology to zoology (Wundt), explaining it by moral instinct, then he forgets that Marx and Engels showed in *On Feuerbach* that man "is only distinguished from sheep by the fact that with him consciousness takes the place of instinct or that his *instinct* is a *conscious* one" [Marx and Engels 1845, p. 43]. In *Anti-Dühring*, Engels calls *both morality and law* equally "*social*" relations, i.e., relations deriving from production and exchange. We should not forget that in a society in which the means of production, the implements, dominate man in spite of the fact that man is in fact living, making his own instruments—instinctive consciousness is essentially different from the instincts of other animals. In *Capital*, Marx wrote that "the Roman slave was held by fetters; the wage-laborer is bound to his owner by invisible threads" [Marx 1867, 1:574]. By this, Marx indicates the way to understand both law and morality. In my book *The Revolutionary Role of Law*, the relation of law and morality is defined as follows:

> Morality is more general, while law is a narrower concept, because law embraces in general only relations of production and exchange. *The morality of the ruling class* in the area of these relations more or less *coincides* with law; i.e., the legal consciousness of the ruling class is also part of the ethics of this class. On the contrary, for the subjugated class it definitely departs from law as the interests of both the opposed classes diverge.

The division of law

Law is divided into branches, and for bourgeois legal theory, which has viewed law exclusively or primarily in statute, this division is very simple. In first place is *basic law*, the law of laws (the constitution—the law of the state); it establishes order in the form of the division of power, and it sets limits on the legislative authority making all law, i.e., for other statutes. It further divides law into substantive (civil, commercial, criminal) and procedural (court procedure, administrative law, etc.). The latter may have as many subdivisions as there are departments in the state.

Our view of the division of the law is entirely different. For us basic law—law in the true sense of the word—must be so-called *civil law or, in the most recent terminology, economic law* defining social relations in the production and exchange processes. For the administration and protection of this law there exists the class state; its essence is defined in the constitution and the law of the state. The system of material *protection* of basic law and the state is defined in the criminal law; this contains the methods of struggle by means of measures of social defense (previously punishments) against persons socially dangerous to this structure and their actions. This category also includes so-called administrative law. Each of these types of law has its own subdivisions by systems so far borrowed from administrative law. One must add *international* law. With the development of relations of international exchange, relations arise that go beyond the limits of a given state, compromises and agreements between whole states emerge on the relations of their "subjects," and certain customs are established for the relations both of private persons living in various states and of the states themselves. People even begin to speak of a "law of war."

Theory and practice of law

Such a contrast actually exists. The opposition between the theory and practice of law in bourgeois society is especially acute. This tendency appears even in our country. We still have not mastered the legal world view; it has not yet been overcome. Instead of waging a serious struggle, we close our eyes to Marxist theory and veer toward bourgeois theory and practice. There is nothing more harmful than such a view. Our revolution, i.e., practice, without our conscious initiative posed the class problem for law and we do not have the right to reject it. To slight this theory invites dangerous consequences. A scientific theory of law— as a class theory it has for the first time been transformed into a science—must become an essential part of the theory of dialectical materialism. And in law, theory and practice must be one, more than in any other area. For "truth is always concrete, not abstract."

13. Legal Relationship

A legal (juridical) relationship is a social relationship occasioned by a specific law. A social relationship has its abstract expression in categories of the science of political economy, and there corresponds to it a *concrete* legal relationship in which living, concrete people formally realize and mediate this social relationship. For example, a commodity is exchanged for a commodity as an equivalent, exchange value, but living *concrete people* as against simple abstractions of people *mediate* this relationship. So we must look at the legal relationship. For the bourgeois jurist, on the contrary, a legal (juridical) relation is *objectively* presented as *an abstract form* expressed in *statute* (legal norm). This is a "*normal relation*" of "normal" people of normal bourgeois society. This normal relation is reduced to the right (power) of one subject and the obligation (duty) with respect to him of another. *In this abstraction, beyond time and space*, independently of all quantitative and qualitative characteristics, *exists the bourgeois principle of legal equality*. For this law, quantitative, economic inequality is legally irrelevant. It is said whether the legal subject buys or sells (a house, bread, manpower), in each given case he has a right on one side, a duty on the other.

Comrade Pashukanis (in his *General Theory of Law*) and Marx showed:

> how the abstract legal form is born in the conditions of a commodity economy. The ability to have *a right in general* is separated from concrete legal claims.
> . . . In the market the person creating an obligation is obligated at the same time himself. From the position of the side of the claimant, he is constantly moving to the side of the obligor. The possibility is thus created of *abstracting from the concrete differences* between subjects of law and placing them under a common concept.

The figure of the legal subject (q.v.) begins to seem not that which he is in fact,

"Pravootnoshenie," *Entsiklopediia gosudarstva i prava* [Encyclopedia of State and Law] (Moscow, 3 vols., 1925–27), 3:440–46.

i.e., not a *reflection of relations* placed on the backs of people, but as an artificial invention of the human mind. These same relations become so customary that they seem to be the necessary conditions of any society. But having discovered the basis of the abstract concepts of bourgeois law, we cannot stop with this. [Pashukanis 1924, pp. 74–79]

Concretely, the matter is different. It is true that a legal relationship establishes a right for one party and a duty for the other, but these are *opposite poles* of the same *phenomenon*, repeating themselves in the great majority of cases along strictly consistent *class lines*. The jurists themselves realized this and introduced the concepts of the active (right) and passive (duty) subject of law. It would be more accurate to designate these opposite poles with the words positive and negative, i.e., the subject of a positive right and the subject of a negative right. For if a "relation" is merely a certain sign of equality (an equation) for abstract law, then in capitalist society the essence of this relation in fact is not equality (*Gleichmacherei*) but, speaking in the words of Marx, "*Plusmacherei*" (quantitative increase, multiplication).

It is *insufficient* to explain that the subject of law is the commodity owner, whose will rules over this thing. What will? Only a bourgeois researcher will limit himself to the abstraction of will deriving from the purportedly innate striving of commodities for automatic mutual exchange. The Marxist knows that *there are different kinds of wills*. These depend on *the class* to which the subject *belongs*. For a subject whose purpose is C—M—C (Commodity—Money—Commodity, i.e., exchange of a commodity for a commodity), the will is directed at *personal* use. For a subject whose goal is M—C—M, or even M + m (Money—Commodity—or even *more* money), the will is directed at profit, rather at *productive* use for the purpose of new profit. Here is the key to the class nature of both law and legal relationship (*cf.* Goal in Law).

Therefore, from this perspective it is wrong to say that "the subject is the simplest, indivisible element of law." This is an illusion created by a bourgeois abstraction, an illusion foreign to us. Only *the relation itself* with its opposites poles is *such an element*: "right—duty," "master—slave," "power—liability," "positive" and "negative" right. To speak of a subject as the single element of law means to emphasize the potential, conceivable possibility of someone becoming an "active" subject of a right, as the *basic characteristic* of the right, i.e., *to discard the class nature of all law*. But the very existence of the opposite poles of a right, mentioned above, is nothing other than the result of the social division into classes as the result of private property, and of the social division of labor, which will disappear only with the final elimination of the division of mankind into classes.

Social relations, or relations of production and exchange, are distinguished from legal relations not by the fact that in the second the will of the parties plays a role and not in the first. Every social relation, although hidden behind the legal relations of capital, of commodities, etc., is a *relation of living people*, i.e., a relation of *will*. To become legal, or to be turned into a legal relation, a social relation must acquire a particular supplementary characteristic: *correspondence to the class interest and its protection by the organized authority of the ruling class*. At first glance this characteristic is purely formal, but *form is not always merely a formality* and it must not anyway be confused with simple reflection or depiction. The social relation is to the legal relation as economics is related to law. Moreover, it is necessary to discard from the concept of law the relationship of people to things, for this relationship contains nothing either economic or legal in itself. As a relationship of man to external nature it relates to physics, chemistry, technology, merchandising, etc. Law deals only with social relationships, however, by the force of authority over things, by possessing them. From the legal point of view, therefore, the *element of form* has the main significance in a legal relationship, but form also signifies a means or a method. Suppose, for example, I wish to make a particular exchange; I cannot choose any form, only a legal form. If I use the means of initial ''purchase'' in Roman law, i.e., simply take the thing (*emere*—to take, later to buy) then this will be in the best case, lawfulness, conversion, or even theft, or robbery, and depending upon the attendant circumstances, I must obey the form, for instance written, even notarial, so that the relationship will be considered lawful in accordance with the statute. This form will be the *only* ''normal'' *method* of exchange by law, etc. There are an infinite number of concrete legal relations, but *typical* groups, of the most customary *types* of legal relations, will be developed—we call them *legal institutions*, e.g., exchanges, purchase and sale, rental, loan, etc. Civil law is essentially limited to providing the distinguishing features of these relations. We are told that, on the contrary, civil law requires some sort of conduct or even *provides rules* for something, but this for the typical bourgeois law has only a very limited importance. The institutes of law establish only the boundaries. The borders formally delineate the *freedom of conflict of interests*, competition and even of class struggle, within the *bounds of which* the ''conduct'' of legal subjects is legally a matter of indifference. Take, for example, the normal contract of sale. What in it is obligatory? A buyer and a seller. Previously when it was possible merely to ''take,'' it was sufficient to have only a ''*buyer*'' (robber). A purchase price is also necessary; otherwise this again would be robbery if one does not have in mind a gift (q.v.) which even jurists say is in fact never without some compensation. But *the setting of norms for prices* is granted to the large *capitalist traders*; an outcry arises against state *intervention* in the relations between sellers and buyers, landlords and tenants, employers of labor and workers, etc., upon every attempt at such intervention. The U.S. Supreme Court declares such intervention *abnormal* and unnatural. *Law* here provides the *form* and not the *norm* for the legal relationship. The norm for this relationship depends upon the ''*results of two wills*,'' upon economic struggle.

But where should we seek the legal relation itself? In life, i.e., in concrete transactions, in the code of laws, in the heads of people? Its seeming, basis is in concrete relations. Ivanov sold Petrov a house for 2,000 rubles by a written contract. This is certainly a concrete legal relation. What do we find about it in the code of laws? The sale of a house is a contract on its transfer by the seller to the ownership of the buyer, for an agreed price, by a notarized contract. This is an abstract relation in the statute. But the contract was concluded in 1920, at a time when the sale of houses was forbidden. Here was a clash of life and law, of the concrete and abstract relation. And in the minds of people, a bourgeois sold; fleeing from the onslaught of Soviet power, a worker bought. For various reasons both then considered the transaction to be legal and just. This is the third, also abstract form of the relation in the minds of men. Now the white guard has returned and on the basis of Soviet law (we will not judge his sincerity), brought suit for the return of the house, because the contract for the house was illegal. He used an abstract legal relation concretely to regain the house. But the court, although it also recognized the contract as illegal under Articles 30 and 137 of the Civil Code, awarded the house to the worker under Article 5 of the introductory law for the Civil Code. If there had not been Soviet power, the bourgeois would have obtained the home, for the worker "used" the "difficult position" of the seller. You can see how the three forms of the legal relationship differ: one concrete and two abstract. In hypocritical, abstract, and bourgeois law, these departures are much greater and constitute a general rule.

We also meet this contrast of three categories of legal relation at every point in bourgeois science: official law (statute), real law functioning in life (the real contract), and the idea of law or justice: sociological law, statutory law, and ideology of law, etc.

In the origin of law in general these relations coincide; they diverge only gradually. A new class, the urban bourgeoisie, arises from the depths of feudal society; within this class (until it eventually gains power) an ideology of law, an idea of equality stands out as a reflection of the contract of commodity exchange on the basis of an equivalent, of freedom of contract, and of bourgeois private property. The dream of turning this *"idea of law"* into an *obligatory norm* became a faith, suppressing out faith in God. The cities clandestinely "introduced" the norms of Roman law (reception). Individual and generally obligatory laws (in England various "charters," in France ordinances) were *bought* by the cities from the kings. But the urban bourgeoisie dreamed of a *free general state law* on the basis of a social contract between people (more accurately, between classes). The statute had to correspond to the concrete contract of life, as the objective law on the basis of the fundamental law (constitution), i.e., expressing the social contract. Thus, the bourgeois faith in law arose. This became a real fetish for the bourgeoisie. The concrete relations (practice) gave way, so to speak, to the background; the naked idea of law (philosophy) lost all faith.

The form of legal relations therefore has a threefold nature: one concrete—a transaction of living people, and two abstract—in statute, and in the impressions of people. Once these forms fully coincided: the *"active subject"* of the concrete relation—of taking the law in his own hands—created the legal relations, for instance, cut out land for himself on a straight boundary; this relationship entered law (purchase and sale) as a precedent or a custom, and the ruling class thief considered this his right, i.e., justice, for it "supports the mode of production." These *three relations* more or less diverged later and now exist seemingly in parallel. Marx defines justice thus:

> The justice of the transactions between agents of production rests on the fact that these arise as natural consequences out of the production relationships. The juristic forms in which these economic transactions appear as willful acts of the parties concerned, as expressions of their common will and as contracts that may be enforced by law against some individual party, cannot, being mere forms, determine this content. They merely express it. This content is just whenever it corresponds, is appropriate, to the mode of production. It is unjust whenever it contradicts that mode. Slavery on the basis of capitalist production is unjust; likewise fraud in the quality of commodities. [Marx 1867, 3:339–40]

In bourgeois society the *statutory*, i.e., *abstract form*, has basic importance (see Statute). The interrelation and the *interaction* of these three forms of relations are understood, but the material basis consists of concrete relations as a mass phenomenon, because *its numerical superiority alone* turns "law into falsehood," deprives law of force: "the law is not in effect."

When referring to legal relationships we usually mean only relationships expressed in law, the so-called *institutes of law* (q.v.). For details on the latter, see Transaction, Society, Contract, Interpretation.

14. Legal Consciousness

Since the October Revolution no term in the entire law dictionary has had such wide dissemination in our country as "legal consciousness." Revolutionary, Socialist, and Communist legal consciousness confront us at every step, but it cannot be said that even a majority of comrades understand them. Only a small minority of comrades have fully grasped the meaning and significance of these terms. Comrade Goikhbarg is obviously wrong to state that these terms mean belief in "some sort of law existing forever from ages ago," etc. This, on the contrary, was a type of *revolutionary protest* against the old law, but in the name of what? In our revolutionary practice this term first appeared in Decree No. 1 on the Court. It was borrowed from bourgeois literature and we know its source was Professor Petrazhitskii, author of the concept of intuitive law as a psychological experience. However, there was still no clarity in its understanding; the term remained, and partly remains today, merely a necessary revolutionary slogan, because how can one understand something for which we lack a proper concept? Law itself was such an incomprehensible concept. It is interesting to note that no one tried to explain those parts of our decrees designated with the term legal consciousness. Everyone sighed with relief, so to speak, when this term was gradually replaced with the terms "legality" or "revolutionary legality."

However, the concept of revolutionary legal consciousness actually represented something fully concrete. Intuitively, we came upon the indicator of the interest of class supremacy which we later placed at the basis of our own definition of law. Thanks to this we rendered the bourgeois concept of legal consciousness harmless, and thus we obtained a fully revolutionary class content. If law is understood as a protected class interest within class consciousness—the consciousness of "the interest of the class as a whole"—then we reach an indisputable conclusion: *Legal consciousness is consciousness of a victorious class*

"Pravosoznanie," *Entsiklopediia gosudarstva i prava* [Encyclopedia of State and Law] (Moscow, 3 vols., 1925–27), 3:446–48.

"which has seized state power" in its own interest. The word "revolutionary" denotes the revolutionary concept of class interest. This is something fully concrete. Lenin expressed this idea very successfully in Decree No. 1 on the Court where he clarified the words "revolutionary legal consciousness": "All laws contravening the decrees [of the Central Executive Committee of the Soviets of Workers', Soldiers' and Peasants' Deputies] and also the minimum programmes [of the R.S.D.L.P. and the S.R.P.] shall be considered invalid" [Lenin 1917b, p. 125]. Engels wrote that "every struggling class must therefore formulate its demands as legalistic demands within a program" [Engels 1887, p. 219].

With this understanding of the term legal consciousness it becomes clear why it must give way to revolutionary legality (q.v.) in our [policy] retreat, i.e., since 1921. The revolutionary retreat was carried out in the interest of the class as a whole and its revolution. However, individual consciousness of class interests was insufficient here. We needed to define the limits (the maximum and minimum of the retreat) in a systematic way through law and its implementation. This idea is expressed in the words "revolutionary legality." Even today, revolutionary legal consciousness has not disappeared, but it does not always coincide with the specific execution of the law (see Legal Relationship).

15. Soviet Law

Broadly, Soviet law is the law of the transitional period from capitalism to communism, from class society to classless society. A new type of state power is now in the hands of the proletariat in union with the working peasant masses. Soviet law may also be called *the class law of the proletariat*, but only in the revolutionary-Marxist understanding of this term. We first met this term in the drafts of bourgeois specialists as a sort of obscenity contrasted to "*general law*," i.e., the law of bourgeois society. It was understood as the denial of all law. Among Communists, conversations were recently heard that this combination of words was somehow unreal. This view has now been replaced by its opposite, and we encounter its too universal concept. We also note that behind this mask is often hidden an old bourgeois or petty bourgeois commodity. We use this term broadly to designate the whole area of law and legislation of the transitional period. A narrower understanding of it is possible in the sense of the formal organization of the system of social relations of the transitional period in which the basic unit is the soviet instead of the family and the individual. This is the law that we now usually term economic law.

When did we first conceive of the *idea* of Soviet law, i.e., of the law of the transitional period (is it not a question of the name)? Our program did not include it. The whole February 1917 Revolution occurred without the "idea" of revolutionary law. It is true that in the Leningrad Executive Committee the Bolsheviks criticized the provisional government for its complete inaction in the area of law, but without result. The Provisional Government could give the same answer that the then German Minister of Justice, Heintze gave in the summer of 1923, with a certain pride to my question about the most important reforms in the judicial branch after the revolution of 1918: "The great revolution brought no change in this area for us (in Germany)." Only with respect to the explanations of the

---

"Sovetskoe Pravo," *Entsiklopediia gosudarstva i prava* [Encyclopedia of State and Law] (Moscow, 3 vols., 1925–27), 3:921–26.

Petrograd Committee and Central Committee of the Russian Communist party from the Kshesin Palace were there discussions on the theme that the revolution would change the laws of the old regime, with a reference to Marx's speech before the Cologne court assessors. In any case, however, the talk here was still *not* of *class* law. Only in his *State and Revolution* does Lenin quote Marx about law in the first phase of communism: "We will indeed have various types of law, but this is still 'bourgeois law.' . . . There is no other standard than that of 'bourgeois right.' To this extent, therefore, there still remains the *need for a state* [emphasis P.S.]. . . . The state still has not completely withered away because the *protection of bourgeois law* continues to sanctify factual inequality. This is a bourgeois state, without the bourgeoisie" [Lenin 1917, pp. 467 & 671]. By means of a rather forced interpretation we can detect here a hint of the concept of Soviet law as "bourgeois" law, but without the bourgeoisie.

The revolution of the law first appeared in the destruction of the old law. The October Revolution relied in principle on the view that all laws of the overthrown governments had lost their force. About this question attempts are sometimes made to contrast the Decree No. 2 on the Court to the [first] Decree on the People's Court in order to show that in the latter this principle was first expressed definitively and categorically. In fact, this is a simple misunderstanding. In Decree No. 1 we read: "Local courts decide cases in the name of the Russian Republic and are guided in their decisions and verdicts by the laws of the overthrown governments *only to the extent* that they *have not been repealed* by the revolution *and do not contradict* revolutionary *conscience and revolutionary legal consciousness*." So what was kept? Just principles such as 2 x 2 = 4. In the draft of the Decree on the Court No. 2, the Socialist Revolutionary People's Commissar of Justice introduced a worse version and the old courts, under this "Court [Decree] No. 2," systematically began to cite old laws. This is why with respect to Article 22 of the "Statute on the People's Court," a prohibition was introduced on "citations in sentences and decisions to laws of overthrown governments." No one will, of course, deny that the old norms remained alive (and even now remain alive) in people's memory. But, proceeding from the principle that the *revolution itself* repealed all laws of the overthrown authorities, we naturally recognized *retroactive force* (q.v.) for this repeal, retroactive to the day of the revolution, although we then were unaware of the experience of the French Revolution in the same spirit (see Bourgeois Revolution). This resulted, simply, from the very nature of our revolution. Crucially, we simultaneously abolish in fact all private ownership of land, and then of factories, etc. This means we undertook the *reorganization of all real social relations* and for this purpose formed our own Soviet power.

From the first day, we acted with an organized-legal order, i.e., by way of general legislation: decrees on power, on land, on the eight hour working day, etc. One should note that there was too great a belief in revolutionary law. We at once started to prepare a code, but this was unsuccessful and the attempt. Life proceeded faster than statutory law and even so-called legal consciousness, not to mention yet theory. In an article written at the end of 1918, for the October collection, I still dreamed of a new code that would include the basic norms of the revolution of law and purely technical rules. About our decrees I wrote that *"proletarian law is above all a simplification, a popularization of our new social order."* I continued:

> The decrees on land, on the eight hour working day, on the family and inheritance, on the separation of church and state, were not all timely, for not all had yet (in 1918) been implemented. But even this opinion is incorrect. We were right to set up these boundary markers. The mere fact that not one of these early decrees has had to be changed, and that one after another they are now being put into practice, shows their usefulness. (Stuchka 1919, p. 68)

It is well known how Lenin evaluated our Soviet legislative work in 1918: "The Soviet constitution was not written according to some plan, was not compiled in offices, was not forced upon the working people by bourgeois lawyers. No, this constitution arose from the developing class struggle in proportion to the maturation of class contradictions." And when it was approved, Lenin stated with relief: "From the moment of approval of the constitution and putting it into practice an easier period will begin in our state structure." This was the first period of the revolution before the brave attack when our decrees were the slogans of war. Lenin later evaluated them as follows:

> At one time we needed declarations, statements, manifestos and decrees. We have had enough of them. At one time we needed them to show the people how and what we wanted to build, what new and hitherto unseen things we were striving for. But can we go on showing the people what we want to build? No. Even an ordinary laborer will begin to sneer at us and say: "What use is it to keep on showing us what you want to build? Show us that you can build. If you can't build, we're not with you, and you can go to hell!" And he will be right. [Lenin 1921, p. 73]

With the period of retreat and the New Economic Policy our legislation and law assumed a new character. We underwent reception; we borrowed bourgeois law. It is untrue that we reinstated the old law; we did not yet have pure bourgeois law before the revolution and eight months of bourgeois revolution *produced precisely nothing* in this area.

Decrees, laws, and codes of this period had another nature. In them we set boundary markers, but *boundary markers of the retreat*. We undertook the reception of bourgeois law and these codes gave the limits of those concessions to bourgeois law to which we then agreed and beyond which we *did not intend to go* in the line of retreat. We *also* noted *those boundaries up to which we nevertheless promise equal rights to all* (Article 4 of the Civil Code) and promised "for a long time and seriously, but also not forever."

But the period of retreat passed. We started a *new attack*, an attack on a new note. The Fourteenth Party Congress defined it as "*an attack in the direction of socialism,*" "*but on the basis of the New Economic Policy.*" During these years we made great strides in the theory of law. Now we have a revolutionary-Marxist concept of the nature of bourgeois law in Comrade Pashukanis' *General Theory of Law and Marxism*. This revealed the secret of the fetish of the "legal subject" (q.v.). Now we have noted the nature of law of the period of monopoly capitalism on the basis of its vain attempts to achieve planning in the anarchy of its economy. We can begin to construct socialism on the base of the New Economic Policy—the conscious development of our Soviet Law, having set our legal apparatus on a new track "in the direction of socialism."

Soviet law, particularly in the narrow meaning of the word, is becoming a serious subject. From extremely diffused, unsystematic legislative material, we must create a simplified, flexible law that all can understand. This does not mean a *rejection* of the reception of bourgeois law. On the contrary, on *its base* we see our construction. But the element of socialist planning must be distinctly added to it, discarding the excess growths of the period of "decay of capitalism" those abuses of economic policy which, in Lenin's words, are "legal in all other countries, but which we do not want to legalize" [Lenin 1922, p. 393].

There are doubts in our country about whether we need a special Soviet law. Is it not sufficient for us to have the phrases that bourgeois law simply will wither away by itself? The analogy of the necessity of a transitional Soviet state has shown us also the slogan of a *transitional* Soviet law. Now this appears in fact. Quantity is transformed into quality. Soviet law has become an accomplished fact.

PART III

Socialist Construction and Soviet Legality

Introduction

Part III of this collection contains essays dating from the end of NEP to the start of Stalin's five-year plans. It shows Stuchka's ability to adapt his ideas to the practical needs of the new era of the building of socialism in one country. Without recanting his basic ideas or breaking with the past, he now shifts his emphasis to the the idea of the importance of law as a means of social engineering and to the long-term need for law. The mild criticisms of the ''commodity exchange'' theory and the scholarly tone of his early writings now turn to polemics, as he realizes that Soviet legal scholars are literally engaged in a life-and-death struggle. Unlike many who maintained integrity at the price of their lives or their lives at the price of their integrity, Peter Stuchka managed to maintain both. The final article, ''My Journey and My Mistakes'' is not the self-criticism that his colleagues had demanded but a defiant statement of his views. ''State and Law in the Period of Socialist Construction'' is to a large extent a polemic with the theories of Pashukanis. In the course of his argument, Stuchka makes a number of points that eventually become established principles of Soviet legal theory. However, two aspects of this article would return to haunt Stuchka in the 1930s.

Pashukanis's theory, as characterized by Stuchka, is that law during the ''transition period'' to communism is ''bourgeois law.'' Stuchka recognizes, as he must, that most of the Civil Code is a verbatim copy of West European civil codes. Nevertheless he argues that the law of the transition period is not ''bourgeois law'' but Soviet law. The main distinguishing characteristic of Soviet law is the use of economic planning in the interests of the proletariat rather than private transactions in the interests of profit. Other specific Soviet elements are the treatment of land and labor law separate from the Civil Code. On all these points Stuchka's views have become Soviet orthodoxy.

From the principle that the Civil Code embodies Soviet law, Stuchka makes an important deduction, which also became part of Soviet orthodoxy. This is that the courts should not take liberties with the principles of the Civil Code to favor the socialist sector of the economy, but rather that favoritism should come through specific legislation, while the code should be enforced in a uniform manner.

On two points, however, Stuchka laid the grounds for specific difficulties for himself. He relied heavily on statements by Bukharin and Grin'ko to buttress his points—and both were destined to fall from favor and become major defendants in the purge trials of the 1930s. Even though there was nothing heretical in their statements upon which Stuchka relied, he would later be subject to guilt by association. Second, he argued that the withering away of the state had already begun. This position would put him in direct conflict with Vyshinsky's and Stalin's theory of the strengthening of the state as a prelude to its withering away. However, the theory would eventually be revived under Khrushchev.

In "Culture and Law," Stuchka makes a number of points that have become accepted Soviet doctrine or practice. He argues that the basic safeguards of criminal procedure developed by "bourgeois law" should be taken over as a cultural inheritance. He goes on to argue that the law should be simplified to the point where anyone could understand it. However, he cites Lenin on the idea that all this should be done "without forgetting the limits of legality in a revolution." Soviet criminal procedure has in fact incorporated most of the principles of prerevolutionary criminal procedure and is simple and straightforward in its operation. The limits of legality are not forgotten, in that political influence remains routine in political cases, however it has become taboo to mention such influence openly. Stuchka argues for a purge of the bar. In fact such a purge did take place in the years immediately following the publication of this article, as the bar was packed with staunch communists, and anti-communist lawyers were removed. It is no longer true, as it was in the 1920s, that punishment by "suffering" is removed from the criminal code. The idea of replacement of punishment by labor education that Stuchka supports here is a dangerous one, particularly when combined with the idea of simplification of criminal procedure and purge of zealous defense counsel. Together they are a prescription for the Stalinization of criminal law. Carried to their logical extreme, as they were by Vyshinsky, they would mean that any unreliable persons could be sentenced to "reeducation" in a procedure that did not involve formal procedural safeguards or the right to independent counsel. In the reaction against Stalinism, Soviet criminal law and procedure have restored many of the elements removed in the 1920s.

In "Revolutionary Legal Perspectives" Stuchka moves away from the idea that the state is withering away and talks instead of perfecting it. He sees this perfection as involving increased popular participation, which is, however, apparently to be more formal than real, for he indicates, for instance, that the lack of reliable people means that judicial supervision of the application of criminal law must be strictly centralized. He returns to some old themes such as the need for simplification of judicial procedure, the need for using labor to reform criminals, and horror at the unmanageable volume of Soviet legislation.

Stuchka moves toward the Stalinist bandwagon in "The Revolution and Revolutionary Legality," which he defines as strict obedience to the commands of central authority, and would allow deviation from legal rules only when necessary to carry out directives of central party organizations. He also makes a very practical suggestion, calling for centralization of legal drafting in an organization with the necessary technical expertise—this may be part of a scheme that would let him gain more control over the drafting of legislation.

As the industrialization and collectivization of the USSR forged ahead, the cultural revolution proceeded on the intellectual fronts. Although in 1928 Stuchka was one of the principal advocates of the cultural revolution of the law, he soon found himself besieged by the very process he had helped to create. At a major conference of Marxist jurists in 1930, a resolution was passed criticizing Stuchka for his "errors" on the legal front. In response, Stuchka promised to undergo "self-criticism." He replied in the form of the long essay "My Journey and My Mistakes" (1931). However, instead of the usual self-deprecating exercise that was the standard fare for these times, Stuchka proceeded to a defense of his positions which was defiant in tone and even contemptuous of his principal critic. The criticism of Stuchka during this conference came mainly from his erstwhile colleague Pashukanis and from a minor Stalinist legal apparatchik, Angarov. Ironically, part of the general thrust of criticism at the conference was that Stuchka had not been sufficiently critical of Pashukanis's theoretical errors—to which he replied by referring his critics to his 1927 essay on his differences with Pashukanis (see this volume, Ch. 16). At the conference, Pashukanis himself (who was already undergoing self-criticism) attacked Stuchka for his role in drafting the Fundamental Principles of Civil Legislation, and for his work as a civil jurist on the RSFSR Supreme Court. In his rebuttal, Stuchka defended his record with considerable skill, assailed Pashukanis in rather strong personal terms, and carried to its logical conclusion his own criticism of the latter's tendency to reduce all law to bourgeois civil law.

However, Stuchka saved his wrath for "Comrade Angarov" who had itemized his alleged twelve "mistakes," refuting each allegation one by one while showering his opponent with contempt.

This essay can also profitably be read as Stuchka's autobiographical sketch of his career as a Soviet jurist, and as a short history of the Marxist school of law in the USSR from its origins in 1917. Stuchka's self-defense was clearly out of step with the Stalinist atmosphere in jurisprudence to which he himself had unwittingly contributed. Times had changed dramatically, but for Stuchka the main issue remained his integrity as a Bolshevik and Marxist jurist. He concluded on a note strangely out of keeping with the emerging Stalinism of the early 1930s—to wit, that he would count on "independent thinking young people to judge his merits fairly." He died a year later, in 1932.

16. State and Law in the Period of Socialist Construction

[W]e might say that we are going through a transition period within a transition period. The whole of the dictatorship of the proletariat is a transition period, but now we have, you might say, a heap of new transition periods. [Lenin 1920b, p. 32]

The Fifteenth Party Conference ended a definite stage in the history of the All-Union Communist party (Bolsheviks) and the proletarian revolution. It completed the work begun at the Fourteenth [Party] Conference and Fourteenth [Party] Congress, and provided a firm basis for the scientific and tactical principle of the Party in this period, the principle of the *construction of socialism in one country*. This idea, which Lenin had expressed theoretically and in general form in 1915, assumed real and increasing importance for the USSR after it became clear that the world revolution apparently was delayed. Lenin formulated this even more definitively in relation to the progress of the work of construction in the USSR on the basis of the New Economic Policy. At the Fourteenth Congress the Party stated that "the Soviet economy would move toward socialism" on "the basis of the New Economic Policy." At the Fifteenth [Party] Conference this was justified more theoretically and turned "into a guide for action" by the Party. At the expanded Plenum of the Comintern, it received *worldwide approval*. In my report after the Fourteenth Congress (see *Revolutsiia prava*, no. 1) I noted that certain tasks for our [law] section followed from the resolutions of the Congress. We must now address these questions more directly and seriously in the area of our science of the state and *particularly of law*; both in theory, and in practice.

However, I must say that I do not plan to present a finished program today. This is not something for an article or even a whole book: this is a program for a whole period. I will mainly concentrate on the question in the *area of so-called civil law*,

"Gosudarstvo i pravo v period sotsialisticheskogo stroitel'stva," *Revoluitsiia prava*, no. 2 (1927) :3–16.

while my other observations will be essentially supplementary to this special task.

Stages of the transition period

Beginning with Lenin's remarks quoted above, we can observe three basic stages in our transition period up to this point: (1) the period of the seizure of power, (2) the period of the struggle to retain power (intervention and so-called war communism), and (3) the period of the construction of socialism. The problem of the socialist nature of this construction process came to the fore especially at the approximate reestablishment of the prewar [economic] level. Naturally, according to the laws of the revolutionary dialectic, each of these stages had to pose new problems for the field of state and law. This was particularly so in the field of law, where the "retreat" to the New Economic Policy evoked renewed hopes for the old "legal thought," which was willing to change temporarily into Soviet khaki in order to preserve its bourgeois essence. Alongside this development even committed communists, adopting the bourgeois forms necessary for the New Economic Policy, declared them to be specifically Soviet, thus unintentionally discrediting the name Soviet and Soviet power.

The construction of socialism

The very idea of socialist construction is new. It was foreign to social democracy even in its revolutionary period. Social democracy imagined that the old society would grow into a socialist one either in a revisionist way (gradually, evolutionarily, and nondialectically) or in a peculiar utopian way by a leap into a "kingdom of the future" already prepared by capitalism. In effect, this would be either a peaceful and democratic or a revolutionary seizure of power for *the continuation of an already finished economy*, with only the necessary formal reorganization of this economy.

But *revolutionary construction in general* is necessary in any transfer of power from one class to another. The very existence of a class is based upon the social division of labor and conditioned by the relation of classes to the means of production. Effecting changes in these relations *requires time*. *The development* of one class society into another requires a definite *transition period*; this is the basis of the theory of various revisionists and opportunists. Starting from the fact of the gradual development of capitalism within feudalism and especially absolutism, they transfer this *analogy in full* to the "society of the future." Given "developed" capitalism, the economic revolution has led to a new political superstructure of capitalism, to a democratic state. When socialism "matures" there will be a *socialist transformation, and not before*.

This notion was categorically rejected by Lenin. It was insufficient to draw parallels between the bourgeois and proletarian revolutions; it was also necessary to note their fundamental differences. The idea of *revolutionary construction* as a specific feature of the socialist revolution—contained in his *State and Revolution*—was developed by Lenin in March 1918:

> One of the fundamental differences between bourgeois revolution and socialist revolution is that for the bourgeois revolution, which arises out of feudalism, the new economic organizations are gradually created in the womb of the old order, gradually changing all the aspects of feudal society. The bourgeois revolution faced only one task—to sweep away, to cast aside, to destroy all the fetters of the preceding social order. by fulfilling this task every bourgeois revolution fulfills all that is required of it; it accelerates the growth of capitalism.

> The socialist revolution is in an altogether different position. The more backward the country which, owing to the zigzags of history, has proved to be the one to start the socialist revolution, the more difficult is it for that country to pass from the old capitalist relations to socialist relations. New, incredibly difficult tasks, organizational tasks, are added to the tasks of destruction.

> The difference between a socialist revolution and a bourgeois revolution is that in the latter case there are ready-made forms of capitalist relationships; Soviet power—the proletarian power—does not inherit such ready-made relationships, if we leave out of account the most developed forms of capitalism, which, strictly speaking, extended to but a small top layer of industry and hardly touched agriculture.[1]

This idea was worked out in detail by Comrade Bukharin in his article "The Bourgeois Revolution and the Proletarian Revolution" [Bukharin 1924, p. 217 and p. 223). Only *"after the conquest of power by the working class does there begin the real* growth into socialism" [ibid., p. 275].

The state of the transition period

It would seem a waste of time to speak of the state during the transition period in general. Lenin theoretically, and in the October Revolution practically, developed the idea of the role of the proletarian state in the transition from capitalism to socialism and communism. Now the importance of the state is "obvious." But not all that is obvious is sufficiently clear to everyone; indeed, often because it is obvious it evokes a condescending attitude. Therefore, I consider it categorically necessary to emphasize that just as in class society, before the proletarian revolution, the *state* was an *unconditional premise* of the existence and preservation of private property and *of law in general*; likewise, the proletarian state is no less an unconditional premise of the transition from capitalism to socialism and communism. The proletarian state is also the premise of the law that corresponds to this transition period.

> Whoever has failed to understand that dictatorship is essential to the victory of any revolutionary class has no understanding of the history of revolutions, or else does not want to know anything in this field. [Lenin 1920, p. 340]

You will not find one article or speech by Lenin in the last years of his life without words of the type: "see how things have changed now that state power is already in the hands of the working class," "after the victory of the proletariat," "on the basis of workers' and peasants' power and the Soviet system," etc. Therefore, we must categorically reject every attempt to revise Marx and Lenin on the question of *the role and significance of the state*. Simultaneously, we must dialectically pursue its development by stages, as forms and especially of the meanings of the state.

The bourgeois revolution led to the *bourgeois state* and to bourgeois democracy. This was a class state without the class of feudal lords or with the bourgeoisification of the feudal lord ("land rent"). Developing according to the innate laws of revolution, the great French Revolution took one step further when the convention (with the cutting off of the Girondist wing) created for the first time a sort of "bourgeois state without the bourgeoisie." But "Thermidor," the reinstatement of a pure bourgeois state (and after it, a temporary restoration) occurred as a result. "Why,"—said Comrade Bukharin to the Twelfth Plenum of the Communist International—"did Thermidor succeed at the time of the Great French Revolution? Thermidor won and *had to* win at the time of the Great French Revolution *because* the major capitalist bourgeoisie held higher economic trump cards in their hands; this bourgeoisie was a representative of *large scale production* while the Jacobin dictatorship protected the interests of *small-scale* production. The contradiction between the great revolutionary political role of the bourgeoisie and its *small-scale* production ideals inevitably led to the *victory of the large scale bourgeoisie*, because at that time the proletariat was still not developed and could not act as an independent and leading revolutionary force."

I will not dwell on the Paris Commune. Soviet power is a developed form of the dictatorship of the proletariat.

We have consecutively defined the Soviet state as a "dictatorship of the proletariat," as a "dictatorship of the proletariat and the poorest peasantry" (Constitution of 1918), as a "workers' and peasants' government," as a "state of workers and peasants" (Constitution of the Russian Soviet Federated Socialist Republic of 1925), and have returned again to the words "proletarian state"— still with a "bourgeois distortion." But in all cases these words mean the state of the proletariat *in alliance* with the peasantry, with the *hegemony of the proletariat led by the Communist party*. This all seemed obvious to us, but then a united opposition appeared and sowed discord. We heard that our state was becoming a peasant one, and that its power has been and is worker and peasant. We must recognize this openly and move to a *two-party government*, etc. This is why this "obvious" question had to be given attention by both the Fifteenth Conference of the All-Union Communist Party and the Seventh Plenum of the Executive Committee of the Communist International. This question has unusual relevance for the problem of law.

Marx's words in 1870

At the Fifteenth [Party] Conference, the opposition cited, among others, Marx's words of 1870 on the possibility in England and America (Engels added Holland) of a peaceful democratic revolution, even with the *buyout* of the private property of "that band," the capitalist class. Lenin, as is well known, recognized this thought as true in relation to the 1870s, but rejected it for contemporary England and America as typical representatives of imperialism and militarism. Why have we now returned to Marx's thoughts of the 1870s? These words create *new perspectives*. If, in fact, a "peaceful transformation" is impossible in general, then is the theory of Kautsky and the Social Democrats possible in the West—the theory that a *coalition of the Social Democrats and bourgeoisie* is the government of the transition period from capitalism to socialism? And what about here? In this case there is nothing dangerous in various *borrowings from bourgeois democracy*. The Western bourgeoisie does not itself argue against such borrowings. On the contrary, it is miserly only with money. In this case, why not continue the *"reception" of more and more institutions of civil law*, even contrary to statute. It was not for nothing that the Ustrialovs argued, under Lenin, that our new policy [N.V. Ustrialov published an anti-Leninist essay in *Smena vekh* (*Changing Boundary Markers*), July 1921, Prague—Eds.] was "not tactics evolution." "In fact, you are sliding into the usual bog" (cf. [Lenin 1922b]). Now the Ustrialovs are much more open.

Here, the task of these enemies is much easier because we have lived for a long period with neither a bourgeois democracy (eight months in all) nor a developed capitalist, bourgeois civil law. Thus, our comrades sometimes tenderly greet, as gifts of the revolution, as features of Soviet law, what are in fact bourgeois legal principles (see Articles 30, 33, 403, 399 of the Civil Code, etc.). We encounter the same, though less often, with respect to the state. Entire theories resurrect old bourgeois theories in a Marxist, Soviet light, and it is difficult to distinguish where naive, but bona fide, confusion ends and malicious intent begins.

The state and the proletarian revolution

The Soviet state of the *first and second* period had as its purpose the seizure and consolidation (retention) of power by the proletariat. Its form also corresponded to this.

The *third period* put forth the task of adapting the state to the stage of socialist construction while Comrade Bukharin stated in 1920 (*The Economics of the Transitional Period*) that *"the process of socialization in all of its forms is, ultimately, the function of the proletarian state."* His words also related to the process of constructing socialism under NEP when socialist construction entailed "the introduction of a still non-existent or insufficient economic base." But at the same time, to a certain extent, *the withering away* of the state *had already begun.* Lenin said in 1921:

> *From now on the best policy is less policy.* Put more engineers and agrono-
> mists to work, study with them, check their work, turn congresses and confer-
> ences not into agencies for meeting, but into agencies for checking economic
> successes, into agencies where we could properly *study economic construction.*

But the state cannot wither away completely so long as there are still classes and law, for, Lenin states, *"otherwise who would enforce the law?"*

What is the nature of the *relation of the state* to revolutionary construction in general and to legal regulation of it. This question must be discussed in more detail, exploring these disagreements among us that relate to practice. I will again use comparative method with reference to the conditions of bourgeois and prole-tarian revolutions and states.

The automaton of bourgeois construction

The bourgeoisie views the bourgeois revolution as if "a person in grey, with the name 'Revolution,'"[1] had produced a *miracle* that realized the principles of natural law, overthrew the hated feudal lords, and established liberty and guaran-teed freedom for private property. Meanwhile, if any rough edges occurred in the form of "revolutionary thefts," terror, and executions, not stopping even before the holy personages of kings, then these were unfortunate accidents to be quickly forgotten (and erased or deleted from history textbooks, etc.). The law, the constitution of the new order, has established a sort of automaton (bourgeois law) regulating civil commerce, which in the future will regulate itself. This automa-ton is provided to everyone in proportion to their means. In place of God— temporarily overthrown by the great French Revolution—law was established ("Law is Reason Itself"), more precisely, the Civil Code (*Code civile*) was established. In the rhythm of this mechanism's motion, the "perpetual motion" (*perpetuum mobile*) of the automaton, *society constructs itself* according to the principles of free competition (*laissez faire, laissez passer*). Demand and supply is the first stage; purchase and sale is its realization. The miracle of the *self-construction* of capitalist society has caused millions to turn a blind eye to the torrents of blood and other horrors that accompany this process. All these are voluntary sacrifices of society. It took no little effort to open the eyes of even part of the millions to the unseen hand of the director, i.e., the capitalist class, the bourgeoisie. Karl Marx revealed the nature of this director—it is the *class dictatorship* of the bourgeoisie. And we now define this automaton as the anarchy of production and exchange and their *juridicization* ("legalization") in the law of property and obligations of the civil codes.

The concept of social democracy

This concept has also migrated to social democracy, in a quite simplified form. Social democracy presents the whole matter as the *economic construction of capitalism*, and in every way supports the maximum development of capitalism. Upon the attainment of the unconditional "maturity" of the economy, a "peaceful transformation" will transform *bourgeois democracy* into *social democracy*, bourgeois law into socialist law, i.e., the capitalist "automaton" will be transformed into a socialist "automaton." In order to do this, it is necessary to replace the class struggle with a policy of reconciliation and cooperation of classes. This will occur either through a coalition between social democracy and the bourgeoisie, or through a Social Democratic government *that conducts the policy of the bourgeoisie*. Even the most recent and most false Social Democratic program—the program of Austrian Social Democracy—goes no further than the peaceful parliamentary victory of democracy.

The state and bourgeois construction

We know that the proletarian dictatorship, the Soviet state, is a necessary condition of socialist construction in the broadest sense. But what role did the state play in the *bourgeois revolution*? "The state has obtained power like it never before had. The state is proclaimed the *very source of rights and property*." This is how the bourgeois writer Sagnac delights in the great French Revolution. Nevertheless, even at the very moment of revolution, the bourgeoisie has assigned the state *merely the task of guaranteeing* the peaceful right of private property. It must not interfere with the actual construction of the state! Marx goes considerably further, and this should be remembered by all who minimize the significance of the state in his teachings, not to mention Lenin's teachings. I will cite only one place from Volume I of *Capital*, also correcting an annoying and basic error in its Russian translation: "But they all [systems of primitive accumulation—Eds.] employ the power of the State, the concentrated and organized force of society, to hasten, *hothouse* fashion *(treibhausmässig fördern²)*, the process of transformation of the feudal mode of production into the capitalist mode, and to shorten the transition. Force itself is the midwife of every old society pregnant with a new one" [Marx 1867, 1:751]. This passage characterizes Marx's view of the role of the state "in the construction of capitalism." The capitalist law of *private property* is itself *inconceivable* without the *guarantee* of a class state. Thus, the state is placed in the role of midwife *at the birth* of capitalist society. It has just as significant a role in the *first* as in the *second* period of capitalism. This role is hidden by the artificial separation of the apparatus of the class state from the ruling class as a whole, and may cause some misunderstanding.

Feudal society and law

In moving to the question of the role of law in socialist construction, we must pause briefly on the significance of law in general. Is there law in feudal society? Both Marx and Lenin answer that there is. Feudal law is characterized by a clearly expressed form of direct domination-subordination. Slavery is domination over people by virtue of landholding for the purpose of their merciless exploitation, but simultaneously the satisfaction—in the most primitive form—of their needs (serfdom). A characteristic type of feudal law is *feudal property law*, mainly feudal ownership. "This feudal system of land ownership had its counterpart in the *towns* in the shape of corporative property, the feudal organization of trades" [Marx and Engels 1845, p. 23].

Bourgeois law

Commodity exchange was underdeveloped in the first period of feudal society. The broad development of commodity exchange and contractual relations begins in proportion to the development of a commodity economy—already occurring in the depths of feudal society, mainly in the cities. Roman private law is a ready-made form of law found in the cities; *the reception of Roman law occurs*. A sort of dual power exists for town and country. (The process of reception facilitates the inclusion of countries where the reception of Roman law has occurred, particularly Germany, in the Roman empire.) Thus, so-called bourgeois law was revived. Its characteristic type is the *law of obligations (contract law)*. This is not commodity exchange in the form of purchase and sale, the material medium of which is *money*; and secondly, which occurs formally by means of *contract*. Contract is the form by which this relation is implemented.

What then is the basis of this feudal exchange? It is the *exchange of equivalents* on the basis of *labor value*: equal quantities of socially necessary labor exchanged for an equal amount of labor. This is the origin of all types of abstract ideas, norms of equality, subjects of law and bourgeois justice.

When Comrade Pashukanis showed in *The General Theory of Law and Marxism* that bourgeois law, with its abstract formula, corresponded to the Marxist theory of value, he solved the riddle of the fetishism of bourgeois law, and revealed the material essence of this formal abstraction.

I will not pause to outline this theory. It is well known to our readers. But since I draw certain conclusions from it, and inasmuch as certain writers contrasted it with my definition of law, I must deal with Pashukanis's theory in more detail, with certain, apparent disagreements. I find that his theory correctly reveals the basis of so-called bourgeois law, deriving it from concrete relations of commodity exchange.[3]

Exchange and consumer value

But having revealed the basis of the fetishism of bourgeois law, one must not stop here. It is necessary not to forget that "a commodity in the first place, an object outside us, a thing that is, by its properties satisfies human wants of some sort or another" [Marx 1867, 1:35]. "A thing can be a use-value, without having value. . . . [A] thing can be useful, and the product of human labor, without being a commodity" [ibid., p. 61]. But *a thing may not be of value without being an object of demand.* "In the use-value of each commodity there is contained useful labor, i.e., productive activity of a definite kind and exercised with a definite aim" (ibid., p. 42]. "Insofar as exchange is a process, by which commodities are transferred from hands in which they are non-use-values to hands in which they become use-values, it is a social circulation of matter" (ibid., p. 104].

The purpose of law is social exchange of things

If the institutes of bourgeois law, or the law of obligations, are a form of implementation of the relations of commodity exchange, then *this law as a whole* is, in essence, *formally defined by* the *social exchange of things. Expedience—the purpose of law* which bourgeois theorists have noted but have not understood-is derived from the nature of the consumer value of commodities. "*The opposition* of consumer value and value are *innate to a commodity,*" "the division between the usefulness of things for direct consumption and usefulness for exchange" remained unsolved riddles not only for the bourgeois jurist but even for the economist. Bourgeois jurists therefore sought the *purpose of law in the definition of the abstract idea of will* in various more-or-less metaphysical constructs.

The abstract will of the legal subject

Comrade Pashukanis begins with Marx's words "on the person whose will rules over things," as commodities, to explain the abstract concept of the subject of bourgeois law. But in this form the will of the legal subject aids that fetishization of the power of the commodity form about which Marx writes:

> But not to anticipate, we will content ourselves with yet another example relating to the commodity-form. Could commodities themselves speak, they would say: Our use-value may be a thing that interests men. It is no part of us as objects. What, however, does belong to us as objects is our value. Our natural intercourse as commodities proves it. In the eyes of each other we are nothing but exchange-values. [Marx 1867, 1:83]

Marx indicates here that this "thought of commodities about themselves" is reflected in the words of economists. Imprisoned by abstract formulas, jurists also risk forgetting living people. "We, as legal subjects, are not concerned with it (i.e., consumer value)" would be how the corresponding words of a jurist would sound.

The class nature of all law

However, the additional conclusion from the above words—and here lies our disagreement—is the denial, the disregarding, or at least the minimizing of the class nature of all law. And since sales and purchases are negotiated solely between particular individuals, "it is not admissible to seek here for relations between whole social classes" [Marx 1867, 1:586]. If we adopt the method of political economy for the theoretical analysis of legal institutions, then we must therefore refrain from introducing the class element in civil law. But this would lead to the very gap in the theory of political economy and the theory of class struggle that we recently experienced here.

I find that for us and for the understanding of bourgeois law it is pointless to deal with an abstract society of simple commodity producers any more than is necessary to reveal the secrets of the abstractions of bourgeois law. Once this is done, back to reality, to the class society of the bourgeoisie. Let every petty bourgeois theory (Proudhonist, etc.) deal with it; we will proceed to study law as a concrete system of social relations.

The class will of the legal subject

We will consider "the person whose will prevails over things." Can one speak of such a will in general? In a society of *simple commodity exchange* the formula CMC (Commodities—Money—Commodities) is in effect; the will of the commodity owner is directed at obtaining commodities (usually consumer goods). This formula is examined in the first chapters of Volume I of *Capital*.

But for *capitalist*, bourgeois society, an *entirely different* formula applies: M—C—M, or more accurately M—C—M + m (Money—Commodities—Money, i.e., more money). Purchase for *sale with a profit*, or for the most part for use in production for *the purpose of new profits*, is the formula of capital. What is the nature of the person whose will rules over things—commodities constituting capital? "As a capitalist he represents only personified capital" (Marx 1867, 1:592). His soul is the soul of capital. "But your law is only the will of your class converted into law, the content of which is determined by the material conditions of existence of your class."

This means two fundamentally *different wills*, two polar opposite subjects of law in class society: as soon as we finish the first chapter of *Capital*, then we "leave this sphere of simple circulation or of commodity exchange" [Marx 1867,

1:176]. The facilitation of capitalist relations constituted by the number of articles is small (Civil Code—6 articles out of 2,000). However, it is facilitated by the number of "transactions," the predominant part of the bourgeois Civil Code "on personal hiring" (labor contract), which however leave their imprint on the entire code, on all bourgeois law.

In addition, I do not share Comrade Pashukanis's view about the relation between state and law because of an inconsistency in his theory. His theory is a somewhat unclear, condescending relationship to the state. It threatens to become the type of *economism* of which I was once accused, in vain, and due to either confusion or misunderstanding by Professor Reisner. One must not forget that the equivalent exchange of commodities, as a more or less generalized phenomenon, *can exist without* the law of private property and, therefore, without the *state*. It is not without reason that the bourgeois theorists usually define the state as a state of consumers. For example: "It is an empirical fact that relations protected by the state are *more securely guaranteed*" (and only that?—P.S.), or about so-called "positive jurisprudence which cannot manage without an intermediary link— state power and its norms." I would be happy if I were mistaken in my evaluation of these words, but here *maximum clarity* is necessary, particularly at the present time (See above: The State and Bourgeois Construction).

Finally, I still disagree about the evaluation of the *process of the withering away of law*. Comrade Pashukanis depicts this as a direct transition from bourgeois law to non-law. I myself assume that as Lenin wrote—on the basis of Marx's remarks about "the bourgeois state without the bourgeoisie," that this state is in fact the proletarian dictatorship or Soviet power—so, inevitably, a *temporary* Soviet law of the transition period is created. This will be discussed later.

Bourgeois law of the second period of capitalism

From the above it is clear that we have no irreconcilable disagreements as our opponents among the "scholarly" jurists suggest. The law of the first period of capitalism—which was also under the veil of an automaton on the basis of equivalent exchange—was essentially a form *of the organization of social exchange of things*, with all the indicia of the elements of domination—by the class of the owners of means of production over hired slave-laborers, with the "bourgeoisification" of feudal property law and feudal property (Marx, *The Poverty of Philosophy*). In the first period, property law—private ownership of the means of production—determines *distribution* (i.e., the bourgeois law of obligations). The start of the period of monopoly imperialistic capitalism signifies a transition to new methods. Instead of free *competition*, i.e., the freedom of demand and supply, as in the previous stage of purchase and sale, *monopoly production* (supply-demand) begins. Its purpose is to replace the anarchy of production (and, accordingly, of exchange) with *planning*—by trusts, syndicates, or state imperialism. But this is, of course, only *limited planning*, subject to violation because of the uneven development of capitalism and the conflicts ensuing from this. This is definitively *capitalist* planning which the legal bards of capitalism and their socialist or even communist followers glorify as a socialist reincarnation of law or so-called juridical socialism, as the juridical transition to a socialist society.

Capitalist planning and law

Like the economists, the jurists also feel compelled to reconsider the theory of law. Such tension in the linkage of bourgeois legal theory is commonplace. Take, for instance, Jhering with his purpose-interest in law. Bourgeois jurists feel that something has changed here or is subject to change, but without starting from the perspective of class struggle, they can proceed no further. But with the development of monopoly capitalism, a number of individuals and schools appear, especially among the petty bourgeois milieu of France, who advocate new aspects instead of the idea of freedom of contract and the element of equality. I consider one of the most interesting theories to be that of Salielles and his group with his idea of the *dictation* of prices and simple adherence (*adhésion*) to them. This is not a simple fiction; it is a fact. "What exists of contract in these legal acts? In fact, they are an expression of private authority (even the order of a private person)."

Similarly, Duguit has attained great popularity. With his theory of the social function of law and property, Duguit is an outright legal apologist for capitalism in the second period. He criticizes the metaphysical theory of freedom of the will of civil law, but he concludes with the same *metaphysical idea of solidarity*.

I also had to deal with these legal representatives of the notion of capitalist planning, because this viewpoint still has not been put forth here (see my article "Jurisprudence" in the *Encyclopedia of State and Law*). We must immediately contrast this with *socialist planning* of the Soviet system and therefrom draw the appropriate conclusion for law.

Law of the transitional period

When Soviet power achieved victory, it had to express its relationship to law. Initially, it was destructive work. It "burned all laws" of the old regime, but retained the function of *courts*, although these were new, *workers'* courts; it also had to provide them with norms of law. Soviet power expressed this in negative form (Decree No. 1 on the Court): "[People's Courts must] be guided by the laws of the overthrown governments (both Tsarist and bourgeois) only to the extent that they are not repealed by the revolution and do not contradict revolutionary conscience and revolutionary legal consciousness." It was clear to all that there was then no distinct revolutionary legal consciousness. On Lenin's initiative it was therefore explained that "all laws are considered repealed that contradict decrees of the Central Executive Committee and also the minimum program of the Russian Social Democratic Revolutionary Party and the party of Socialist

Revolutionaries.'' (The government at that time included Left Socialist Revolutionaries).

Next, we pursued a frontal attack, and there was no talk of civil law. When I formulated the results of and future proposals for our work for the October collection of 1918, I pointed to the proposed Code of Social Law that consisted first of all of family and labor law. Further:

> After family law comes property law, or rather the repeal and limitation of these laws; here the repeal of the right of private ownership of land, the socialization of land, the nationalization of production facilities and city buildings, and the procedure for the administration of nationalized property; finally, the permissibility of using the vestiges of private property during the transition period.
> . . . Certain remnants of contract law will continue, most likely the limitations on the freedom of contract.

As is well known, the period of so-called war communism indeed followed this path. But bourgeois law, the principle of contract, was more powerful and continued to exist illegally (''underground''), not even to mention its survival in the head of every communist. In 1919 the power of concrete relations helped to effect our association with the so-called sociological, or rather materialist concept of law: ''a system (or order) of social[4] relationships (in the sense of relations of production and exchange), which corresponds to the interests of the dominant class and is safeguarded by the organized force of that class.'' This did not imply a contrast between law and decree, ''of sociological'' law to ideological; it merely *stressed* actual relations and not their reflection. In my note in *Revolution of Law: Collection No. 1*, I pointed out Comrade Lenin's attitude toward the decrees of Soviet power. He described the decrees of the first period as ''a form of propaganda.'' ''Our ideas on policy were given to the simple worker and peasant in the form of decrees.'' However, this form of propaganda was waged not only by means of persuasion, but also by *coercive state power*. Lenin did not acknowledge the possibility of law without the state and its coercion.

Comrade Lenin wrote about so-called civil or bourgeois law in 1917 (*State and Revolution*) on the basis of Marx's criticism of the Gotha Program—that in the first stage of the transition period, to the extent that private property in the means of production was replaced by common property, ''*to that extent*—and to that extent alone—'bourgeois right' disappears'' [Lenin 1917, p. 467]. However, it persists as far as its other part is concerned: it persists in the capacity of regulator (determining factor) in the distribution of products and the allotment of labor among the members of society'' [ibid.]. ''An equal amount of products for an equal amount of labor,'' is also already realized. But this is not yet communism, and it does not yet abolish ''bourgeois right,'' which gives unequal individuals, in return for unequal (really unequal) amounts of labor, equal amounts of products'' [ibid.].

Marx wrote that this "defect" is inevitable in the first phase of communist society. Without lapsing into utopianism, we cannot think that having overthrown capitalism, people will at once begin to work for society *without any legal rules*. The abolition of capitalism *will not immediately provide* the economic prerequisites of *such* a change. But there are no rules other than those of "bourgeois law." To this extent the need remains for a state that protects the common property in the means of production, the equality of labor, and the equality of division of products. To the extent that there are no longer capitalists, no longer classes, and no class whatsoever that can be suppressed, then the state will wither away. But the state still will not have withered away entirely, for there will remain the protection of "bourgeois law," sanctifying factual inequality. "For the complete withering away of the state, full communism is needed."

The matter is apparently clear: bourgeois law, and only that. But Comrade Lenin also talks of the "bourgeois state" without the bourgeoisie: "As a result not only does bourgeois law remain for a certain time under communism, but the bourgeois state as well—without the bourgeoisie."

And now we know that the bourgeois state (bourgeois democracy) without the bourgeoisie is Soviet power or proletarian democracy.

Comrade Lenin enters a reservation here:

> But democracy means only formal equality. And as soon as equality is achieved for all members of society in relation to ownership of the means of production, that is, equality of labor and wages, humanity will inevitably be confronted with the question of advancing farther, from formal equality to actual equality, i.e., to the operation of the rule "from each according to his ability, to each according to his needs." By what stages, by means of what practical measures humanity will proceed to this supreme aim we do not and cannot know. [Lenin 1917, p. 472]

Soviet law and socialist construction

The significance of Soviet law has already been repeatedly discussed. The term was already formed during Comrade Lenin's life and with his full approval. But it is not a matter of the name alone (and least of all of the name), but of its nature. If the Civil Code may be called the political economy of the given age or the economic policy of the given class state laid out in paragraphs,[5] then Soviet law narrowly construed must be the political economy of the transition period, *the economic policy of Soviet power laid out in paragraphs* (in the broadest sense of the word, i.e., not of a single law). To *contrast* it with direct measures or considerations of expedience of individual persons or institutions, etc., constitutes a petty-bourgeois anarchist survival of the protest *against organized* legal action by means of general norms. From the first day of the October Revolution, Comrade Lenin bitterly derided comrades who did not know how "to think in governmental terms.'' (See my article in *Revolution of the Law* no. 1.)

Lenin's remarks on bourgeois law should, of course, not be understood *literally*, but revolutionarily-dialectically, because: (1) they were written before the October Revolution, and (2) in our proletarian state the *bourgeoisie* has been partly tolerated along with NEP. But the essence of these words was correctly interpreted by Comrade Pashukanis in the sense that *the basis of labor value has not been transcended*—the exchange of commodities by the principle: for an equal amount of socially necessary labor, an equal amount of the same labor. It is true that here we must introduce a doubt expressed by Lenin—is the concept of commodities applicable in general to the product of a socialist factory?

The economics of the transition period of socialist construction

If we proceed from the concept of so-called civil law as the laying out in paragraphs of the political economy (or economic policy) of a given period, then we should listen to the opinions of economists about this period. In the most interesting polemic between Comrade Bukharin and Comrade Preobrazhensky, unfortunately interrupted, Bukharin recalls Marx's words that the law of labor value is only one form of the general ''law of *labor expenditures*,'' consisting in the fact that ''under all possible social-historical formations'' ''for the respective different masses of demands for masses of products, different and quantitatively determined masses of total social labor are required,'' to which corresponds the necessity of dividing social labor into definite proportions. Bukharin concludes from this:

> From this viewpoint it is obvious that the process of the victory of socialist, planned bases is nothing other than the processes of eliminating from the law of labor values of its sinful value lining, i.e., the process of transforming of the law of value into the law of labor expenditures, the process of the defetishization of the basic social regulator.

These considerations are even more valuable for the jurist. In the same discussion, Comrade Bukharin indicates the obvious difference between ''a society of simple commodity producers, where demand and supply, the competition between simple commodity producers brings forth progressive movement,'' and a developed capitalist society where prices fluctuate around concentrated assets of production, ''around *production* prices (costs of production + average profit).'' ''The average norm of profit is the specific soul of this mechanism.'' I already pointed out above the formula $M—C—M + m$.

Comrade Bukharin continues:

> Consider socialist society. Here, the objective law of labor expenditures

corresponds to the consciously applied norm of labor expenditures. Fluctuations occur first along the lines of statistical errors (but, as is understandable, the nature of these fluctuations is not the same: these are not fluctuations up and down like the fluctuations of prices around value); second, the basis here is the conscious and a priori established constant raising of the productivity of labor (with the corresponding change in measures of labor). The mass of labor is applied in a concentrated manner. The stimulus for movement is *not profit, but meeting the needs of the masses with the greatest savings of living labor.* The latter fact sharply distinguishes the whole mechanism that serves as an intermediary for the appearance of the law of labor expenditures from the corresponding mechanism under a capitalist system. . . . The capitalist and socialist mechanisms through which the law of labor expenditures acts, as we see, are sharply different. Thus, the type and tempo of development are different. But the law of labor expenditures continues to remain the basic regulator of the whole process, and even in its *maximally "pure"* form.

Finally, Comrade Bukharin also touches upon the *transitional period*, when the "process of rebirth of the law of value into the law of labor expenditures takes place."

> Further—in the analysis of capitalism one may digress from all the noncapitalist elements. Marx analyzed "pure capitalism." However, for the theory of the transition period the most abstract formulation of the question can only be a formulation that assumes state industry and the simple commodity economy of the peasants, and finally . . . the complicating element of private capital. Thus, we have *various* forms of action of the law of labor values—both as the law of labor expenditures, and as the law of value, and as the law of production prices, i.e., a modified law of value.

Under *a plan*, prices in their "semi-fictitious" function . . . are formed quite differently than when they take shape spontaneously. . . . This is prior anticipation of what under spontaneous regulation would be established (only) *post festum.* . . . Figuratively speaking, we here force the law of values to serve our purposes."

Here before us is a ready-made diagram of the law of the contemporary transition period. Its paraphrasing is sufficiently simple that I will not do it here. However, *the plan* in the context of proletarian state power ("the state planning commission") must be strongly emphasized. It is here that the transition occurs from the legal system of domination and subordination to the legal system of *socialist economic planning.*

The Soviet Civil Code

Elsewhere, I considered different bourgeois civil codes and noted that the same grouping of chapters (property, obligations, commercial law) or institutions of law points to the pecuniary features of each of them. Comparing any of them with our Civil Code, we see a profound difference in two senses: first, labor relations and pure land relations are *excluded* from our Civil Code. At first glance, this simple formal abridgment of content introduces a significant change in the nature of the whole code. In practice we also protect the Land Code and the Labor Code from infiltration by the norms of the Civil Code, but some aspects of labor law— e.g., compensation for injury, housing law for the working people, cooperative law, etc.—still remain in the Civil Code. Secondly, a fundamental change in the *property law* of the Civil Code has taken place as a result of Art. 15 of the Constitution of 1925 concerning the state monopoly of the means of production, transport, and foreign trade. The code does not emphasize this clearly enough, although this provision must be considered to be the dominant element because, as in any bourgeois civil code, the principle of private property rules.

The Soviet legal "automaton"

With these differences it would seem that our Civil Code is an automaton for free demand and supply (or supply and demand), for freedom of purchase and sale, as the form of facilitating our social exchange of things. The means of large scale production have been taken over by our society; it is true that for NEP, exceptions have been made for part of large-scale production and for all of small-scale production leaning toward the formation of cooperatives. But the percentage of private production grows smaller. According to Marx, each member of society, having contributed a certain amounts of socially useful labor

> receives a certificate from society that he has furnished such and such an amount of labor (after deducting his labor for the common funds), and with this certificate he draws from the social stock of means of consumption as much as costs the same amount of labor. [Marx 1875, p. 18]

We have departed and returned to the monetary system. But the money paid out for labor—so long as it constitutes only a *means of payment*—can be considered to be the same certification for a certain quantity of consumer goods. But here a new feature is inserted into the framework: *socialist planning*.

The construction of socialism and the Civil Code

What changes must the thesis of socialist construction effect in our attitudes toward the Civil Code? This is a very serious question, causing doubts and disagreements. Does it not mean an intensified legal, or procedural attack on the "private entrepreneur"? Certain comrades have oversimplified the matter and they believe that it is now necessary to emphasize this "reinforcement" of the application of Articles 1, 30, etc. of the Civil Code. They forget that at the Fourteenth [Party] Congress it was resolved to move toward socialism *on the basis of NEP*. In legal language this means *on the basis of the Civil Code*. We do not refuse to allow *competition* between the private entrepreneur and *socialist* production, or between the Soviet state and the cooperative trade apparatus. In commerce, the private entrepreneurs retain all the rights provided to them by the Civil Code. The struggle against them is by economic means (differences in selling prices) or by political-administrative methods (differences in railroad tariffs or rates, etc.). But legal *instability*, for example, in the court, is unprofitable for commodity exchange in general, and can destroy the planning in which the production of peasants and concessionaires, etc. is also included. This is *not a matter of the artificial, absolute* reduction of private capital but of its proportional, relative reduction (in comparison with the socialist economy), i.e., of the much more *rapid* growth of the socialist economy. In general, this is not a matter of an individual court official *himself* acting expediently; this expediency is already being implemented when necessary, in an *organized* manner, i.e., by means of the law and the governing institutions.

Capitalist and socialist planning

Marx and Lenin said that "bourgeois law" will remain. But which bourgeois law—of the first, or of the second period of capitalism? To the extent that state planning—based upon state monopoly of the means of production and exchange (Art. 15 of the Constitution of 1925)—replaces the *capitalist planning* of the private monopolist or the financial imperialist—bourgeois law must be *purged of the outgrowths of the second period*. In bourgeois law, capitalist planning has introduced, in place of freedom of will and equality on the basis of equivalency, the coercive element of monopoly in the interest of profit for capital. In contrast, *socialist planning* by means of *socialist rationalization* of labor and production, and the compulsory reduction of prices, acts in the interests *not of profit* for private capital, but of the working class (as a whole) in the sense of *expanding consumption by the masses*. In capitalist countries we see simultaneously the lengthening of the working day (even by means of law in England and Italy), the intensification of labor, the reduction of real wages, and increases in prices of consumer goods. In our country, on the other hand, we see the retention of the eight-hour working day, falling prices, and an increase in real wages.

I am not developing this thought in detail here, but just noting certain practical conclusions. Socialist planning even more so than capitalist planning, of course, also violates the principle of the individual free will of the legal subject. In the bourgeois sense, what freedom is there in the collective contract for a whole branch of labor, or for enterprises with fixed maximum wholesale and retail prices, whether in the form of a decree of the People's Commissariat of Trade or a general contract of the Central Union of Consumers' Societies with the All-Union Council of the National Economy? What kind of freedom can there be with fixed prices for habitable premises, with standard contracts for construction and [state] bank mortgages, with standard charters for various companies, with the state insurance monopoly, or with limitation of testamentary freedom to the circle of heirs? It seems that we have already extensively furnished our legal sphere *with actual and real, rather than abstract "norms,"* to the extent *we have standardized* (reduced to simple forms), that this whole area has already been reduced to *a simple technique* understandable to the most uninformed citizen. But, in fact, our laws are uniquely distinct. Nowhere else in the world are there so many specialized legal counsels. A manager would rather give up his typist and write by hand, or even his engineering specialist, than give up his specialized legal counsel. Simplify our laws! This is the basic task at this time.

Moral or labor equivalence?

However, as a consequence of all these norms (in the real sense of the word) we are left with the area of "free consent." How should we introduce a basic principle for general guidance? Here, we must use the valuable work of Comrade Pashukanis and *consciously introduce the labor principle of equivalence* (of labor expenditures), as the basis of the legal principle of bourgeois law—*for equal labor, equal compensation.* The second period of capitalism, with its capitalist planning, is reducible to the dictatorship of the strong over the weak, to the former's conditions and the monopoly power over the means of production. This situation evokes the protests of "scholarship" in the name of humanity, morality, etc. I have before me a 400-page French book on *Moral Rules in Civil Obligations* [*La règle morale dans les obligations civiles*] by George Ripert. Here you will learn about the elimination of clearly immoral contracts, protest against the so-called principle of adherence (*adhésion*), interference by the court in contractual relations, the abuse of right, the refusal of judicial protection, the liability of the enterprise for hazards to the workers (our Civil Code, Art. 404), unjust enrichment (our Civil Code, Art. 399), fraud, and even responsibility in a civil suit for crime, etc. For them all this is morality. How much morality is there in any civil code!

If one is to introduce a general principle, then the conscious introduction of the principle of labor equivalence will be the most suitable principle for the first period of socialism and the most "just." In Chapter XIII on obligations arising from causing of damage by death and bodily injury, this principle (social insurance and general liability not above the labor norm) are introduced, but unconsciously. The Supreme Court of the RSFSR has specially to decipher it. Rejecting

"slippery profit" (Art. 117) in the speculative sense, the same court unconsciously applied the same labor principle. Speaking of the labor use, of the labor
communality of family property (still before the new Code on Marriage), the
Soviet Court acknowledged the same principle. But there is still no general
analysis of our Civil Code *from the point of view of the labor theory* of law.

Soviet and bourgeois law

But in such a case what is specifically *Soviet* in our Civil Code? When
Comrade Goikhbarg developed theses (actually one thesis) three years ago (in
1924) at the congress of officials of Soviet justice, he was unusually helpless (and
I will say openly, we all were). These theses explain Articles 1, 4, 30, 33, 59 and
notes, 147, 156, etc. That's all. However, since no general guidance was provided, we had no small struggle against the (*incorrect*) broad application, especially of Arts. 1, 4, 30, and even 33 (on conspiracy). What (aside from the
application of Art. 59 on the confiscated property of the bourgeoisie) is specifically Soviet in these articles? We saw that these and other statutes are all adduced
by a French author (and he is not discovering anything new) as principles of
morality in civil codes. And Art. 1 repeats the *bourgeois* theory of Duguit, who is
by no means a socialist.

The parallel between bourgeois and Soviet law

In the bourgeois code we noted the *struggle* between the principle of freedom
of competition and freedom of will on the basis of equality of equivalence on the
one hand, and capitalist planning on the other. In our Civil Code it is therefore
possible to characterize it as the parallelism *of socialist planning with the labor
principle of individual freedom and equality*, with the victorious expansion of the
first principle. Then the "socialized" Art. 1 is received in a new light, not as a
simple explanation of Art. 4, but as an article on the permissibility of free,
individual competition in the interests of development of productive forces.

Soviet law and socialist construction

What legal conclusions result for Soviet law from the economic thesis of
socialist construction? First, of course, there is the intensification of the planning
factor, of socialist planning. In the area of the Civil Code both of these principles
have to struggle against the legacy of bourgeois law of the second (monopoly)
period of capitalism. This occurs in the form of speculation, the raising of many
prices, etc. We noted above, with Comrade Bukharin, that in the economy there is
simultaneously the effect both of the principles of labor expenditure and labor
value, and of the principle of capitalist profit. But socialist planning must subordi-

nate all these principles to it. *Here, quantity is naturally transformed into quality: bourgeois law is transformed into Soviet law of the period of socialist construction.*

I draw here only certain general practical conclusions, although a mass of them is demanded:

1. Our Civil Code is in general a reprint of bourgeois law and, in an unsophisticated way, we should use it as such, borrowing even further all that is needed for its formal understanding and realization.

2. However, the deletion alone from the Civil Code of a whole series of mass relations (the Land Code and the Labor Code) and the introduction into it of Art. 15 of the Constitution on the state monopoly of the means of production and transport and of trade, fundamentally modify our Civil Code.

3. At the same time, socialist planning appears even through the simple fulfillment of the barren formula of freedom of contract with concrete material norms: the eight-hour workday, housing rates, the setting of norms (reduction) of prices, etc., become the guiding principle of the Civil Code. The abstract norm everywhere assumes concrete form.

4. Because the entire ideology of bourgeois law (both ideas and the law) have now received correct interpretation from the perspective of value—wherever this does not contradict socialist planning (i.e., where a firm norm has not been established)—we must proceed from the principle of the labor theory of equivalence (equal for equal), restrictively interpreting all the articles on profit, etc. (for instance, percentage of damages, etc.).

5. Having discarded the hypocritical principle of morality or Duguit's theory of social functions, etc., based on the solidarity of classes, an analysis of the Civil Code must be made on the basis of the theory of labor expenditures.

6. The opposition in bourgeois theory between the idea of "is" and "ought" should be replaced with a confrontation between the notion of labor equivalence and the idea of socialist planning.

7. We have two tasks: to create law adequate for the simplified social relations, and in turn to simplify that law. This will be the best method of defetishizing law and statute.

8. The fact that the relations of the Civil Code are protected by the class state and the class court of the proletariat already gives this code a Soviet character, not in words, but in fact; quantity is transformed into quality.

Notes

1. This personification of "Revolution" is found among the best poets of the bourgeois revolution. For instance, in Freiligrat, and later in John Mackay and others.

2. This place in the translation of Comrade Stepanov (p. 775 of the 1st edition) reads merely "in order to facilitate the process," etc. The word *treibhausmässig* is entirely omitted by mistake. And from this edition both "Proletarian" and, in the form of a

quotation, also the collection of Comrade Razumovskii, were printed.

3. I fully realize all the difficulties of including in this article a polemic on our disagreements. But my work on civil law, where I deal with them in more detail, is now delayed, and at the same time our disagreements are being used in certain circles to create schism in our group. I am of the opinion that these disagreements, if there really are any, can be easily eliminated, but at the same time I suppose that clarity is necessary in this matter.

4. My critics sometimes omit this little word "social" and its explanation in Marx's words, i.e., production and exchange relations, and they talk of relations between people in general. This clearly distorts my thought. . . . [This definition of law originally appeared in the Collected Decrees of the RFSFR in 1919. Stuchka used it extensively in his *The Revolutionary Role of Law and the State—A General Doctrine of Law* of 1921—Eds.]

5. To paraphrase Comrade Lenin: "We do not yet know socialism that can be embodied in clauses and paragraphs" (Lenin, 1918f, p. 515).

17. Culture and Law

Improvement of legality . . . teach people to struggle *in a civilized way* for legality, without at all forgetting the limits of legality in a revolution. [Lenin 1921b, pp. 549–50]

After the Fifteenth Party Congress of 1927 we were entirely under the influence of cultural revolution. Why did Lenin's words of 1921 on the "cultural upheaval, on the cultural revolution which now confronts us," not become the real slogan for broad practical work until 1928? Lenin himself answered this question when he repeatedly stated, "to be cultured we must achieve a certain development of the material means of production, must have a certain material base" [Lenin 1923, p. 1475]. But Lenin also repeatedly recalled that for the achievement of our high tasks a certain level of culture was necessary. The great economic upheaval, and the rapid growth of the economy, have created the basis for a cultural revolution; for it to be successful, we must have an elemental understanding of the cultural sphere. This is the state of the problem of the relation between economic growth and culture, or, speaking more simply, the relation between material and ideological culture, between the economic base and the cultural superstructure.

All questions are most complicated when they concern the area of law and morality, and so too is the question of a cultural revolution. On the one hand there is a completely negative attitude toward culture: what does culture have in common with law? If it does have something in common then it is as a bourgeois element, as superfluous rubbish, or even as a harmful bourgeois element that should be discarded. On the other hand, we are threatened with a deviation from *Changing Boundary Markers* [name of a White Russian emigré publication—Eds.] or the "Ustrialovs" [Ustrialov wrote in *Changing Boundary Markers*—Eds.], and the area of law is especially fraught with this danger. Only a consistent, revolutionary dialectical method will show us the true direction and the right measure of our work. Vladimir Ilich taught us the need not only of trade, but *of*

"Kul'tura i pravo," *Revoliutsiia prava*, No. 2, 1928:15-20.

trading in a cultured manner if we want to progress to socialism, in the above quoted words he provides an unsurpassed model of the dialectic on the question of the relation between culture and law—to struggle for legality, *to struggle in a cultured manner* for it, while simultaneously *not forgetting the limits* of legality *in revolution.* Here you have in two lines the solution of one of the most complex problems of the proletarian revolution, revolutionary legality, the solution of this—at first glance—irreconcilable internal contradiction. But we have already posed this question in the problem of political freedoms in the creation of our constitution, in the problem of proletarian and bourgeois (or "pure") democracy, and in recent months in the problem of criminal law and procedure, etc. At first, we avoided this question, and rejected it as irrelevant. But the questions did not go away, and we must now formulate and solve them. Once, it was asked: Why should we build a new state if it is destined to "wither away"? Now they ask: Why should we conceive and justify a new, Soviet law if it will later disappear? But we must and will have to construct a new state and law despite, and even because, it is destined to perish. Such is the logic of the revolution.

I do not intend to write a scientific tract on this theme. As usual, I will merely evoke or pose the question. I always remember the famous words of Hegel and Marx that the correct formulation of a problem is also its solution. The correct formulation of the problem is especially valuable for us in the area of law, where each day brings forth new facts depicting the current state of affairs in a most unfavorable light.

Has the problem of cultural upheaval occurred in previous revolutions? Unquestionably, yes. Without turning to dimly known times of old, we see how the rising and then emerging bourgeoisie, the capitalist class, was involved in an acute class struggle under the catchword of culture. This we term the Church revolution ("The Reformation"), because the oft-repeated struggle of the "democratic" state against the power of the Church in general or against a particular church—e.g., the Catholic church in England, the so-called "*Kulturkampf*" in Germany, in Mexico, etc.)—at least *partially* took the form of a cultural revolution. To the extent that a national struggle acted as a liberator from a "foreign" landowner in some countries, it also encompassed a struggle in the guise of national culture for the cultural uplifting of the peasant masses in general. However, in all these cases the objective outcome was reduced merely *to culture for the minority, if this was not actually a conscious goal.*[1] Literacy was a rare exception even for the knights of the Middle Ages.[2] For the factory worker under capitalism, it was valued merely as an indicator of the productivity of labor. Again, Lenin convincingly demonstrated that only capitalism (for the bourgeois equated culture with civilization) created the conditions for the actual possibility and then for the necessity, of a cultural revolution *for the great majority of the population* and, afterward, for all of mankind.

When the bourgeoisie writes about culture or civilization (for the bourgeoisie, the latter term is usually equated with the former), it, as the very word civilization shows, speaks only of bourgeoisified culture (literally "civil—ized"), which also means "commodification." Thus, the bourgeoisie often equates civilization with capitalism itself. Its theorists of the state equate the *Rechtsstaat* with capitalism itself. And its scholarly jurisprudes in their turn equate *law with culture*. The excessively loquacious Social Democratic Professor Radbruch writes:

> Law relates not to the domain of nature, or of values, or of religion; it relates to the domain of culture. Jurisprudence, accordingly, is the study of culture and is misunderstood as the study of norms.[3]

For Radbruch even the very "essence of culture consists not of its historical concept"; for him "culture is the *totality of absolute* values."[4]

For us, culture is of course a historical concept. To the extent that it can be reduced to a sum of objective achievements, it is handed down in certain degrees from period to period. "Without the legacy of capitalist culture we could not build socialism. We have nothing with which to build communism other than that which capitalism left us," (Lenin 1920a, p. 284). "Proletarian culture must be the logical development of the store of knowledge mankind has accumulated under the yoke of capitalist, landowner and bureaucratic society" [Lenin 1920a, p. 287]. But this does not of course signify a simple copying, a peaceful taking *of the whole inheritance*. On the contrary, this is the goal of cultural *revolution*.

But the essence and course of every revolution has been sufficiently studied by us. The destructive and subsequent constructive process is the merciless discarding of everything that has turned out to be unsuitable for the newly built and new construction [process]. To the "outside" observer this might seem a wild expenditure of effort, but there is no other way to victory. We can see this best of all in the example of the state. Marx clearly showed in "The 18th Brumaire" how the bourgeois state grew. This is counting on *complications*. One is forced to recall Struve's famous prerevolutionary article, during the period of legal Marxism, where even the necessity of democratic or political revolution was deduced from the principle "life is becoming more complicated." To this Lenin juxtaposed another concept of development:

> Capitalist culture has created large-scale production, factories, railways, the postal service, telephones, etc., and on this basis the great majority of the functions of the old "state power" have become so simplified and can be reduced to such exceedingly simple operations of registration, filing, and checking that they can be easily performed by every literate person. [Lenin 1917, pp. 420–21]

"Capitalism simplifies the function of 'state' administration, permits the discarding of 'management' and reduces the whole matter to the organization of the proletariat (as the ruling class), in the name of the whole society hiring 'workers, watchers, bookkeepers.'" Only this conception can lead to the Soviet state and proletarian democracy in which the whole working people participate in administration, and in which every cook must know how to run the state.

Toward this end we eliminated the bourgeois state; we smashed its apparatus into little pieces. However, the newly constructed apparatus turned out to be rather, indeed extraordinarily, bureaucratic. Lenin wrote in 1917 that "abolishing the bureaucracy at once, everywhere and completely, is out of the question. It is a utopia" [Lenin 1917, p. 425]. But the time has come when it is necessary systematically and with the help of theory to take up this work of construction. It is necessary "to select the minimum, to check the serious situation, to continue work only so that *it truly stood on the heights* of modern science *and gave us all its support.*" What is now noted in regard to the state is also fully applicable to law. Here, we also have traveled the same road: "have burned the old laws," have written new ones, again "have burned" and again have built. The time has come for *serious*, consciously Marxist construction on the basis of all the achievements of science and culture.

We find a very instructive example in recent events. When we considered reforming the Criminal Procedure Code which we put together six years ago, and which was suddenly recognized as useless everywhere, two deviations were argued against us. To simplify I will just say briefly: one deviation came from "nihilism," or the throwing out of everything bourgeois, while the other was from "Changing Boundary Markers," or the extraordinary preservation of everything bourgeois. Of course, in both cases the deviations were *unconscious*. But it is worth considering a whole series of conclusions made in localities from the proposal to throw out the "remnants of liberal-bourgeois procedure," to be convinced that a certain deviation had taken place. Too radical proposals to throw out all the constituent parts of the adversary process ("formal" referral to the court, public hearing, defense and debate, and likewise also appeal) forced us to pose the question more profoundly, and scientifically. As a result, we concluded that we are dealing here with a "*cultural conquest* which we must recognize among other cultural conquests even in the class state of the proletariat." But a deviation was also noticeable in the other side, toward the preservation of these guarantees in an extraordinarily pure form. We must insist on a "cultured form of conduct" in court cases but not forgetting, in Lenin's words, *the boundaries of legality and revolution.* I therefore added to my theses on the Criminal Procedure Code the phrase "eliminating all in it that is excess, harmful or contradictory to the interests of the working people." I would now formulate this phrase even more definitively. Taking into account Lenin's notion that capitalist culture enables the simplification of all relations, Soviet power should eliminate all *excess* complications, *thus simplifying both law and the court* to the extent that a mill worker and a peasant—if not from behind a wooden plow then from behind a steel plough—would be able to participate in a case in court.

The participation of a defense counsel in criminal and in civil procedure continues to be hotly disputed. Derogatory things are said about the [institution of] defense counsel and I must agree that its present form is in fact most unsatis-factory. It follows that we must purge and reorganize the ranks of the defense counsel *rather than abolish them*. Such reorganization should assist the *simplifi-cation* of the conduct of cases and not complicate them by introducing red tape, and other more harmful elements. From the data published recently, it is quite possible, although difficult to detect, certain points of departure for a rational reorganization of the defense counsel. As I already said, Lenin warned us against getting carried away over a special proletarian culture. "We would have enough real bourgeois culture for the start, we could get along for the start without particularly double-dyed types *of culture according to the bourgeois order*, i.e., of bureaucratic or serf-owning culture, etc. In questions of culture, haste and bold motions are the most dangerous of all." Lenin's words, written five years ago, have not lost relevance, and may be fully applied to the area of law and the court.

Under such conditions, in what should our cultural revolution in law consist? For us, law and culture are not identical concepts. The conquests of culture will survive the transition into the future society (of course, not in "pure," i.e., in current form), but law will not survive the transition; it must "wither away." The culture of the future is a new way of life, new habits, *without any* legal coercion. But for now *law* and coercion have significance in our life. Both class property relations come to court in the form of a legal dispute and also purely personal relations, e.g., an insult. The question has now been raised of removing the latter from the jurisdiction of the court. How did Lenin look upon this with respect to the future society? He wrote that

> We are not utopians, and do not in the least deny the possibility and inevitabil-ity of excesses on the part of individual persons, or the need to stop such excesses. In the first place, however, no special machine, no special apparatus of suppression, is needed for this; this will be done by the armed people themselves, as simply and as readily as any crowd of civilized people, even in modern society, interferes to put a stop to scuffle or to prevent a woman from being assaulted. [Lenin 1917, p. 464].

Is it a significant proposal to transfer cases of assault to the decision of comrades who will simply "pull people fighting apart"? No, so long as there is a question of Comrade's *Courts* in place of the general People's Court. This means that there is still also a question *of law*. But this is done only in the interest *of more cultured forms* of influence.

The problem is posed even more sharply in the area of the punitive activity of the state. We, so to speak, have made real inroads here. We abolished the very word punishment, and replaced it with the phrase social defense. We have re-moved all suffering from the Criminal Code. On checking, it seems that our houses of detention were filled far above capacity, and the mere existence of deprivation of freedom negates the elimination of all suffering. This time, it seems, we took matters seriously in hand. This, perhaps, will become a new page in the culture of the revolution. But one should not confuse culture with laxity. We are conducting a struggle for culture by eliminating illiteracy. We already have enormous successes and will have more of them. But one must note that not far from Moscow this struggle was conducted by forced labor sentences. The Supreme Court had to explain the illegality of such an approach, even though committed with the very best of intentions. The firm establishment of cultured social life, of so-called social discipline, cannot do without measures of coercion. But here we will set for ourselves the task of selected *cultured* methods of *coercion*, by applying deprivation of freedom not as a general measure, but as an exception; moreover, it will be an exception under such conditions that a maximum of a element of culture could be introduced (treatment, adaptation, labor education) into it. Of course, "*not forgetting the limits set for us in a revolution.*"

Our task—the task of Soviet jurists in a cultural revolution—is, first, the rational and scientific reception of bourgeois culture with respect both to the law and the court. For this, however, we must carry out a rigorous scientific analysis of these bourgeois cultural conquests. Further, this decision should be strictly critical with the application of our tested revolutionary-dialectic method, i.e., "not forgetting the limits" set for us by the revolution. One of the basic slogans must be Lenin's slogan about the simplification of law. Cultured law must be simplified law. I claim that we have already begun this work and have formulated it correctly. But this work is unusually difficult and drawn out, and *we have to fight for every inch of ground*. We are still far from perfected scientific accomplishments. Setting ourselves the goal of teaching others, we simultaneously must "study and then verify that our science is not a dead letter or a stylish phrase." There is no other path to a true cultural revolution in law.

Notes

1. "Capitalism provides culture only for the minority" [Lenin 1919a, p. 70].
2. "A certain knight was so educated that he even read books." This was written when literacy was still the privilege only of the clergy.
3. Radbruch, *Gründzuge der Rechtsphilosophie* (Leipzig: Quelle & Meyer, 1914), p. 184.
4. Ibid.

18. Revolutionary Legal Perspectives

The Sixth Congress of RSFSR Justice Workers opened on February 20th of this year. It has been five years since the previous congress. During this period many changes occurred, but it is actually the present period, 1929—replete with new tasks and promising a radical upheaval in the whole structure of Soviet law of the Republic—to which we should turn our attention.

We have often met arguments about whether legal rules are a revolutionary or a conservative (preservationist) element. In such an absolute formulation, both sides to the dispute are wrong. Both sides equally lack a dialectical conception of law. In my short book *The Revolutionary Role of Law*, I contrasted the law of *two struggling classes*, the revolutionary and the counterrevolutionary. After this we went through the period of "retreat" in which even our law became partially "preservationist," because it defended revolutionary achievements against the claims of former owners (for instance, the famous note to Art. 59 of the Civil Code), indicating to them the limit of our retreat: to this point, but no further. But at the same time, our *law* as a whole remained revolutionary. On the other hand, it continued our destructive work against the so-called juridical world view, which had appeared not only in its present light, but also in various artificial illuminations, even pseudo-Marxist. On the other hand, after this destructive work (in part, simultaneously with it), however, comes research and creative work. For the first time, we have a scientific basis for law without which it is impossible consciously to use *law*, especially Soviet law, for revolutionary purposes. I have already repeated this by indicating the exceptional significance of the Fourteenth and Fifteenth Party congresses. The truth that "quantity is transformed into quality" is well known to all of us. This is an objective process, whether or not we are conscious of it, or have realized and recorded it. It is clear to all that only by recognizing the fact of transformation can we correctly orient our further work.

"Revoliutsionno-pravovye perspektivy," *Revoliutsiia prava*, no. 2 (March-April, 1929), as reprinted in *13 let bor'by. . .*, pp. 193–98.

This is very difficult in those branches of knowledge in which ideology plays a significant role. This is of course true for sociological and legal questions. Lenin wrote in *State and Revolution*: about the replacement of bourgeois democracy with proletarian democracy: "Here 'quantity turns into quality': *such* a degree of democracy implies overstepping the boundaries of bourgeois society, and *beginning reorganization*" [Lenin 1917, p. 472]. Is everyone aware of this transformation? No. The bourgeoisie abroad and the Social Democrats who serve them, do not recognize this process and even curse the thought of it. Doubts and hesitations on this score are found even in our ranks, among the panicky or opportunist communists.

All accomodationalism (*Ustrialov-shchina*) amounts to this. And certain facts support it, for instance the power of the remnants of bureaucratism. If one adds to this the objective or subjective blindness of bourgeois science, then we understand why you can never explain to the bourgeois scholar the difference between a council of ministers and a council of people's commissars, between bourgeois and Soviet law or justice, between bourgeois-democractic and Soviet electoral law. He would be unable to comprehend this because of his class interest and class consciousness. However, once we have grasped this *objective* law of development, then with our proletarian interest and understanding of the world, we can consciously "use" it for accelerating development. We have transcended the limits between necessity and freedom. In 1921, Lenin introduced an *amendment* to the old, conventional conception of the relation between base and superstructure. He often returned to this new notion of "subsuming the previously inadequate foundation (base)" to an elementary socialist superstructure. But this was only on condition of the existence of a proletarian dictatorship: "Our last, but most important and most difficult task, the one we have done least about, is economic development, the laying of economic foundations for the new socialist edifice on the site of the demolished feudal edifice and the semi-demolished capitalist edifice" [Lenin 1921a, p. 57]. Or: "Either we lay an economic foundation for the political gains of the Soviet state, or we shall lose them all. This foundation has not yet been laid—that is what we must get down to" (Lenin, 1921:73).

This simple thought is *one of the clearest conclusions* from Lenin's brilliant dialectic, which we value fully only now when, with unbelievable difficulties, but nevertheless *openly* for the whole proletariat, we broaden its basis daily. This is why with such disillusioned hearts all the lackeys of the bourgeoisie, all the Dans, Dallins, etc., etc., try in unison to convince us that we are nevertheless only building a capitalist prison and not a socialist temple of freedom. It must be acknowledged that ideologically this upheaval is still far from being brought to an end among us, that the new order is still being born *in old forms*. We still see this in the area of law and state construction. But we also see something *else*: the improvement on questions of state and law is being transformed from rhetoric to reality. The ice has broken, the flood can no longer be stopped. At such moments it is sometimes advisable to turn away from the special, particular, and more elevated pedestal, and to view the entire movement as a whole, to sketch the general rough outline of the plan of the whole real movement. Against this general background we can see more clearly both particularity and peculiarity.

For anyone unclear about the revolutionary role of law condemned to wither away, conversations on "perspectives" in the development of law will seem useless or even "heretical." I will therefore begin with the state, the fate of which is completely analogous to the fate of law (or rather, vice versa). For the proletarian state, that which is "almost not a state," must be developed to its perfection and only then can it finally disappear, completely "wither away."

What do we see now in the life of our state? We are now living through *a fundamental break* in the area of Soviet construction, in the sense of the realization of *real proletarian democracy*. I here give the example merely of our directly *revolutionary struggle for truly Soviet elections*. What is this if not also *the placing of the previously insufficient foundation in the localities* under the strong soviet authority in the center. Our worst enemies—the bourgeoisie and especially the Social Democrats—note with malicious pleasure that the number of *non-communists* elected to the soviets is increasing. But we, on the contrary, are exultant that we have succeeded in bringing into the soviets a more significant number of *non-Party-members*. These are not kulaks, of course, but working people.

To overcome the old state, i.e. "to struggle with bureaucratism to the end, to full victory, is possible only then when the *whole* population will take part in administration," says Lenin. He continues:

> What we have done, was to remove these hindrances (legal, as among the bourgeoisie—P.S.), but so far we have not reached the state at which the working people could participate in government. *Apart from law, there is still the level of culture*, which you cannot subject to any law. The result of this low cultural level is that the Soviets, which *by virtue of their program are organs of government by the working people, are in fact organs of government for the working people by the advanced section* of the proletariat, but not by the working people as a whole. [Lenin 1919b, p. 183]

What Lenin said in 1919 remains quite relevant today. The cultural revolution which Lenin also proclaimed is just developing. And part of this revolutionary struggle consists of our preelection campaign for the purpose of the real—not merely verbal—involvement of the broadest masses in the soviets. This struggle is very difficult. In the countryside it takes on the force of a fierce class war, the terror of the kulak elements, etc. But simultaneously, it has success. Not only do the urban soviets grow, but even the *rural* soviets are being turned into reality.

With this struggle goes the *broadening of the soviet base* by the involvement of the working masses in sections of soviets, at first urban and now rural soviets.

Recently there was an inspection of sections of urban soviets that demonstrated the huge growth of their work. The rural soviets, of course, are still behind, but [overall] one must evaluate what this enormous progress [in soviet construction] means for the development of the Soviet state, for the realization of the principle of "administration *through* the working masses," including the complete involvement of all the working people in administration. Only then, having attained its highest development, will the Soviet state have created the conditions in which it will become unnecessary, superfluous, and will wither away.

But can anyone doubt that our successes in the reestablishment of the economy, and its reconstruction based on an accelerated industrialization program, has for the first time created favorable conditions for the Sovietization of the country, its backwaters, and especially its ethnic national areas? [By contrast] it would be ridiculous to argue that the restoration of "capitalist" relations, rather than the formation of socialist relations among us, strengthens soviets of workers and the Soviet order.

One more factor has enormous significance; this is the repudiation of superfluous bourgeois centralism not just in the area of *economic* jurisdictions but at the same time in the regionalization of general administration, including the court.

Are these thoughts correct? Of course they are correct. But if this is so, then we must make the same conclusions about the *class* (Soviet) *law* protected by the class state. The struggle is still significantly more difficult here, for if administration of the state has come about for the working people through *the leading stratum* of the proletariat itself, *legal work* by and large is conducted by strata who, for one reason or another, remain prisoners of bourgeois-legal "thought." But it is not only this that has delayed us. Without a material *base*, *without* a material (more accurately, an industrial) *foundation*, the best laws, the best formulations of law will lag behind—even if they could emerge in name only, "without speaking." We had clear examples of this in the past, as Lenin noted. But when there were appropriate data, law, statute was turned either into a serious hindrance or into a significant *revolutionary lever* depending upon their content.

I will start with the centralism of our legal work. We *were* centralists and the majority of us, theoretical "revolutionaries of the law" (i.e., struggling under the banner "Revolution of the Law"), probably also fully support this viewpoint. On the one hand, Marx's economic theory contributes to this; on the other hand, it is largely explained by the fear of dissipation of our forces. We now struggle at the center for our revolution; we certainly are successful, but for the time being only among young people. But we are far from victory at the center. Five years of struggle were necessary to effect the already approved creation of a legal department of the Institute of Red Professors; two more years passed to get that group underway. Now it is proposed that we expand our work to the whole Republic, to the whole Union. But this is a dissipation of forces. Even without this, however, we remain a drop in the sea. The same tendency exists in the practice of the one leading judicial research institute. We oppose the provincialization of judicial supervision. Why? Because we do not have enough manpower for this, but we must move toward the *simplification* of our legal relations in contrast to the bourgeois tendency to complicate them. If we jump from a country pony to a steel horse during industrialization, then here it is rather the reverse: we do not need a steel "law horse," just the unavoidable servicing of the central branches of trade. Only the revolutionary perspective would be correct.

We begin our survey with formal (procedural) law. In the RSFSR we see the following: the almost total provincialization of supervision over judicial procedure; the further broadening of the People's Court with a final decision for the People's Court in such a small locale as an *okrug* [administrative district]; the retention of the newly reorganized centralized supervision superseding the former *random* nature of appeals and protests; and a systematic *scientific-research* approach to the typical isolated phenomena of legal life (the study of the realization of individual legal relations of groups of crimes, etc.) with appropriate conclusions drawn from them. No *court anywhere has done* such work previously. We have set this task for ourselves and have started it. Where does all this progress lead? Leaving complex norms in force to the extent that they are necessary *for external* relations, i.e., not only abroad, but with the remaining capitalist elements in general, with the *bringing* to the possible limits of the simplification of these relations for our *specifically new order*. We now must march in step with Soviet construction.

We are approaching a real simplification *of the judicial process*. This is not just the simplification of the criminal and civil procedural codes respectively, but their actual merger. I will not mention the Criminal Procedure Code; enough has been said about it in our journal. The revision of the Civil Procedure Code, in particular, even the elaboration of the All-Union fundamentals is still in the future, but not in the distant future. This, of course, is only the beginning. For now all attempts to simplify the court (all sorts of comradely courts, etc.) even more *are crystalized in judicial form*. Nevertheless, the way is noted, as even here, to involve the entire working population fully in cases when, as Lenin said, it is necessary simply "to put a stop to a scuffle or to prevent a woman from being assaulted" [Lenin 1917, p. 464].

We are taking a decisive step *in criminal law*. The historic joint session of the RSFSR Council of People's Commissars and the Presidium of the All-Union Central Executive Committee was the first time divisive voices spoke out in the highest administrative body, recalling that with regard to criminal acts that we are *Marxists*. When the resolution was adopted on the radical reconsideration of our repression policy in criminal cases—on the one hand in the sense of merciless class struggle, on the other against the senseless continuation of bourgeois *prison* construction—it became clear that we were still deeply entrapped by the bourgeois world view with our faith in the "place of confinement" (I almost said: prison). However, I will not speak of the group of compulsorily isolated class enemies. Finally, it seems we have taken—at least in practice—a decisive step toward a new organization of a sensible socially [useful] work *influence* on the nonconscious, socially undisciplined, unstable, or declassed part of our working society, discarding the pseudo-humanistic phrases and approaches. The period of our not knowing how to organize the work tasks of prisoners on the basis of payment, so to speak, is behind us. If we learn how to bring this task to a conclusion, then we will not only be doing a revolutionary, necessary deed, but we will achieve savings so as to turn to *a more effective struggle* with the still unbelievable darkness and disrespect in the dark corners of our socialist society. The results will be in the future, but the fresh breezes can already be felt. Until now we have had excellent discussions on crime and criminals. It seems to me that now for the first time we are sternly but *correctly approaching* a resolution of this problem. If even the "criminal" part of our country will be *included in the working* ranks of our socialist construction, then we must not accuse ourselves of fighting against phenomena which *we ourselves created*, i.e., crime, since this struggle is not reducible simply to a class struggle. Along with the acceleration of the process of the industrialization and socialization of the country, a differentiation—the destratification of society by compelled isolation from it of the temporarily unemployed, the declass, etc., also occurs. This [occurred] everywhere during the transition period. The struggle is now necessary, but this *struggle must not be*, as it has largely been until now, *senseless*.

The most notable step in the legal field is directly related to the progress toward socialism in the countryside proclaimed by the Fifteenth Party Congress. I refer to the publication of the "General Principles of Land Use and Landholding." The new principles proclaim in Article 1:

> [T]he basis of the land order of the USSR ensuring *the possibility of socialist construction in agriculture* . . . is the *nationalization of land*, i.e., the abolition forever of the private ownership of land and the instituting for it of exclusively state ownership.

With this premise for the possibility of socialist construction, however, "*the voluntary nature of the transfer* to collective (and other cooperative) forms of farming is maintained" (Art. 29), but every kind of assistance concretely indicated in the "Principles" is being rendered for this transfer. Certain advantages came with progress in agriculture (the obligatory nature of the majority decision for all members of village land societies, the right of a minority to leave a land society in order to engage in collective farming, etc.). *At the same time, however,* the possible *progress* of individual farms of poor and middle peasants *is being ensured*. Finally, legislative progress is being made toward the formation of large and very large "grain factories" of giant state farms. Everyone remembers Lenin's words that we (at that time) still did not have the objective and subjective conditions for the success of state farms. *These conditions have been attained, and we are again setting up state farms on a broadened base.*

We also have before us the development of a new *Civil Code* and have *already* drafted All-Union principles for it. I will not elaborate on these principles here. This issue of the journal also includes my theses on this subject. We still have a serious struggle ahead of us here, for civil law is to a certain degree *the last refuge* of bourgeois legal thought. We can now clearly see two paths before us: first, toward separating the regulatory principles of the socialist sector of the economy, land, and labor relations from civil law; second, toward the simplification and contraction of the scope of purely civil relations. This is the picture before us of the *general reorganization* in the sphere of our Soviet system. It represents a great step forward and, moreover, a step that is possible only now after the consolidation of the previously inadequate foundation. Simultaneously, this advance guarantees a more genuine revolutionary influence on the most fundamental construction.

One area remains *to the side*, although it is a "most necessary, most urgent matter." This is our *legislation*. Floods of new laws, waves of old ones, batches of individual articles as supplements to the codes, all threaten to inundate us. I read an interesting article on how the paper famine stemmed this flood (it held back the printing of laws) and I smiled with malicious pleasure. However, paper was found and the work continued. You can read, in *Revolution of the Law*, the note by Comrade Prushitskii on the complaints by the former German Minister of Justice about such waves of laws and his thoughts on the elimination of some of these laws. However, that is taking place in bourgeois Germany. Here I received a shipment in two volumes of 1,128 and 1,144 pages, in all 2,272 pages (I do not know the weight), "a parcel without value," under the name *Systematic Collection of the Laws of the RSFSR in Effect on January 1, 1928 (November 7, 1917)— December 31, 1927)*, in all 2,078 pieces of legislation. I read (No. 812) about renaming the settlement Vasil'evskaia Artel' as the village of "Isaevskii"; (983) the village of Durakov was renamed Koltsovo; and the village Bardakovo became Serzhino (984), etc., etc. Of course, all these laws *are in force*, even if *at the place they do not know* of the authorized new names, but if one recorded all the renamed streets in the cities and villages, then the number would run into millions. I remember also the necessity of changing unsuitable names, such as Tsarevokokshaisk. But why put 1/100,000th of them in a systematic collection of laws in force? *Simplify laws, simplify, and simplify again*. This is our slogan. But in fact one institution in 1927 alone registered over 7,000 laws, legislative acts, and decrees. We have red Speranskies writing laws; when will red Voltaires burning them appear?[1] I am not an opponent of law and legislation in general, but it is necessary to keep in mind proportion. We must above all, at least in publications, distinguish *statutory law* from purely technical departmental regulations and instructions establishing particular procedures for these regulations. Agronomists, engineers, beekeepers, etc., also have their technical rules, but they do not include them in a series of legal acts. Laws of nature are in force without even being published. Why is an exception needed for jurists?

Note

1. Reference is to Voltaire's well-known dictum that it is necessary "to burn old laws." We have obeyed it, but unfortunately we have to an even greater extent followed the second part of his advice: to write new *ones*.

19. The Revolution and Revolutionary Legality

There is a certain gap between our practical successes and the development of theory. Moreover, it is necessary that theoretical work not only follow practical work but even move ahead of it, arming our practical workers in their struggle for the victory of socialism. [Stalin 1929b, p. 148]

Comrade Stalin's words must become the *leitmotiv* of our work. They are particularly valuable for us as Marxist jurists. I have often indicated that legal theory has experienced difficulty and great delay in catching up with legal practice, which in its turn has "confirmed" only that which has been won (codified), or approved or disapproved that which was finished or left incomplete (judicial work). But what can be said if less than a month after these words we read: "However, at the present time it is impossible to express precisely in law the basis on which the legal form of relations of production and distribution must be constructed. These relations occur in agriculture, urban industry, and even in the organization of consumer supply."[1] This is the model of the helplessness of the "legislator"—despite his external "revolutionary nature" abrogating his *basic* role: to provide *direction at the present time*. Law exists for him as a conservative rather than a revolutionary element.

But this is only one fact taken at random. In the first issue of this journal I polemicized on this theme with a group of students and their sympathizers. Subsequently, such a leading institution as the Moscow Regional Court issued a ruling simply repealing the laws of the NEP. The Plenum of the Supreme Court had to reverse this ruling of the Regional Court. The Regional Court in its ruling had added one word—"bourgeoisie": "The Party and Soviet power have decided to liquidate the kulak and the *bourgeoisie* as a class." From this "supplemented" text, conclusions were drawn in the form of local "legislation" repealing the laws of NEP.

"Revoliutsiia i revoliutsionnaia zakonnost'," *Sovetskoe gosudarstvo i revoliutsiia prava*, no. 3, [1930], pp. 15–22.

At the same time, courts in other cities are issuing similar resolutions in the same spirit while at the conference of heads of the court and Procuracy of the autonomous republics, it is proposed that the majority of the participants should essentially consider the slogan of revolutionary legality as a *survival*, almost a right deviation. As a result of certain directives from central governing agencies, this tendency has weakened somewhat, but it is far from overcome. In some places there is unparalleled lawlessness, not toward the kulak, but toward the middle and poor peasant, who are being assailed with the epithet "kulak or semi-kulak." In cities and large villages this assault is directed against NEP and commodity exchange in general. The latter fact has had an adverse effect on the fragile economy and this is readily apparent in the marketplace. It is at best utopian to declare that exchange is a survival of the past when in places (for instance in the Far East), the consumer cooperative includes less than half or a little over half the available supply of commodities. It is not sufficient to discourage the abolition of commodity exchange through local or departmental decrees. In this regard Comrade Stalin has already said that, in his opinion, it was still to early to abolish NEP. This means also that the time has not yet arrived to repeal the law of NEP, let alone laws and legality in general. I recall that nine years ago, in a different context, I wrote my book *The Revolutionary Role of Law and State*. In that book I defended the theses of the class nature of all law, the revolutionary role of the law of the emerging class, and the victory of the transformation of its program into "positive" law into legislation. The book was successful. Soon, every Marxist "jurisprude" affirmed that he, of course, also recognized the class nature of law. And I myself received the "title" of the "head of the revolutionary Marxist school of law in Russia" or, in another version, "the leader, or one of the leaders, of a certain *school* of law." But the problem of the class nature of law and its "relation" to other theories is sufficiently complex that many people breathed more freely when, in their opinion, the first "signs" of the rapid "withering away" of law appeared. Why continue to struggle theoretically over the nature of law if tomorrow it will "disappear" entirely? Similar pleasure was shown toward the disappearance of the concept or slogan (I myself do not know which term is more accurate) of "revolutionary legality," which in general was treated more as an icon than with a full understanding of its real character.

Because it was out of date in many respects, I decided not to reprint my book. However, as you see, the present state of affairs inevitably gives rise to the thought—pull out the old book from its dusty archive, sit down and rework it, keeping in mind the basic goal, to recall again the slogan—the revolutionary role of law. It is true that history does not repeat itself; thus the question is posed on a new plane. "Revolution *or* revolutionary legality"—this is in fact the form that my slogan of the revolutionary role of law (which I have discarded) has assumed. However, we *now* have before us a more definitive formula: revolution *and* revolutionary legality.

What is the basic difference between these formulas? In the first case we argued roughly that a revolution both occurred and succeeded and now, in place of revolution, revolutionary legality taken precedence. This understanding of revolutionary legality pushed aside and displaced revolution. Add to this formula the bourgeois view as a conservative element which would bring forth a revisionist version with which any bourgeois "turn of the century" specialist would have gladly agreed. However, it simultaneously became the prevailing view of legal, mainly *procuratorial*, as well as *judicial, practice*. Naturally *my book of 1921 did not teach this*.

My slogan was and still is: "revolution *and* revolutionary legality." For anyone using the logic of the revolutionary dialectic, rather than law, there can be no other view. The power of the proletarian dictatorship consists of the fact that it is *simultaneously* both a state and a revolution. The bourgeois revolution is distinguished by the fact that having formed the new bourgeois state, *the revolution is declared dissolved*. The state becomes a mechanism—almost a kind of automaton—within the limits of, or on the basis of legality serving the bourgeoisie, for whom the sanctity of private property and freedom of contract need to be protected. But this automaton is a *bad* automaton; it is directed by the "unseen hand of the 'class' stage director" and when the open stage director—fascism—takes its place, this is merely the natural course of development.

For the bourgeois state the picture is clear: *behind the letter of the law*, stands the fetishism of legality. This is legality in general, for there is *only bourgeois* law. Every new law falls under suspicion: does it serve the bourgeoisie? Therefore the logical conclusion is retroactive force because law itself is criminal. This is the type of concept of legality that we have inherited rather than revolutionary legality.

Revolutionary legality is an entirely different matter. It is by no means the opposite of revolution, nor is it meant as the *restraint of revolution* in general. It appears to be a restraint only to overzealous and extreme leftism. The essence of the proletarian revolution consists of the fact that its *victory*, and the institution of the proletarian dictatorship, puts another *new and powerful weapon* in the hands of the revolution—state power. The exercise of state power in part consists of law influencing the course of development *in an organized manner through a legal process*, mainly in the course of the class struggle. "The dictatorship of the proletariat does not mean the cessation of the class struggle, but *its continuation in another form, with new weapons*" (Lenin 1919, p. 435).

Thus the combination of revolution and revolutionary legality merges into a unified whole. In order to give a small explanatory example, we might say: bourgeois legality depicts, for instance, a judge *sitting with his back to the future* delving in the sources of the law for the thoughts of the mystical "legislator." Conversely, we can represent revolutionary legality as a judge sitting with his face *toward the future*, understanding the law not merely historically, but *dialectically*, from the perspective of the present period. I demonstrated this in the Supreme Court with Art. 1 of the Civil Code. It speaks of the "social and economic purpose" of rights (this is a somewhat illiterate repetition of a phrase found in bourgeois theory). As a dialectician, Comrade Lenin approved of this phrase as a whole in terms of the future (thus he stressed: "It will do"). What *purpose* did Art. 1 have? It was, of course, not the purpose of that day, but of the *future*, of the time of application of the law. If this was initially a time when competition was permitted and even state property was scattered among individual artificially created subjects of law (trusts, stock societies, syndicates, etc.), then, with the change to full-scale collectivization, the "social and economic" purpose of the means of production was transformed along with the subjects of law. The latter went in an opposite direction, lost their rights to the means of production. Their rights lost the basis for protection and were converted into assets of the collective farms, of course, only where these farms were formed. This was done by the revolutionary masses and afterward was confirmed by the *law* of Soviet power (the Central Executive Committee and Council of People's Commissars).

Of course, mass collectivization in the countryside did not exist before Art. 1 of the Civil Code; neither that nor any other article could have stopped that elemental movement which constituted a leap ten years forward. But even then there was no break between the revolution and revolutionary legality because the movement was carried out on the basis of Party directives and formalized in Soviet law. Violations of revolutionary legality derived from distortions of the basic political line. Dekulakization did not signify the abolition of NEP in general; local agencies, even those of justice, tried to "supplement" the slogan prematurely, bypassing central agencies, as if socialism could be constructed in one district, in one region, in one autonomous Soviet socialist republic.

Thus began the abrogation of contemporary revolutionary legality. This was not central law but *local* law of the local court, of the local Party committee. As a result, there were excesses that went beyond the usual limits, with senseless violations of revolutionary legality, shades of 1918. This directly contradicted the current revolutionary slogan of dekulakization calling for the *transfer* of the means of production to the *indivisible* inventory of collective farms, etc. by transforming dekulakization into a means *for gathering household items* in the form of baby's diapers of the kulak and the middle peasant as well. Once the satirist Shchedrin characterized a moment of his age with the words: "Those who had *two* awls informed on those who had *one* awl" (as an unreliable "proletarian element"). Here, it has come to the point in some areas that those who have one awl see a kulak in those who have two awls. There is now a practical demand to speak out against the open and secret opponents of revolutionary legality in such a situation. Most resolutely I affirm that this slogan is *still destined to play* a role in the creation of the new order and a new society.

Of course this problem too will be posed differently. We have previously failed to remember the persistent *linkage* between the revolution and revolutionary legality, but in the future we must not forget that revolutionary legality is a continuation of the revolution. From this it follows that legality should be truly revolutionary; it should not retard the revolution but lead it forward. Revolutionary legality, however, does not mean *individual* arbitrariness, but *organized* work *under directives* from the center or with its consent. But it means something else as well: more intensive influence by the revolution on law itself, or as one likes to say, on the legislator. The law must *become something else*. This means relying on revolutionary law rather than anticipating the rapid withering away of law.

If I were asked "Where should the question of revolutionary legality be assigned?" From the point of view of our institute, I would reply that it is, so to speak, a *connecting link between law and Soviet construction*. In one of my previous articles, I showed that a statute may be law, but it can provide only a technique. But a characteristic feature of the state, particularly of the bourgeois state, is its *legislation*. Vladimir Ilich, who in a well-known dispute supported and developed the idea of a *state of Soviets*, assigned great significance to revolutionary law. More than once he admonished those of us who did not share his belief in the decree: You "do not know how to think in a governmental manner." But at the same time he supported the idea of a dictatorship, as he pushed forward the revolutionary work of the Cheka, and with no less zeal he supported the revolutionary decree.

In issue No. 1 of the collected essays *Revolution of the Law*, I tried to show how at various stages Lenin understood the significance of decree and law differently. With the coming to power, the Party program was for him transformed into decree-law. Then came laws as "declarations, statements, manifestoes, decrees," in general as a "form of propaganda which could not always be transformed into action. The material "base" was inadequate. The retreat to NEP brought to life a new type of law—a code, whose significance as a regulator resembled bourgeois law and its concept. Of course with reservations. Vladimir Ilich did not live to see the full unfolding of the revolutionary offensive, although he did proclaim it. What should the type of law be for the new revolutionary offensive? Lenin did not say, and he did not create this type, although a suggestion can be found in his slogan "Better less, but better."

One thing is clear: on the one hand the new revolutionary law will have to a significant degree a *directive* character, while on the other hand it will provide "standards" for the form of mass relations. When the Central Executive Committee issued a decree on dekulakization, for example, it indicated that its effect applied only to districts of *full-scale collectivization*. This also relates to the individual laws deriving from this decree and to the repeal of the law in force (e.g., the Land Code, the Civil Code). But this means neither that this law was not in force nor that it was merely a form of propaganda. On the contrary, this is a harsh reality for the enemy. We live in *other conditions*, and have a firm material base. Lenin's words of 1921 are also now practiced: "We have any number of laws! Why then have we achieved no success in this struggle? Because it cannot be waged by propaganda alone. It can be done if the *masses of the people* help" [Lenin 1921, p. 75] [emphasis P.S.]. Now this "help of the popular masses" occurs only if the matter is not limited to administration alone as has, in some places, been the case. And here *particularly* the role of *Soviet construction* emerges as one and the same with the establishment of the new legality.

Are we now approaching such work? Unfortunately, we still are not. At the start of this article we saw how the "high" and responsible commission, instead of providing a directive in the area of civil law—a directive now more necessary than ever before—has gone to sleep until, they say, everything is under control and it will be apparent what to write, until we have *finally* come to a halt. Indeed, this can be drawn out until the complete victory of socialism—and then law itself will not be necessary. The "legislator" of the revolution should perhaps, like a model journalist, have in his portfolio material for an article in the event something important occurs. But, in any case, the revolutionary law, *barring a retreat*, must pave the way for a further advance. We took a step forward and learned to fear using the words "socialist," etc. in law. However, the problem does not lie in phraseology, but in content. For law is not simply an order; it regulates or protects a system of *social relationships*. Revolutionary law must also be approached in this sense. In bourgeois society, these relationships were realized anarchically and imperialistically within the framework of the norms of the Civil Code which, of course, provides only bare forms for "free contract" "social exchange of objects" (simply according to the forms of purchase and sale). Without restricting the working people, Soviet revolutionary law must in the future give defined, general directives for development to socialism. The economics of this development will be defined by the socialist state plan of production and distribution. But Soviet power will ensure the conduct of this plan both in the struggle *against* class enemies and in the struggle for strict social discipline, until "people become accustomed to observing the elementary rules of social intercourse . . . without force and without coercion" [Lenin 1917, p. 462]. These two tasks: struggle *against* . . . and struggle *for* . . . in essence constitute the two tasks of every revolution: destruction and creativity. In the Criminal Code, where these two aspects of the struggle have not been recognized and have been insufficiently separated, this division must henceforth be more clearly expressed. Of course both these tasks are intertwined, for even part of the working people ("subkulaks," "bourgeois yesmen") were under the *influence* of the class enemy. In the countryside, collectivization has brought about a great upheaval, depriving the estate-owner and then the kulak of his material power and creating the basis for the birth and growth of consciousness amongst the most backward farm worker, *under whose influence* the middle peasant also must fall in the future, before he is transformed into a conscious worker. This upheaval will, of course, be a long one; it requires time, intensified agitation, and a correct evaluation in the future of the so-called subkulak.

This upheaval in the countryside must entail another and even greater change in life-style: *the liberation of women and the family from the shameful survival from the times of slavery—the household family*. During dekulakization we had to exile the kulak's family along with the kulak himself. This was a necessary deed. But to a certain extent this is a tragedy of which we are guilty as well. If you look at the theses on marriage and the family (published by our section in 1926), you will find an exhaustive theoretical analysis of the question of the household (Theses XV - XXX). Our authorities were then trying to "preserve" the work of the Ruling Senate of the Tsarist government, by coming out against *the dissolution and even the fragmentation* of this first (according to Marx) and last locus of slavery. *Economic* considerations forced us to do this so that there would be no reduction in the level of agriculture and so that the size of the proletariat would not increase too quickly. Now the *labor* element is disappearing in households that have gone into collective farming; here the household is, in essence, an *urban* proletarian family. Life has also brought the class struggle to the peasant household-family. In a rather abnormal, and probably not always candid form, this appears in all the frequent newspaper advertisements to the effect that such and such persons have broken ties with their fathers, families, etc. We should go to the aid of this struggle by the *legal untangling* of the family from the eternal slaveowner, "the father of the family"—the "man of the house." There are no longer bases to encourage the household even when there is no collectivization. May this *last refuge* of slavery quickly disappear! And we should assist this process through revolutionary law.

What will happen to the Civil Code? One wit stated that perhaps only Articles 1 and 4 of the Civil Code remain in effect. To the extent that these words were intended seriously, they merely display their author's ignorance of theory. Rather, it could be said that—at least for the countryside—Article 1, *this guarantee* of private ownership of the means of production, has played its role and has become unnecessary. From Article 4 it is possible to delete the words, beloved by many, "for the purpose of development of productive forces." We do not need the help of a "subject of law" to develop the forces of production; production, we think, has been freed from the web of civil law. But we must more vigorously strive to attain the real *goal* of civil law, *supply* on the basis of commodity exchange, so long as it is still impossible to conduct *full-scale organized* supply. As Lenin indicated, the law "equal for equal" (equivalent) remains in effect for now. But, we must add, this differs sharply from bourgeois law, where equivalency was exclusively contractual. Revolutionary legality understands equivalency as primarily labor equivalency, based mainly on plan and less on contract.

Some will say that I am sidetracked by trifles. Does not this objection recall that Soviet construction in the localities was called a minor detail after the great step forward to dictatorship? Everywhere such objections are unfounded. It seems to many that revolutionary legality is just a "bombastic" phrase—that it is not designed for relationships of the future and that it occupies a sort of exclusive position in the state system. But revolutionary law is called upon primarily to protect the social *relationships of millions* on a civilized basis, to defend them from being attacked, trampled, and maimed while, of course, not forgetting large scale "legal relations" as well. "Red"—"do not interfere with me"—is also an inheritance bequeathed us by semi-bourgeois and semi-feudal Russia. This attitude has frequently laid behind disrespect for revolutionary legality.

It would perhaps be more rational to reduce these thick volumes of laws to scrap paper, leaving a few copies in the archives, but by no means reprinting them in new codified editions, or in six or seven languages. To what will this lead? In the report on the inspection of Kazakhstan, a complaint by a Kazakh people's judge to the following effect was included. They do not have a translation of the current collection of codes (1,160 pages), and *to print such a translation* it would be necessary to suspend the political newspaper for half a year! And Kazakhstan is a relatively large republic. What if one "put aside" this collection of codes and wrote small, simple, and thin revolutionary codes? This is still a dream, but a worthy one to which we should devote some time instead of criticizing revolutionary legality. That would be a really revolutionary law. Now, as we have seen, we have lived through a crisis of revolutionary legality. It has been preserved and has obtained a new, but more real mission. The struggle for revolutionary law remains. There is perhaps no greater misfortune for our state than the historically established "departments" with their departmental and interdepartmental relations. At all times, both convenient and inconvenient, these departments issue, as if in the form of rockets, their drafts of new laws, for each of these departments has their "writing machines," their legal or legal counsel departments. The same department also exists at the Council of People's Commissars. These drafts flow together along with their legal counsel authors. There, after the struggle of these fighters for law, these drafts are adopted or rejected. This is real cottage industry production, standing in the sharpest contradiction to our plans of socialist rationalization. The capitalist country of England, despite all its ideological backwardness, is served by a small group of clerks (attached to the Exchequer) who prepare the drafts of all laws on departmental initiative. I am not offering the legislation of England as an example, but its *economy* of legislative efforts is indisputable.

I have mentioned Lenin's statement that the struggle for our law will be successful only "if the masses of the people help" [Lenin 1921, p. 75]. How are these words to be concretely understood? I propose that they must be compared with Lenin's own words about *the participation of each and every person in administration*. At the present time, the mass participation in administration assumes the forms of direct influence on the state apparatus in the course of its daily work. The development of the system of patrons of enterprises, the activity of workers' brigades, the development of working executives—these mean that representatives of the working people, not breaking with production, enter directly into the operational work of the state apparatus both as controllers and as direct participants. In these circumstances, Soviet law should especially become a form for organizing the initiative of the masses and for guiding the mass participation of the working people in the administration of the state. Aiding the struggle for revolutionary legality is only one aspect of participation in administration. It is true that this is one of the hardest and least understood tasks and that it requires, on the one hand, a high cultural level and, on the other, a genuinely revolutionary law. Simultaneously, it is necessary to transcend the prejudice that all law is *conservative*.

But, I am told, the revolution advances faster than law, rather than lagging behind it. One must do everything possible to keep law apace with the revolution, but the fact that it does not must be taken into consideration. The Civil Procedure Code provides an escape from this position by the application of Article 4: "To be guided in these instances by the general policy of the Workers' and Peasants' Government." It is time to show the real concrete significance of these words. From where can this general policy be learned? In recent years we have increasingly received detailed and purely *instructional* decrees from the Soviet authorities. But this is not enough. While Lenin, as I showed above, dialectically understood the formula: the program of the Party until victory—the decree of its government after victory, this dialectic in no less degree should relate to the party of the proletariat that has come to power. The trust that broad strata of the working people have for the Party, convinces them that the political directive of the Party, and the law as the formal expression of the will of the ruling class as a whole, must not and may not differ. Today's Party directives are *tomorrow's, even today's, revolutionary* law. Of course this refers fully only to *central* directives, because only central laws are generally obligatory. Only in this context can we comprehend the slogan: revolution and revolutionary law. Within the proletarian revolution, revolutionary law and the revolution are *mutually complementary* and by no means exclude one another. To the extent that the revolution takes the form of a dictatorship under the hegemony of the proletarian party, *the proletarian dictatorship acts through revolutionary legality*. The more law becomes *truly* revolutionary, the *more* revolutionary legality *becomes* obligatory and a matter of course. Now millions of peasants are rapidly converting to a new means of production, to a new order of labor. Can we conceive of this conversion without a new, and initially strict discipline? We find the answer to this in industrial life, where the *legal principle of one-man management* alternates with mass *voluntary*, or even *contractual socialist competition*. Analogously, does this not remind one of the "left" deviation in the countryside of abolishing and transferring their powers to the collective farms? The legal essence of these deviations has now been revealed, and this undertaking has now been eliminated. But the fact itself should be correctly evaluated.

The thoughts that I have hurriedly written down here should be developed further; but first of all people must take an interest in them. At the time of Dneprstroi and other giant projects, who wants to dedicate himself to such trifles as revolutionary law and revolutionary legality? Of course, these projects are creating the [economic] "base" without which we would to a certain extent be floating in the air. However, even those construction projects take place *within the framework of law.* One must not forget the interaction between base and super-structure. Socialist construction is not only economics, it also requires an appropriate ideological superstructure.

Note

1. It is interesting to note the fact that the ultra-left communist and old bourgeois specialists concur in this type of statement. This is peculiar consensus, of course, for different reasons. The left is delighted that this repugnant law is dead, and the specialist sees a confirmation that we in Soviet Russia do not have and have not had real law.

20. My Journey and My Mistakes[1]

"Go on . . . go on . . . go on"
—Serafimovich, "The Iron Torrent"

I.

I have been reproached for not yet having admitted my mistakes. I have been cast in the role of one of the two little boys in the famous advertising picture "This boy eats Hercules [breakfast cereal] and this one doesn't." This one admits his mistakes while Stuchka here has still has not. Conclusion: the more mistakes you admit, the better. The best is even to *overadmit* or to stop work, to do less: he who does nothing also makes no mistakes; or the less you do the better. Unfortunately, I can do neither. *I cannot not work*, but I cannot and will not *admit mistakes* where *I do not see them*. Possibly because *it was so hard for me to find my way*, I cannot lightly throw out or condemn that which I did, while *I in no way can change that which I reject*. But if I have found a truer, more correct decision, then I have *never consciously delayed* in simply and easily *replacing the old with the new*. I do not know how to repent; I am neither a nobleman, loving to repent, nor a bourgeois who does not recognize mistakes in principle. About the latter I wrote in 1918 (and even earlier in 1905) wrote: "It (i.e., the proletarian revolution—P.S.) does not fear mistakes or temporary misfortunes. Simultaneously, as the bourgeoisie loses *one* excess *hope* with each misfortune, the *proletariat*, as an ascending class becomes *one experience richer* with each mistake."[2] My slogan has therefore always been: do not repent, do better and correct [the mistake]. This is how I understand *self-criticism*, which in practice I have applied to myself more strictly than anyone.

In fact, starting from 1917 (with my very first works on legal subjects) if I had

"Moi put' i moi oshibki," *Sovetskoe gosudarstvo i revoliutsiia prava*, no. 5–6 [1931] :67–97.

frightened myself with the question: "what will posterity say;" if at each step I had stopped and asked myself, suppose something did not work out and suddenly became an error—would my work have been successful? Why for a long, *too long time* I was *alone, all alone,* and if it had not been for the support of Vladimir Ilich then I would have been forced to abandon this work. When I presented the draft of the first Decree on the Court, and met with the warmest support of Vladimir Ilich (who also personally *worked* on the draft and added his famous observation to Art. 5), we met with great resistance not only from the Left Socialist Revolutionaries (it was no accident that the question was raised only in the Council of People's Commissars and not in the All-Russia Central Executive Committee), but also from communists. As a result, for two days Vladimir Ilich "diplomatically" removed the question from the agenda and asked Comrade Lunacharskii to write his well-known article in *Pravda* in support of the decree. But we did not foresee that the decree, after thirteen years, would be evaluated as a "liberal bourgeois draft," although such a thought has already been explicitly stated in one article sent to the editors of our journal. The same may be said of every one of my articles. Each of them must be considered in the context of *revolutionary-dialectic development*, i.e., *of movement*, and not by today's standards. My one basic position the whole time in the area of law was: look to the future. Conversely, for bourgeois law, the basic slogan is: face the past, "Quieta non movere" do not touch that which has stopped.

Only with such a future-oriented slogan, could I arrive at *the establishment of the three basic* foundations [text has "kitov"—"whales"—from an old myth that the world is supported by three whales—translator's note] *of our general line* on the legal front: "The revolutionary role of law." Where could this thought be found if not in the revolutionary dialectic of our revolution. When I received the *proposal* from the Party's secretariat, on behalf of the Central Committee, to write a small book on the theme of "the general theory of law and state," without a moment's hesitation I gave the book this *title*. It is true, somewhere recently the accusation was voiced when I not long ago mentioned the revolutionary role of law in the press, that I purportedly *am preaching the idea of some new* revolution. In another place that I spoke *of the coming phase* of the revolution as *communist* (an innocent play on words), meaning again a "new" revolution. Dear comrade pedants, albeit red pedants, the talk was always of the same *continuing revolution in various areas of life at various stages*. If you like the role of "red" Bekmesser (from Richard Wagner's famous opera, "Die Meistersinger"), keep it up.

II.

During the entire first period of my work on the legal front, which to a certain extent was the decisive period—I was alone. When on January 31, 1921, I received from the Orgbureau of the Central Committee of the Russian Communist Party (Bolsheviks) an assignment to write a *Textbook on the Theory and*

Practice of Soviet Law in the course of two or three months, this at first seemed impossible. But I devoted myself *exclusively* to this work and only thanks to my well-known obstinacy did I finish it in June, i.e., in four and a half months.[3] I had to work intensively and take into consideration a rather large quantity of material. But of course I could not have succeeded with this work if I *had not been helped by the revolution itself.* The twenty-seven volumes of Lenin's works, particularly all that happened after 1917, *did not then yet exist.* His *State and Revolution* served as the basic guide. However, this title, the unprecedented scholarly combining of these two concepts, the consideration of the concept of the state *in the process of class struggle* replaced for me a whole literature on the revolutionary dialectic. The revolutionary concept of *class struggle*, inevitably leading to the dictatorship of the proletariat, was the basic *leitmotif* of all my work. But we also had a practical legal experience, the objective dialectic of the revolution in the form of the Decree on the Court, the "burning" of the *old* laws and the promulgation of the *revolutionary* decrees of Soviet power. Only from the conception of law as one of the forms of class struggle, namely, in the stage of seizure of power by the new, previously *oppressed* class in the form of the dictatorship of the proletariat, and from the revolutionary dialectic as the exclusive method of analysis and development of this question, was *The Revolutionary Role of Law and State* possible. But one element was still missing. This was to remind people of Marx's old notion that, in the *study of law*, we must proceed from real "social relations" (of course in Karl Marx's sense of the term rather than my most recent critics). Here the *revolution* again saved us, since we lived the first period *almost without laws.* I have been accused most recently of having been under the influence of the sociological school of law (Muromtsev, Korkunov and, in part, Jhering and others). This naturally was so; but I took from then *only the result* of their studies and by no means the bourgeois-*class* attributes of their science. In this respect, I stood firmly on the *Leninist point* of view. Recall Lenin's speech of October 4, 1920, at the Third Congress of the Young Communist League. It would not hurt to reread this even today, in 1931:

> Proletarian culture has not sprung from somewhere unknown, it is not something thought up by people who call themselves specialists on proletarian culture. This is total, complete trash. *Proletarian culture must appear as a natural development of those stores of knowledge which mankind has developed under the weight of capitalist society, of bureaucratic society.* . . . A model of how communism has appeared from the sum total human knowledge is *Marxism.* . . . "If I know that I know little, I will seek a person who knows more, but if someone calls himself a communist and says that he needs to know nothing substantive, then nothing resembling a communist will come from him. . . ." We must learn how *to take for ourselves the whole total of human knowledge.* . . .[4] [Lenin 1920a, pp. 287–89]

Engels's article (written with Kautsky) of 1887, in the Social Democratic journal *Neue Zeit* on *"Juridical Socialism,"* had a decisive significance for my work. It was printed *anonymously* and only by chance did I learn (from the jubilee 25-year index of the journal) that it belonged to Engels. By accident, therefore, I discovered it; only two years later did it appear in Russian translation. From it I drew the *basic direction* for our struggle, the direction of the *"legal world view* as the class *world view* of the bourgeoisie." In the preface to my work, I placed this at the *center* of our attention. Today is cited by all and is recognized as one of the basic arguments for the necessity of our new concept of law.

One more event helped me. In a letter of 1890, Engels wrote that now (i.e., in 1890) "all history must be studied afresh" [Engels 1890a, p. 484]. Thus, with the victory of the *proletariat*, the entire past is seen in a completely *new light*. All revolutionary events of the past, all history as a process of uninterrupted class struggle, etc., has obtained a new meaning. I was helped *in taking account of this direction* by such conclusions (beyond "basic whales" which are repeated by all until now, such as: on the changeability, the fluidity of law, on natural law as a political platform of the emergent and rising bourgeoisie, on the most recent bourgeois theories of law as the *superstructure* on the base of the monopolist imperialist period of capitalism in which *changes in this base could not help but be reflected*.

Thus, the fundamental basis appeared for our revolutionary-Marxist concept of law, which (in a weakened and castrated version) lay on the platform of the newly created Section of Law: the class nature of all law instead of its bourgeois-democratic concept; the revolutionary-dialectic method instead of formal legal logic; material social relations as the basis for explanation and understanding of the legal superstructure instead of explanation of legal relations from the law or legal ideas.

In my work, I was always true to the method of the proletarian revolution as characterized by Engels:

> The essence is not in this, but in the method—*in the principle of general movement and general interaction*, in the appropriate approach to the study of an object, *not allowing thought to be pacified*, but forcing it to most truly *reflect reality in its motion and in all its complexity*.[5]

These are the bases that I have consistently adduced, which give me the *right* to answer the accusations that I lacked a dialectical method, and allegations of various sins "of a mechanistic nature" with the words of Kuzyma Prutkov: "If you read BUFFALO on an elephant's cage, don't believe your eyes."

III.

The year 1922 opened a *new stage* both in my own and in "our" work. I was not alone for there were three of us: myself, Comrade Adoratskii, and then Comrade Pashukanis. We came together by accident. Comrade Adoratskii somehow gave me his prerevolutionary manuscript on the state, which I found most interesting from the point of view of our orientation on the question of law. This was published. As for Comrade Pashukanis, in the legal field, we met for the first time at a conference on the legal program of Sverdlovsk [Communist] University [in Moscow], and later at my report before the Communist Academy. I found that our views coincided on basic questions, and I invited Comrade Pashukanis to collaborate in *joint work* on the theory of law at the Communist Academy. He consented. Even then I noticed one disagreement between us: this was his under-evaluation of the role of the state for law—which, as it later turned out, was *not accidental*. Meanwhile, the *state* already played a central role for law in my first work.

I greeted the first edition of Comrade Pashukanis's. *The General Theory of Law and Marxism* as the most outstanding work of the period. However, I have been unjustly criticized during the discussion for *not having criticized the book's mistakes*. Given our extraordinarily collegial struggle against "the entire world" of jurists, I could not openly engage in sharp criticism of Pashukanis while our opponents were watching for disagreements among us. Furthermore, I was awaiting a convergence of our views: this was very possible from my point of view. I nevertheless emphasized from the outset that Comrade Pashukanis's conception encompasses only bourgeois law and, by declaring it to be *law in general*, he blurs the *class nature* of law, i.e., he denies the existence of feudal law and now the law of the transition period, Soviet law, as well.[6] In the article published in *Revolution of the Law*, No. 2, 1927,[7] I definitely laid out *all the basic* elements of a critique of his theory, such as: concealing the role of the state and as a natural result of this—the disappearance of the class nature of all law, the correlation of law exclusively with relations of exchange, the denial of the concept of Soviet law, etc. I pointed out the exceptional abstractness of his theory[8] and called upon him, having uncovered the true state of affairs of the bourgeois essence of law, to return to the real world and to the concrete phenomena of law. I went still further and more than once noted the danger of economism (deviation in the question of the significance of the state, i.e., of politics), of petty bourgeois ideology (see my citations from Marx on Proudhon and in general on petty bourgeois ideologies). Only by having tied this theory to the revolutionary class struggle right up to the dictatorship of the proletariat was it possible to cut off all compromises of excesses.

The extraordinary abstractness of his work was recognized by Comrade Pashukanis himself and we more than once bantered over his students or follow-ers who were more "Pashukanisite," than Evgenii Bronislavovich himself, who had to a certain decree the inclination of an ivory tower scholar, but who never lost feeling for concrete struggle. For instance, we were always supporters of the demand to study revolutionary periods in history, so as by a correct understanding of them to support the strengthening of our proletarian revolutionary dialectic.

But we spent too much time on abstract work, on the development of a theoretical program. Of course we had to study, to begin with, all the questions of law in our own way, in a new way. For this we went through the stage of publication of an *Encyclopedia of State and Law*. It arose somewhat accidentally. In 1922 the Communist Academy ordered the publication of a large revolutionary Marxist *Encyclopedia of Social Sciences*. A broad commission was created and a division for state and law was also included in the plan and assigned as the work of our section. The commission conducted preparatory work according to the "state of the art," rules of planned development (I will not undertake to say whether there was conscious sabotage or simply laxity, but the realism of the plan was immediately doubtful). For our division of the project, we [jurists] had nevertheless and already noted something, already become proficient so I audaciously set the task: to publish separately our special *Encyclopedia of State and Law* if the entire project was not to be realized. Our "daring" was initially met with doubt by the leading circles of the Communist Academy mainly because, it seems to me, we planned to publish this *Encyclopedia* without Goikhbarg's participation.[9] In spring 1924, our proposal was finally accepted. A prospectus was published in summer 1924, and the work (twice as large in size as was proposed for subscription), although late, was finished by the end of 1927. We had to overcome unbelievable difficulties, bringing in a mass (110) of authors, but this work was necessary for it forced us to work out our own opinion on every question. With the unusually swift tempo of our revolution, the *Encyclopedia* became outdated. Now one might even question whether or not it paid off idea-wise (financially it was a huge success). Such thoughts, however, are engineered by an insufficiently firm revolutionary dialectic. Even the well-known "theoretician" Il'inskii wrote at that time that an *Encyclopedia of Law* cannot be published during a revolution, only after the revolution, i.e., when there will no longer be either law or a state. Our *Encyclopedia* should be evaluated as a work corresponding to a certain stage of the revolution, no more, no less.

The journal *Revolution of Law* (1927) and before it the collection with the same name (1925) opened a new era. The very name, proposed by me, at first brought forth objections that it was too daring. I insisted on it and quickly became attached to it; and only recently did people begin, in the word and concept "revolution of law," to see some sort of deviation or excess, for assertedly our revolution had already ended with victory. Yes, we took stage by stage victoriously and irreversibly, but—the revolution of law still continues.

The new stage signified that our section would go out onto a broad road. For this it was necessary to leave behind the stage of a sect and to move closer to the broad masses and their movement. Accordingly, starting with the Fourteenth [Party] Congress and each congress and conference thereafter, I had to call the "men of law" to the respective struggle. Already in the report of 1925 to the Communist Academy,[10] I stated:

In fact this change has taken place: workers are hired for work at *factories* exclusively belonging *to the class of working people as a whole*; commodities are the product of this *collective labor* and exchange is made namely by this product. I noted that quantity in the given case turned into a new quality, perhaps incomprehensible at first to the outsider but swaying over the minds of the very creators of these riches "of the working people," on the bases of the law "of the working people themselves?" But I added with some annoyance, "our 'class ideologues' however still have not penetrated this consciousness." Our poets have so far noticed and noted only the noise and rhythm of the factory and the external discipline corresponding to it, but not the *destruction* of the ideology of the masses. . . . Our jurists still repeat borrowed old abstract formulas, and still have not yet found new forms.

Proceeding from the resolution of the Fourteenth Party Congress "On Attaching on the Side of Socialism" on the basis of NEP, I drew a conclusion also for our work on questions of Soviet law. The Fifteenth Congress had as its result the issuance of the "General Principles of Land Use and Land Tenure," proceeding from the possibility of socialist construction in agriculture, thanks to the nationalization of land. The Sixteenth Congress sanctioned the liquidation of the kulaks as a class and approved a plan for the victory of socialism in the countryside,[11] discarding the general principles as out of date. In connection with the excesses, "Dizzy with Success" (1929/1930)—it was necessary to call for revolutionary legality as the broad task of involving the working masses in administration, etc.

As a result, we set out on a new journey, or rather on a new stage of our journey. But the position at the base of my work of the first period remained intact. The task was set even before the Congress: in the theses on each branch of law to give a whole conception of this area, but by no means as parallel to the corresponding branches, but as constantly interwoven. As Engels said: "In a modern state law must not only correspond to the general economic condition . . . but must also be an *internally coherent* expression of it, which does not, owing to inner contradictions, reduce itself to naught"[12] [Engels 1890, p. 492].

After the decision of the Congress, I drew conclusions for the work of the law section which I included in the report "Tendencies of Development and Perspectives of Soviet Law" published in this issue. This about-face, from the ivory towers of abstract science to the floodgates of mass movement and concrete legal work, was not achieved easily and at once. Still, some prefer a "tempest in a glass of water" at the discussion table.

IV.

I had to become specially acquainted with civil law, to become something of a civil law "specialist." [The term "specialists" was used in the 1930s mainly to refer to persons hired for their technical skills rather than their loyalty to Party policy. Here it is used ironically by Stuchka—Eds.] It is true that from the very first moment of speaking out on the legal theoretical front, I indicated that I considered civil law to be the basic law and the remaining areas of law merely offshoots or subsidiary branches. (There was not yet talk among us of "State Law" but only of the "Theory of the State.") I had expressed my preference for civil law in the preface to my first work. But against my wishes I had to be occupied with this branch of law in practice, with my appointment from January 1923 as President of the Supreme Court of the RSFSR. I then posed the question of our task dialectically, as "the proletarian court and bourgeois law." In this context I conducted my work. Once more, in answer to all slanderers, I daringly affirm that I did not ignore the class role for nine years, not for a minute, not for a single case.

But it must be said that decisions on civil law of the first period demanded great attention given the full scale "legalism," right deviations and "left" excesses in localities. In the Civil Code which on its very appearance was officially regarded as being unsatisfactory and was sharply criticized in competent circles, there were indications of the bourgeois approach itself (Articles, 117, 403, etc.) and only individual articles, like slips of the tongue, from the perspective of the interests of the working class. I succeeded in introducing some of these in the Civil Code in the commissions of the All-Russian Central Executive Committee, for instance Articles 5 and 6 of the Introductory Law for the Civil Code.

By judicial practice there was gradual success in turning even this (civil) law into Soviet law. Thus, the judicial practice of the Supreme Court introduced the principle of preference (presumption) for state property instead of the presumption of bourgeois law always in favor of the actual possessor, i.e., usually of a private person. In bourgeois law, state property was in essence simply the right of "private property" in the person of the state; thus, by my proposal the word "socialist" was added to our Constitution of the RSFSR in 1927. I introduced into judicial practice instead of the application of prescription also to state property, the complete denial of such prescription, as deriving from the absence among us of the institution of prescriptive acquisition, for if no one could obtain ownership by prescription, then property would be left without an owner, i.e., would again become state property.

The class perspective of the court appeared in very high relief in defense of the interests of working people in case of violation of a contract on sale of small homes by virtue of the new principle of "labor use," i.e., of use by the working people (at the start, incorrectly: possession).

Further, the practice of the Supreme Court originated a new point of view on compensation for damages, etc. Many of the explanations of the Supreme Court became law; as a result there was achieved a full transformation of all civil law in the direction of class Soviet law. Courts could be accused of a "distortion of the class line" only by ivory-tower scholars unacquainted with practice, or by malicious slanderers.

On the basis of five years' experience I began preparation of my textbook; the preparatory work was published in journal articles, in theses, in a report and brochure *The Class State and Civil Law* in 1924, etc. In the preface to Part I of the *Treatise* on civil law of June 10, 1927, I wrote: "I pose the questions; you find the answers yourselves. Throughout all my work are scattered ideas requiring elaboration, further development, or disproof." I did wait until these ideas were further developed, but I had to wait through three and a half years of wild accusations. They will be discussed below.

In order to make civil law a subject of science rather than of commentary or direct reprinting of laws, it was necessary to "put it on its feet;" to turn from the area of abstract formulas to concrete forms of relations. Two thousand years have been used to find the most abstract formulas, most successfully to hide and concealing the concrete, i.e., before all the class contradictions of this law. I was the first to show this in practice. Of course we have basic foundations in the works of Marx, Engels, and Lenin: we ourselves also have the experience of the outstanding work of Comrade Pashukanis. However, he drew conclusions which in their degree of abstraction stand beyond all competition.

I posed, first of all, the question of the concrete goal of civil law (and of law in general), moreover of a fully practical goal. I had previously indicated to Comrade Pashukanis—who built his theory on exchange value alone—that a commodity simultaneously has a consumption value as well. This means that civil law is a form of facilitation[13] of so-called social exchange of things, i.e., speaking in nonscientific language of supply of people with commodities or products necessary for production. There can be only three possibilities: supplying one's own family in self-sufficient household and farming operations, communist supply ("to each according to his needs"),[14] or contract, civil-law supply. I assert that by this, I introduced great clarity into the practical understanding of the meaning of the Civil Code for every judge, rendering it understandable for every working person. But I simultaneously applied Marx's formulas for the unmasking of the so-called abstract subject of law: C—M—C (simple commodity exchange) or M—C—M+m (exchange for the purpose of profit). The answer to these questions provides a true class evaluation of every plaintiff and defendant in court, i.e., of every subject of civil law. If I provided nothing more than this, my work would still be useful.

I further divided the significance of the division of civil law into *two parts* from the perspective of class (hidden by bourgeois law and particularly by its theory): to the law of things (the sphere of domination and subordination) and obligations, contracts (the sphere of freedom-exchange). The law of inequality and the law of equality. This is a contradiction, unsolvable for bourgeois society, which will finally be solved only under communism. He who does not understand this does not have a real idea of the revolutionary dialectic, or he is simply a pseudo-politician.

Proceeding from the ever stronger position of state property and contrasting

its *polar* opposite—the ever narrower jurisdiction of the law of private property—
we really have obtained *something new* in Soviet civil law, in which for the first
time in history the word "socialism" is actually heard.

I used the work of Comrade Pashukanis to solve the problem (unsolvable for
the bourgeoisie) of the *equivalent* contract of commodity exchange, namely, as
the labor equivalent of exchange value according to Marx's *Capital.* For bourgeois civil law this is definitely true in the form of a *general equivalence* of
money, while in Soviet civil law the *planned element* is playing a more and more
decisive role.

But where should the State Planning Commission start: with the provision or
supply of the whole population, as the right deviations proposed, or with the
planned supply of a class or even part of a class standing in the most responsible
place of construction?

> There has also been a discussion about the distribution of products in future
> society, whether this will take place according to the amount of work done or
> otherwise. The question has been approached very "materialistically" in oppo-
> sition to certain idealistic phraseology about justice.[15] But strangely enough it
> has not struck anyone that, after all, the method of distribution essentially
> depends on how much there is to distribute, and that this must surely change with
> the progress of production and social organization, so that the method of distri-
> bution may also change. But to everyone who took part in the discussion,
> "socialist society" appeared not as something undergoing continuous change
> and progress but as a stable affair fixed once for all, which must, therefore, have
> a method of distribution fixed once for all. All one can reasonably do, however,
> is (1) to try to discover the method of distribution to be used at the beginning,
> and (2) try to find the general tendency of the further development.[16] [Engels
> 1980a, p. 484]

Engels' very *clear* and wise words remained forgotten in our disputes. Those who
imagined themselves to be great dialecticians did not notice this simple truth.
Comrade Stalin correctly evaluated this truth in his plan for the supply of the basic
part of construction on the one hand; and on the other, for the powerful movement
of shock workers and socialist competition from below, adding from above all
sorts of rewards on the basis of "*labor equivalence*, replacing the abstract labor
of a commodity economy with *concrete* equivalence according to the quantity of
labor."[17] Labor is a concrete measuring rod.

The State Planning Commission is also subordinate to social relations on the
basis of civil law. But the State Planning Commission continues to use *money,
cost of production, productivity* of labor, *piecework wages, economic accountability, self-sufficiency,* etc.

In the last part of my work, and even earlier in various theses on this theme, I
demonstrated the *great fluidity* and mutability of civil law. But these themes

should be developed by action, and not merely by simple conversation. In particular, it is interesting to follow *the process of abolition* of the remnants of the norms of bourgeois law, of the sphere of *economic-judicial* arguments, with their *replacement* by new forms of supply, i.e., of regulation of relations of supply. But the full *withering away* of Soviet law will occur only when the state withers away. Here is what I had written in 1918 on the topic of proletarian law which was *assigned* to me.

> Understanding law in the bourgeois sense, we cannot even speak of proletarian law; the goal of the socialist revolution is to abolish law and to replace it by a new socialist order. For the bourgeois legal theorist, the word "law" is inseparably connected with the concept of the state as the agency of protection, the weapon of coercion in the hands of the ruling class. With the fall, or rather the *withering away* of the state, law in the bourgeois sense naturally collapses or *withers away*. We can only speak of proletarian law as the *law of the transitional period*, of the period of dictatorship of the proletariat or of the law of socialist society in an *entirely new sense of the word*. With the elimination of the state as the organization of class coercion of social relations, the social order will be regulated *not by coercion but by the conscious good will* of the working people, i.e., of the entire new society. [Stuchka 1918, p. 20]

This sounds rather timely.

When we now consider the ever decreasing sphere of civil law the question arises, has the "game been worth the candle"? Was it work expending so much *energy*, and (keeping in mind the "events," we will add) *nerves* on the theory of a civil law that is clearly withering away? I assert that this was necessary. Without a correct understanding of bourgeois *civil law* there could not be in general a correct viewpoint of the significance of law; and this law still is a basic element of the bourgeois, and petty-bourgeois *world view*. This struggle is still continuing.

V.

Thus, I briefly view *my way* both in the *past* and also the direction of this path in the *future*. This is the path of uninterrupted struggle along the prescribed *general* line. Never losing a close connection with the *practice* of life, with *concrete* tasks along a *firm class line*, without *right* deviations and without *left* excesses.

After this statement of my way, I must deal with those *mistakes* that were attributed to me during the discussion—to the extent that I have still not corrected them and have still not recognized them. It was not my fault that *I could not attend the whole conference* and that *therefore on the evening when I was there I could reply only to that part of the speech of Comrade Pashukanis that I had heard.*

I must start with a particular accusation, that of *direct counterrevolution*.

Comrade Pashukanis writes: "How, comrades, may this be *qualified*, I ask you? It seems only a *distortion of the class line*, which was conducted by the introduction into our civil law of this very *systematic.* . . (?) principle of labor equivalence? *And this principle was introduced* by P.I. Stuchka not only in the practice of the *Supreme Court of the RSFSR* but also in the 'Fundamental Principles of Civil Legislation.'" And in what does the position of the draft "Fundamental Principles" consist? Or the words "deprivation of property and of civil law rights without compensation *is allowed only* in cases specially provided by law." From where did I take this "criminal" principle? It was taken from the RSFSR *law in force* on confiscation, kept in force and repeatedly approved by the Soviet government during the time of the excesses of 1929–30 even when the kulaks were being liquidated as a class by a revolutionary process (and not a judicial process). *This liquidation* was approved by a decree of the Central Executive Committee of the Union.

And the decree on "Requisitions and Confiscations" of *April* 16, 1920 (now replaced by the codified law of March 28, 1927) also has an *interesting history*. When *after a special* proposal by Lenin, the Executive Committee of the Council of People's Commissars wrote the draft of this decree (obviously with the same attitude as my current accuser) it compiled the decree in *moderate* form. But Lenin rejected this first draft in a very *sharp* way, *categorically* demanding that it be formulated: "*No property whatsoever* may be requisitioned or confiscated other than by the procedure provided by the present rules" (Art. 1). "The right of compensation belongs to the *agencies of authority* indicated in the previous article and also the presidium of the All-Russian Extraordinary Commission, revolutionary tribunals, and people's courts applying this measure as *punishment.*" The decree was signed personally by Lenin.[18] So, who was it who introduced this principle constituting a "distortion of the class line"? It is true that Comrade Pashukanis always showed a certain "devil-may-care" attitude toward statutory law.

And what is the nature of Comrade Pashukanis's views about equivalence? When the commission for the drafting of All-Union Fundamental Principles of Civil Legislation began its work, then I was assigned the drafting of general guiding theses for the work in the commission. In these theses we read, incidentally, that "*the uncompensated alienation* of property or the deprivation of property rights of private persons or organizations for the use of the state is allowed only by the procedure and in the instances provided for in All-Union statute (for instance as a result of the expiration of the period of limitations, of an illegal transaction, etc.)." In all remaining situations, "*compensation for all unrecovered expenditures according to the principle of equivalence*" is required.

These theses *were adopted* on May 22, 1927, in the Section of the General Theory of State and Law with the participation of E.B. Pashukanis.

These fundamental theses of the Section of Law were introduced as guidance in the Drobins Commission attached to the Council of People's Commissars and were approved there—again *with the vote of Comrade Pashukanis*.

A *subcommission* was formed *under my chairmanship* for the drafting of "general provisions." This subcommission presented to the Drobins Commission a program for the general part, also approved by Comrade Pashukanis, in which Para. 6 reads:

> Transformation into state property *without compensation* shall be only *by the procedure of the criminal and civil legislation* of an All-Union nature; *in all other cases* alienation of property or deprivation of property rights shall be *with compensation for the equivalent* of the thing *or of unrecovered expenditures*.[19]

These articles were approved by the Drobins Commission (November 2, 1927, Minute No. 4) with *the participation and the vote* of Comrade Pashukanis.

With Comrade Drobins's departure, the Commission of the Council of People's Commissars continued work under the chairmanship of *Comrade Antonov-Saratovskii*. A new subcommission was elected for the coordination of the separate parts of the draft, under my chairmanship, consisting of Comrades Brandenburgskii (People's Commissariat of Justice), Pashukanis (Communist Academy), Bernshtein (Council of People's Commissars of the USSR), Raevich (Council of People's Commissars of the RSFSR). This commission, at its session of January 23, 1929, with the participation and *the vote of Comrade Pashukanis* decided:

> To state Para. 3 of Art. 5 in the following form: the uncompensated deprivation of property rights shall be allowed only in instances specially provided by law. In all remaining instances the deprivation of property rights shall be allowed only *with compensation for the value* (the equivalent) by the procedure and within the limits established by the statutes of the USSR and the union republics.
>
> To adopt Para. 4 of Art. 6 in the wording of the draft saying at the end instead of "*compensation for its equivalent*," "*compensation for its value*."

On the theme of equivalence, the subcommission at the session of March 20, 1929, decided:

> In the voting on Para. (c) of Article 56, the votes were divided; Comrades Stuchka and Pashukanis were for the adoption of the provision "transactions concluded that are clearly *extraordinarily disadvantageous* for one of the parties"; Comrades Bernshtein and Raevich were against the formulation and supported the previous text of Para. (c); Comrade Brandenburgskii abstained.

On July 12, 1929, with *the vote of Comrade Pashukanis*, the following article was adopted in the chapter on unjust enrichment:

Art. 85 is adopted in the following language: "A person who has obtained or has used property belonging to another person without sufficient basis deriving from law or contract, and without compensation for value must return what has been obtained unjustly to the person suffering from this."

"The second and third subparagraphs are adopted in the language of the draft."

It seems clear and consistent. What are these votes if not a *conscious approval* of this same incriminating article? Did this occur unconsciously—"As if it happened in a dream?"

Is all this to be designated as a *distortion of the class line*? By whom? Comrade Pashukanis himself. Of course this *was not* then, and *is not* now a *distortion* of the class line. Comrade Pashukanis, "repenting," abjured his very valuable work, which he did not and could not *bring consistently and usefully to an end*. And now his accusation is simply a poor application of polemics against a comrade. We will return to the question of equivalence itself below.

What led Comrade Pashukanis to this *panic*? I read:

Comrades told me how, in the course of *almost two years*, *a struggle* was waged in the *Ukraine* between the *Civil Division* and the *Plenum* of the *Supreme Court*. The *Civil Division* rendered a decision for the *uncompensated seizure* of certain means of production,[20] but the *Plenum* of the Supreme Court *reversed* this decree relying upon the principle of labor equivalence and on the authority of the Supreme Court of the RSFSR.

This is an almost literal repetition of a well-known passage from *The Three Sisters*, the play by Anton Chekhov: "The contractor was saying that in Moscow it was 150 degrees below zero." Listen to what really happened. I am little acquainted with the work of the Ukrainian Supreme Court, but some readers must think something is wrong here. First, what of the *benign* Civil Division and the *evil* Plenum of the Ukrainian Supreme Court struggling in such a manner with one another? Why the Plenum of the Supreme Court consists of this very same Civil Cassational Division as well as the Criminal Cassational Division, which usually includes in its composition judges with more working class background who are more steadfast in their class orientation. Nonetheless, it was only in the Civil Division that someone in the Ukraine was found to be unsteady in a class sense. And what kind of "means of production" were involved? Not taking means of production from a *middle peasant* in the form of *windmills* with those blades Don Quixote once fought,[21] or that windmill about which the poet sang: "here is the windmill, it has already collapsed"? All *other mills*, i.e., mills capable of being a *means of exploitation*, are considered *nationalized* and for them, according to Art. 1 of the Civil Code, there is nothing to take. Or was it a question of suits on violation of *rental contracts* for windmills? In fact there were cases when the basis of the suit was that in fact *repair* had been overdone. I *cannot* of course be as open as Comrade Pashukanis on this question, but I must say that these claims were *nevertheless granted*. They were not granted under Art. 1 of the Civil Code, but on the basis of contract with consequences under the contract and the law on rent. As for the decision of the Supreme Court of the RSFSR on compensation under Art. 147 of the Civil Code cited by Comrade Pashukanis, one should not forget the words he cited: "in case of absence of bad faith."

But what *labor* equivalence can be spoken of here? For the entrepreneur is not a working man. For him the formula of our law of compensation is: return of *unused expenditures* for improvements. But even this provision, *upon my proposal*, was supplemented in a limited manner with respect to entrepreneurs, by the words: "and with the subtraction of all his profits." No one may accuse me of *class lack of self control* even in civil cases if he does not resort to conscious or lightheaded lies. All fully recognize the responsible role that was assigned to me by the Party and Soviet authority as President of the Supreme Court and I am now fulfilling it with honor for the ninth year.

Nevertheless, I became more deeply interested in the Ukrainian Supreme Court. What did I find? *The situation turned out* to be *directly opposite* to that which Comrade Pashukanis wrote. This is what in fact the Plenum of the Ukrainian Supreme Court wrote already on November 23, 1926:

(1) To consider that on the basis of Articles 1 and 4 of the Code it is possible to take an owner's property which is classified as means of production. (2) Such property may also be taken from the owner when the latter uses his right to this property in contradiction to its social and economic purpose. (3) Compensation in such a case for property taken, as a general rule shall be obligatory, with the exception of property transferred by the procedure for denationalization.

This explanation, of course, is *fundamentally incorrect*, but moreover it was compiled *before our theses*, before our drafts, and before the rulings of the Plenum of the Supreme Court of July 4, 1927, as well. It was *this* interpretation of the Plenum of the Ukrainian Court that its Civil Cassational Division *did not follow*, and in its decree of December 20, 1927, the Plenum of the Supreme Court of the USSR again writes:

Bearing in mind that the decision of the Civil Cassational Division of the Supreme Court of July 4, 1927, in the suit B. vs. L. District Executive Committee on the return of the *cistern* (and not a windmill) *contradicts* the decision of the Plenum of the Supreme Court of November 23, 1926, on the question of the limits of application of Art. 1 of the Civil Code, the above-mentioned decision of the Civil Cassational Division is reversed. . . .

Comrade Pashukanis's exceptional ignorance of judicial practice and its "distortions'' is not limited to this. He adduced as an innovation the example given by Comrade Slivitskii at the conference in Kharkov ''on our concept of *support payments* as a surrogate (surrogate is not entirely correct, this is *a historical form* of support) for social security.'' This as all know is *my* statement of the question (see the article ''Family'' in the *Encyclopedia*, and also ''Theses on Marriage''). But ''we have entirely abnormal decisions, recovery for past time, and other distortions (of what?) in *our judicial practice*,'' so spoke or so wrote Comrade Pashukanis in January, 1931. But on January 18, 1926, *on my proposal*, the Supreme Court of the RSFSR had issued *an interpretation* that:

> [A] suit of one parent against another for his expenditures for *past* time as a general rule is *not allowed* with the exception of cases when the plaintiff shows that he, the plaintiff, went into debt for these expenditures and that they were necessary, . . . for a suit for support should not serve as a means of accumulation.

The exception for cases of indebtedness was necessary in the interests of the weaker party, the woman. Comrade Pashukanis *could not fail to know* of this explanation, since it was published. *Of what distortions is* Comrade Pashukanis *now complaining?*

The Congress did not follow in the footsteps of the speaker and did not decide to raise Comrade Pashukanis's concrete indictments against me. Comrade Pashukanis nevertheless considered it necessary (reducing the remaining part of his talk to a minimum), to immortalize his escapades against me in full, both in a journal and in a separate publication. I am therefore obliged to answer him just as openly, and I *have the right* to demand, after this statement of reality, that he *either admit his mistake* or give the *concrete facts* of my purported *class-harmful* work on the Supreme Court. *Otherwise, I have the right to declare him a malicious slanderer.*

VI.

But let us move to the basic theoretical and principal practical question—*on equivalence* in general in civil law and after that also in Soviet civil law. In the previous paragraph I disproved the accusation against the RSFSR Supreme Court. I will not attempt to say whether ignorance or bad faith was predominant in this accusation.

The problem of equivalence requires a detailed development and not a frivolous approach. I will deal with the question only briefly here.

How does Marx describe the first stage of the transition period in ''Critique of the Gotha Program''? He writes

> [T]he individual producer receives back from society—after the deductions have been made—exactly what he gives to it. What he has given to it is his individual

quantum of labor. For example, the social working day consists of the sum of the individual hours of work; the individual labor time of the individual producer is the part of the social working day contributed by him, his share in it. He receives a certificate from society that he has furnished such and such an amount of labor (after deducting his labor for the common funds), and with this certificate he draws from the social stock of means of consumption as much as costs the same amount of labor. The same amount of labor that he has given to society in one form he receives back in another. [Marx 1875, pp. 17–18]

I interrupt the citation here because the rest is known from Lenin's *State and Revolution*. I translated this long citation because people usually confine themselves to individual phrases of Marx's unusually simple plan for distribution of the means of consumption. But we must *define flexibly* the stage in which we find ourselves *during the time of the NEP*. Comrade Stalin gives us very clear guidance: "The NEP is freedom for private trade within certain limits, within certain boundaries with the proviso that the role of the state as the regulator of the market is guaranteed" [Stalin 1929a, p. 46]. "As long as NEP exists, both its aspects must be retained" (ibid. p. 67).

This means that it must be kept along *with the plan and contractual* basis, although in a complex "plan-contract" order. But both bases still rest on *the same equivalence*. For an equal quantity of labor, an equal quantity of product. In one case this proportion is determined by the plan and government regulation—in another, simply contract or contract on the basis of plan regulation.

Lenin concludes from Marx that: "*in the first stage* of communism differences, and unjust differences, in wealth will still persist, but the *exploitation* of man by man will have become impossible, because it will be impossible to seize *the means of production*"[22] [Lenin 1917, p. 466].

In our country there still exists the possibility of obtaining and transferring means of production, even in the countryside after the liquidation of the kulaks. This complicates both the concept of exchange and in particular the legal relationships of this exchange.

In my *Treatise*[23] correctly taking account of all this, I wrote:

> [W]henever one must be guided by "justice" *on the basis of our code* even for us *the principle of equivalence* there remains *in force. The gradation of equivalence* is defined by law (defined prices), by *contract* (agreed equivalence), by the costs of production plus *average profit* (equivalence of bourgeois exchange), and *in principle* by labor equivalence (equivalence of simple commodity exchange). Which of these equivalences it is necessary to take into consideration *must be dictated by the dialectical logic of the judge* in each individual case, considering both the force and purpose of the given section of the contract, *the factual circumstances of the conclusion of the contract* as well as the *factual relations of the parties*.

It is clear to everyone that we speak of equivalence in defense of the weak party, in defense of the working person. But for disputes between the Nepman and the government we enter a correction also in the equivalence of bourgeois exchange: not the costs of production *plus* the average profit, but the unused expenditures minus the profit (see below).

In our country, as the factory worker receives wages, so also the collective farmer is awarded an *income* at this stage *proportional to the concrete labor expended, extending to piecework.* How is this connected with the State Planning Commission? The State Planning Commission means not *an arbitrary decreeing of equivalence*, but its calculation, on the basis of the real quantity of labor (raised wages depending upon innovation and raising the productivity of labor, etc.). And if in our country the significance of labor equivalence is improperly raised, then this means that we have forgotten, or do not understand, the deep significance of Marx's words cited above. It would be interesting to know how my critics themselves understand *equivalence* if they reject *labor* equivalence. Do they understand it as simply a *maximum part*, or as an arbitrarily designated amount or a *leveled* wage? They are silent on this.

I cannot acquaint the reader with all my work on the Supreme Court but I can cite *all* my book on civil law. This explains it very clearly. I have recognized and condemned the essential incorrectness and the unforgivableness of the citations from an article by Bukharin, and discarded them from the second edition (although it was printed without additions as a supplementary first edition). I restored Marx's text, but I did not change my basic conclusion. In fact *I had to* finally put *as the starting point* Engels' revolutionary-dialectical notion that it is possible to distribute *only what is available*, that it is necessary to establish only *a basis and a general direction of movement* of further development (see Ch. IV). This mistake—without outside suggestions—I fully recognize. In the future I will correct it.

But "Ukrainian comradely stories" disturbed other comrades and they went to further generalizations. A small mistake, if developed, can become great. In the second edition of Part I of the *Treatise*, I wrote (p. 177): "Socialist planning on the basis of the New Economic Policy is increasingly limiting the sphere of free action of the New Economic Policy and *of civil law.*"[24] And the contractual principle *on the basis of labor equivalence* relates only to this sphere which is not subordinated directly to plan regulation, while both for the socialist sector and its relations with elements of the "nonsocialist sector," planned regulation and its norms are always in force. Such must be the direction of Soviet civil law.

And in a footnote I wrote: "That labor equivalence relates *only to relations of the working people* is apparent from a whole series of examples in Part II of the *Treatise*: (1) p. 300, a second example, or (2) p. 262: "application of one-sidedness to a state agency is impermissible," etc., or (3) p. 306: "this result not of the work of the factory owner, *but of the unpaid labor* of the workers,' etc., etc. In fact, who could think of a *labor* equivalence for the private employer or, on the contrary, agencies of the dictatorship of the proletariat? 'Between what lines' is this read?''

But this does not satisfy our ''extremists'' or ''superextremists.'' Several more weighty arguments must be introduced against them.

Comrade Molotov says in his paper at the Eleventh Congress of Soviets, as if in answer to these superextremists says: ''In this respect the following words of Lenin from the book *State and Revolution* are extraordinarily significant:''

> In the first phase of communist society (usually called socialism) ''bourgeois right'' is not abolished in its entirety, but only in part, only in proportion to the economic revolution so far attained, i.e., only in respect of the means of production. ''Bourgeois right'' recognizes them as the private property of individuals. Socialism converts them into common property. To that extent—and to that extent alone—''bourgeois right'' disappears.
>
> However, it persists as far as its other part is concerned; it persists in the capacity of regulator (determining factor) in the distribution of products and the allotment of labor among the members of society. The socialist principle, ''He who does not work shall not eat,'' is already realized; the other socialist principle, ''An equal amount of products for an equal amount of labor,'' is also already realized. But this is not yet communism, and it does not yet abolish ''bourgeois right,'' which ''gives unequal individuals, in return for unequal (really unequal) amount of labor, equal amounts of products.'' [Lenin 1917, p. 467]

Lenin's statement has *today a special practical significance*.

Take an example from the creation of the collective farms.

In the theses on collective farm creation presented for consideration by the Congress, it was stated that the most important shortcoming in collective farm organization was the distribution of the collective farm income *not by quantity and quality of labor expended, but per capita. Elimination of this most important shortcoming is one of the immediate tasks of today.* Full *clarity* is needed on this question. It must be recognized that the Bolshevik concept of creation of collective farms requires the distribution of collective farm incomes in true *correspondence with the quantity and quality of labor expended*, and not on a per capita basis as the kulaks and echoers of the kulaks are now attempting in the countryside. Without now closely linking the receipt of a share of the collective farm output with the labor expended and with its real productivity—without such a connection we will not have a ''collective farm movement.''

This means that *for the kulaks* the principle of labor equivalence on the collective farm is *unprofitable*. Comrade Molotov expresses almost the same idea about industry, e.g., on *economic accountability, on the real cost* of production, etc. Do I need to add citations from the speeches of Comrade Ordzhonikidze and Comrade Molotov *on contract*, on contractual penalties, on contract discipline, etc.? Or will our superextremists finally think things over and cease their comments on the harmful ideas of Stuchka—"about the *idea* (!) of material labor equivalence of the contract of Soviet civil law"?

It would seem that the question of labor equivalence is solved for us quite easily—we recognize money, according to Marx's *Critique of the Gotha Program* as the *universal equivalence of labor.*

But do we still need money or have we already transcended this stage? About this, People's Commissar of Finance of the USSR, Comrade Grin'ko, has said:

> One must say directly that the successes of socialist construction sometimes *turn people's heads.* Some begin to think that it does not befit us, standing with both feet on the road of socialist construction, to save money. Some of our young scholars prematurely begin to eliminate money in theory. *We must decisively rebuff these ideas*, because they are opposed to the interests of socialist construction at the current stage. *Finances are still a powerful organizer of accumulation in the country, a powerful lever for the development of socialist construction. Therefore, we must eradicate a carefree attitude toward money*, an underevaluation of the role and significance of the financial system. We must have, and we will have, the strictest financial discipline; *we will set up supervision by the ruble* of the course of our economic construction. In practice, we will base the expenditures of each organization directly on how it fulfills its production and financial plans. [Grin'ko 1931]

In his speech at the Congress of Workers in Finance, Grin'ko expressed himself even more critically against such conversations as *disturbance of the internal currency*.[25]

Comrade Pashukanis has abjured his abstract theory and condemned it, but he does not so easily free himself from its influence when he discusses *concrete* legal questions. Here it's gossip, rumors, or general opinions (so to speak, off the wall), where concrete study is needed. In this respect, shortcomings are apparent from his conclusions about the civil law of bourgeois society and about the civil law of the transition period of the dictatorship of the proletariat. For him the civil-law relations of the bourgeoisie are *stable*, for they correspond to the law of "*completed* socioeconomic formation." Comrade Pashukanis asks: "why does the system of bourgeois private law develop into a *completed*, frozen legal system?" He himself replies:

> Because the principles of *free* private property and free contract reflect relations, in essence, nothing other than the legal facilitation of capitalist exploitation. This is the source of the closed *and immobile nature of the system* of bourgeois law and its seeming independence from politics.

All the old mistakes of Comrade Pashukanis appear here more than anywhere else. He ignores both the role of the class state and the class nature of law, and adheres to *a dogmatic* conception of civil law *under an abstract form of equality and freedom* which completely conceals the concrete content *of inequality and domination-subordination.*

"My viewpoint," Marx says, "is that an economic social formation *develops* as a *natural-historical process.*" This means *the movement* of commodity capital formation developing from a simple commodity economy is an *all-out movement*, and that to correspond *to all* these different stages of development of the economy, bourgeois civil law is *more and more abstracted* right up *to the purest normativism* in the formula on "impersonal instrumentality" (the invention of former Professor Shreter). This was aided also by the development of the economy which created corresponding to the abstract subject of civil law a still more abstract subject in *the anonymous impersonal subject*: the anonymous (it is called in French) or stock society as only one form of *bearer* rights. This also is the *abstract* concept of legal subject held by to Comrade Pashukanis: "*The legal subject* is *the abstract commodity owner* elevated to the heavens. His will—will understood in a legal sense—has *its real basis in the wish to alienate in acquisition and to acquire in alienation*" [Pashukanis 1924, p. 81].

I have said that our Soviet civil law has not developed as indicated by Pashukanis's abstract theories on the subject of law. But it has sharply raised the question of *unmasking and openly declaring the class nature of the subject of law according to his goal* (C—M—C or M—C—M+m). Our Soviet civil law destroyed even the bearer shares, etc. allowed at the start of the New Economic Policy. It also unmasked the "hidden" kulak. The court also dealt very well—contrary to the *scandalmonger* informers of Comrade Pashukanis—*with the class line* with respect to all these subjects of laws.

But for other purposes, Comrade Pashukanis insisted on an argument on the purposefulness, the systematic nature of *immutable bourgeois* civil law and in contrast to it, *changeable* Soviet law. In my opinion, during the discussion on his paper, he somehow simply made a slip of the tongue, *denying a system in Soviet law*. I made a "Zwischenruf" (remark from the floor), and then Comrade Pashukanis "ex promptu" *raised* the wild theory with which he now addresses me on *the impossibility of a system in Soviet law.*

Does this mean that the Soviet authorities are following a general plan of the economy, the state plan, but that law is not only *unplanned*, but in general it cannot and must not "be reduced to a system." And what about the state plan? Does it not of itself introduce a *legal* order or, as it is expressed in Pashukanisite terms, "by the application of legal form," in the case of a given law (and the state apparatus)? I answered by relying on Engels' words on law (cited above) as "an internally consistent expression," that the coordination of every new political step with the law already in effect is absolutely necessary, and I cited as an unprecedented revolutionary example the famous Decree of the All-Union Central Executive Committee on Dekulakization. As is well known, even in theory Comrade Pashukanis "does not like" a statute; he is more sympathetic to "*direct actions.*" But he ignores Lenin's attitude *toward* law, as will become even clearer when his notes to Comrade Bonch-Bruevich as head of the Council of People's Commissars are published. Comrade Pashukanis was not satisfied with this. He considered himself obliged to accuse me of yet another sin, that I *hid* part of a citation from Lenin on the *permissability of reform (i.e., of the influence of statute)*. Comrade Pashukanis forgets that according to Lenin himself, the dictatorship of the proletariat is in fact a *continuation* of the class struggle, but by "*other*," "*newer*" and more powerful means: for instance, the revolutionary law of Soviet power. Comrade Pashukanis finds that the *most interesting thing in this* citation begins at the point where I stopped quoting. And what does it say there? Only that "a breathing space is required when forces are under maximum load." That *I hid nothing* is apparent from the fact that I give the page of the citation. But I had *something entirely different in mind*: I was speaking *of the procedural influences on law*, and not of revolutionary influences.

I *wrote a great deal* about Article 1 of the Civil Code (in full agreement again with Comrade Pashukanis). I summarize this in Part I of the *Treatise* (p. 120).

It is true, even Lenin approved the text of this article, but not from a philosophical perspective. At the sessions of the All-Union Central Executive Committee (October 31, 1922), with respect to the Civil Code Lenin spoke of "*the abuse* of the New Economic Policy—the things that are legal in all other countries, but which *we do not want to legalize*" [emphasis P.S.], but "we shall leave ourselves a perfectly free hand in this matter. If everyday experience reveals abuses that we have not foreseen, *we shall forthwith introduce the necessary amendments*" [Lenin 1922, p. 393]. But how? By simple interpretation of Article 1? No, by *legislation*. "In this respect, you all, of course, know very well that other countries regrettably do not know *speed of legislation* like ours."

I do not know why Comrade Pashukanis needs to question my revolutionary character. Whether to apply one revolutionary method or another—mass actions or statute—depends upon *concrete circumstances*. But Comrade Pashukanis vainlyconsiders it necessary to present "dekulakization" merely as an *elemental movement*. *This revolutionary slogan* had been presented by Lenin. On a page in the passage[26] of mine earlier cited by Comrade Pashukanis (in 1929), there is a discussion of the Directive of the Fifteenth Party Congress and the Plenum of the Central Committee *on the attack on the kulak*. I speak in the same place "*of the firmly determined direction of expected changes*." Thereafter, the leader of the revolution, Comrade Stalin, put forth the revolutionary slogan of liquidation of the kulak class through full-scale collectivization. Finally in January 1930, the decree of the Central Executive Committee of the Union was published. This legalized[27] a revolution *already* achieved *and one also still to take place*.[28] The Supreme Court concurred with this movement. And when after this, for instance, *a further step* was taken in the Moscow city council, and *Nepmen in general* began to be included as kulaks, then I had to speak against such an excess on the part of the Moscow Regional Court; this happened in the Plenum of the Supreme Court (coincidentally, on the same day, February 4, 1930, when an article by

Comrade Stalin was published on this theme). But Comrade Pashukanis *transferred* these moods of January 1930 to *January 1931*. And from this I was accused of a right deviation.

VII.

When I wrote my first theoretical work on a legal question, I was faced with the task of theoretical formulation *not so much* of the concept of law itself as of its nature, its characteristics, etc. At that time *everyone* lived under the bourgeois concept of *law* as statute. But we did not have statute law. I wrote in 1918:[29]

> "For the bourgeois revolution it was sufficient, considering its decisiveness, to change the form of the organization of state power rather than putting in power one or a combination of classes. *Thus the means of subjugation* freely *changed* even without essential changes in the text of the law. *The constancy of the law* appears to be the most essential pillar of human society, to the extent that it is based upon the exploitation of man by man." [Stuchka 1931, p. 25]

However, in 1919, when we needed to draft something in the form of a *criminal* code (in place of the draft of Shreider, the leader of the Left Socialist Revolutionaries, which we had rejected), the question *confronted us directly*. At that time the question of a struggle over the attitude ''no law—no punishment'' unconsciously arose. Crime was still understood as a violation of law. But what was the law whose violation could be discussed if there was no statute? This is how *life forced us to find an answer* ''to the accursed questions.'' Now it is *easy to speak* of formulations and to criticize them. It was not so easy in 1919. Nevertheless, our definition *was correct*: it contained both the base, real social relationships, and the class nature of every law in the form of protection (and not only protection!) of the base by the *class* state as the interest of the *ruling class*. For us it was clear that law is a *form*, but we *did not have* a fully clear Hegelian *understanding of form and content*. We could not accept Stammlerism, which among us appeared as an understanding of law as (this is my word play) a ''pillowcase'' for economic relations. We spoke *of the system or order* of these relations which (system of order) was supported by the state. For criminal law we reached *a valuable conclusion*: violation not of *a statute-law* but of *an interest* supported by the state and *of the order* established by it. *This was an achievement*, was it not?

But turning to the development of theory, I was actually faced with *three kinds* of relations: (a) relations actually formulated—in a *concrete* form (especially contract); (b) abstract form [of two kinds]: (1) statute (in particular the abstract provision of civil law), (2) legal consciousness—an ideology or idea of law, etc. The necessity of solving this problem arose from *actual* life. This is an example of the gap between principle and practice, *an unavoidable contradiction of bourgeois society*, *which cannot be resolved* in that society. But the problem was not *in the principle of law* which must disappear even during the phase of the dictatorship of the proletariat.

It seems to be a simple, fully dialectic thought, but it corresponds to the *objective dialectic*.

The first public statement against me came *from the camp* of *Comrade Bukharin*, in the person of comrade Podvolotskii, with allusions to some "trinity," etc. These were cheap jokes. Later they found "mechanism" in this wholly *objective* dialectic. In the second edition of my *Treatise on Soviet Civil Law*, I stated that "this problem still awaits solution." But help, give your interpretation of *the fact*. For instance, is it a fact that in the bourgeois state the actual and written constitutions diverge, while here the formal and unwritten constitutions fully correspond to one another? Comrade Pashukanis, for instance, now speaks of concrete-relations (February 17, 1931):

> I consider that a turn from abstract scholasticism *to the study of the concrete reality* of the current tasks of socialist construction in the area of *Soviet law* must be attained, by the way, also in the sense that *from the study only of legislative acts*, norms and legal relations *to go to that which occurs in reality*, and accordingly to the study of how the apparatus *brings* this very Soviet law to life.

I do not here adduce citations on the two abstract forms—"statute" and "legal consciousness," "idea of law," etc.—*enough of them can be found, particularly in Engels*.

The problem must be solved, in essence, in terms of Hegel's definition of the relation between form and content: "When form and content are contrasted, it is most important to take account of the fact that *content is not formless*, but has *immanent form which at the same time is something external* . . . so that *content* is nothing other than *the transformation of form* into content, while form is *the transformation of content* into form." A further development of this notion with respect to law may be found in Adoratskii's article "Ideology (Legal)."[30] In it there is a discussion of the same "unequal" development of form and content about which Engels also speaks. "As soon as the new division of labor which created *professional lawyers* become necessary, another new and independent sphere is opened up which, for all its general *dependence upon production and trade*, has also a special capacity for *reacting upon these spheres*"[31] [emphasis—P.S.] [Engels 1890, p. 492].

I have been accused of *confusing relationships with the form of these relationships*. This accusation already has an *eight-year history* behind it; it came from the late *Reisner*, but it was based on a misunderstanding. In our definition, I defined *law* as a *system* or *order* (now a form or rather a whole system of forms) of these relations. Since Marx [Marx 1846, p. 518] at first called *production relations* social relations, but later also *relations of exchange*,[32] I also derived the form of production relations (according to Marx's expression: "in the legal language'' of relations of ownership) and the forms of relations of exchange, i.e., in general the so-called law of obligations. I propose that what I have said *on the form and content of law*, on law and economic or social relations here is sufficient. By itself, these questions of the history of the origin of law do not presently have special significance and "can be deferred."

But I am less interested here in *the mistake I have admitted* in formulation than in *the matter of substance*. Because of unclarity about this we suffer great inconvenience both of a theoretical and of a practical nature. If we put forward the possibility and, hence, the desirability of the *unity of these three forms* in our stage of the transition period, then we are approaching purely theoretically, *a new method of legislation*: the deepening *of the concept of revolutionary legality*. We should outgrow our casual attitude *toward the Soviet decree or law*, which is possible only with a rational standard presentation for our legislation so that, on the one hand, not to force judges and other institutions to ignore law as outgrown, and on the other, so that law was formulated not as *polemics* with the past, as landmarks for outgrown relations, but also contained *a direction for the future*. Thus, I also posed the question of my own legal theory and practice in the future. It was then possible to transcend the lack of coordination between our theories and *the old narrow concept of law* as statute, that understanding which today even *among communists* includes not less than 99 percent. But this requires serious work and development. I can only say about Soviet *decree and law*: back to Lenin. When I wrote on the decree on dekulakization as an unprecedented fact, Comrade Pashukanis saw it as an attack on him. I cannot otherwise explain the angry tone of his paper. "Can there be a system *only* in decrees? Does it mean that all movement before publication [of the decrees] was chaos? Does it mean that there was no system in it and that system began only then when the decree was issued? Comrades, this is in fact just the same narrow legal point of view." Yes, if someone so understood decree and statute, then this would be not only narrowly legal, but even according to the method of Shchedrin's "pompadour" who ordered the river to change its course from downstream to up. [M.E. Saltykov-Shchedrin, in his story *"Pompadury i popadurshi"* used the term to mean an autocratic administrator—translator's note.] Long before the decree, by means of the slogan calling for an attack on the kulak, we were preparing ourselves for liquidation of the kulak as a class. But we know also that as a result of left excesses, the well-known "chaos" in fact ensued. Because of it—a certain retreat, and then *a decree brought order* into this chaos, a decree issued moreover according to plan and not without the knowledge of the Party. And here we also diverge in the concept of law, for in law Comrade Pashukanis saw only the phenomenon of the anarchy of bourgeois contractual commodity exchange. I see in it an organized means *of action and influence* of the class *state*. But the *means*, the method of this influence consists of *legislation*, of the creation of "rules of law" and in their defense. As Lenin says, they are "enforced through a special apparatus called the state" [Lenin 1917, p. 462]. Once we have begun *the planning* of socialist economic construction, we *must introduce* this same system and planning *into Soviet construction and law* as well.

Comrades, it is finally time *to dissociate ourselves* from past mistakes; recognition of them alone is not enough.

VIII.

The accusation against me of mistakes, the accusation made by my critical friend, Comrade Angarov, is of a somewhat different type, and is "softly made." He is a methodologist and Hegelian by profession, and he even has a speciality: the struggle with neo-Kantianism, *specifically* with Comrade Galanza.

After his admitted failure in a struggle against the rural Soviet (in favor of its replacement by the administration of the collective farm), Comrade Angarov *took up the study of civil law* (from my *Treatise*) and discovered in my work a *whole catalog of mistakes with twelve entries*. Its basic *leitmotif* was: "there are many *mechanistic positions* in Comrade Stuchka's work." How could it have happened that my achievements: "emphasizing (it seems to me somewhat more!) the class role (?)[33] and the revolutionary significance (only?) of law and the state" were turned into *full-scale mechanism*? In my opinion if there is anything not connected with the mechanistic understanding of history and social development, it is the *revolutionary class struggle*. And I am true to this point of view to the extent that I evoked puzzlement among my closest comrades when I first spoke of class struggle in even civil law.

But let us begin. *Mistake No. 1.* The same approach for reprinting an article by Comrade Bukharin, which I recognized above and for which I should be particularly attacked, since I know the citation from the letter of Engels which I cited above. I corrected the mistake, and reinstated both the text and thought of Marx himself. But I would beg Comrade Angarov to become *more closely* acquainted with the text of Karl Marx and not through Bukharin alone. *After this* he and I can talk about the "mechanistic position" (what terminology!) on the question at hand. I affirm that he has misunderstood either the mistakes of Comrade Bukharin or the thoughts of Marx himself.

Mistake No. 2. Purportedly, in certain places I made a "formulation about organized capitalism" which is allegedly "in the closest manner connected with his (i.e., my concept) of law of inequality—law of equality and then again the law of inequality." This of course, as the English say, is "sophistication" (i.e., falsification) of my thoughts. And the concepts "law of inequality" and "law of formal equality" were taken by me from Lenin. But Comrade Angarov mentions the law of (real) inequality and the law of (formal) equality, only thus, in passing. His basic accusation is different: attributing to me the mistakes of Comrade Bukharin committed by him in another article, which appeared significantly later than my book, namely, in the article on organized capitalism. Comrade Angarov states that this notion is very clearly present (in my work), thus:

The start of the period of monopoly and imperialist capitalism means a transition *to new methods*. Instead of free *competition*, i.e., freedom of demand and supply as in the previous stage of purchase and sale, there arises a *production monopoly*. Its purpose is the replacement of anarchy of production (and accordingly also of exchange) with *planning* by way of trusts, syndicates or state imperialism. [34]

I formulated the notion of organized capitalism *more than once*. [35] But Comrade Angarov in a strange manner *has omitted* for instance, pages 32 through 35, where we read my *basic concept* of the monopoly or imperialist period of capitalism:

Imperialism arose as the development and direction continuation of the basic features of capitalism in general. But capitalism became capitalistic imperialism only at a certain, very high stage of its development, when certain basic features of capitalism were turned into their opposites, when on all lines features of the transition period from capitalism to a higher socioeconomic order were formed and appeared. The economic basis of this process was the replacement of capitalistic free competition with capitalistic monopolies. Free competition is a basic feature of capitalism and goods production in general: monopoly is the direct opposite of free competition, but this latter in our eyes has begun to turn into monopoly.

Even "half a century ago, when Marx wrote *Capital*, free competition seemed to the majority of economists to be a 'law of nature.' The official scholarship tried, by a conspiracy of silence, to kill the works of Marx which demonstrated by means of a theoretical and historical analysis of capitalism . . . that free competition . . . at a certain stage of its development leads to monopoly. Now monopoly has become a fact." This is how I *understand* the question of the "monopoly or imperialist" nature of capitalism. As noted in the text, *these are Lenin's words*. [36] In this passage, I *continue with extracts from Lenin*. One can be forgiven for dozing off [37] while leafing through a book, and for missing several pages, but we should know *Lenin's thought in our sleep*. But in Part I of my *Treatise* (e.g., p. 54) there was *a direct qualification*, that this "capitalist planning" is a vain illusion, "which the legal bards of capitalism and their *socialist or even communist followers* sing of as a socialist rebirth of law." In its second edition which was in print before the paper by Comrade Pashukanis, I again purposely and *definitely* characterized the theory of Bukharin's "organized capitalism" with which *I never had anything in common and have nothing in common*. This simply does not correspond to the truth—in legal language, it is a "slander" on the part of those who really agreed with Comrade Bukharin.

Mistake No. 3. "Comrade Stuchka particularly *emphasizes* (just emphasizes?) the class nature of law and the state. *This is good* (very pleasant). But, in emphasizing this class nature it is necessary to apply it consistently in concrete analysis. *However*, dealing with the nature of statute, Comrade Stuchka writes the following: "This means that statute in essence is the result of victory of a class, but between the rule[38] of two classes there exists a transition *period of dictatorship not recognizing any statute*" (p. 169). And further he affirms that "this dialectical concept of statute is obligatory for anyone who wishes (a word left out: *scientifically*) to take an interest in law in general, and in civil law in particular." "It follows, that dictatorship is a period of non-class rule. *This is at a minimum* mechanistic."[39] It is necessary, Comrade Angarov, to know Lenin. I hope in the first place that the reader will read the whole (I say without excess modesty) very interesting section on statute (pp. 167–73). But the "mechanistic" (at least) thought again belongs, unfortunately, *not to me but to Comrade Lenin*. Comrade Angarov, as a specialist in the state, *should have* known (i.e., "could not have failed to know") that I wrote one more work on the theme *Theory of the State*, and there (sixth edition, p. 29) this thought is developed more fully with citations from Lenin: "We read in Lenin that the transitional stage between the state as an agency of the rule of the capitalist class and the state as the agency of rule of the proletariat is the *revolution*."[40] The specialist in the state must know, at the very least, Lenin's notion of *dual power*.

Mistake No. 4. "We (who is this "we"?) have gone through a tremendous struggle to support the view that statute is not a compromise of class interests. But Comrade Stuchka ("we" and "you"?) writes the following: "Thus *law* is always *to a certain degree a compromise* between the "*idea of law*" *and the economy*, and in the class concept—the interests of the classes, but *with clear and defined* predominance *of the interests of the ruling class*" (pp. 16-17). "And in such a form the formulation of the author offends Marxist-Leninist theory." It may not be said that my brief formulation (with the words "always to a certain degree") was very clear: I even removed it in the new edition. But the author should *also* read the *preceding words*. The *thought* itself, incidentally *is taken from Marx, Lenin, and Engels.* Comrade Angarov, take vol. I of Marx's *Das Kapital* and read the remarkable pages *on the victory of the working class* over the law on the ten-hour work day. The law was a *bourgeois law*, but it was a concession, *a compromise in the face of a working-class victory.* Did this not compromise the ruling class? Then read Lenin's article "On the Significance of Gold." If these passages are not enough, I can give you as many citations as you wish.

Mistake No. 5. I allegedly "smear out (?) struggle with normativism." I do not know where you would have waged this struggle. You will find my struggle right in the same book.[41] In my article on jurisprudence[42] I even predict the role of Bentham for the normativists. But in the cited passage,[43] I merely show how, *in the language of lawyers*, a norm "from the middle of that which is ("existing") is turned into that which should be ("ought")." It is necessary to read without "distorted" glasses.

Mistake No. 6. It is simply *decreed* by Comrade Angarov: "I *suppose* (?) that this is so and that this is mistaken." I spoke of the *monopoly* right of ownership of land. I followed Lenin's example. He used the word "monopoly" rather often (foreign trade, for bread, etc.) not having the purpose of "clothing our socialist construction in legal relations." And if Comrade Angarov already *contrasts* socialist property (see Art. 15 of the Constitution), then he has somewhat "run ahead." Compare his former plan for abolition of the rural soviets.

Mistake No. 7. On the communist revolution. I already wrote of this, see above. "So," Comrade Angarov exclaims, "the communist revolution is still in the future, the socialist revolution will grow into it. This *is at the least* (!) *unfortunate*." But *at the most what*? The *revolution is continuing* here in fact. That I accidentally termed the stage of communism at the last stage is *irrelevant*, but it is correct (see the *Communist Manifesto*, the thoughts of Marx and Lenin *on two phases* of socialism: socialism and communism, etc.). I apologize that I have had to waste so many words.

Mistake No. 8. I began my *Treatise* with a paraphrase of Lenin's words of 1918: "We do not yet know a socialism that can be embodied in clauses and paragraphs"[44] [Lenin 1918f, p. 515]. I stated that Soviet civil law *(more accurately* the code of civil law) *now* must be rephrased in paragraphs of economic policy. But what did Comrade Angarov infer from this? "Here is given the position (again a position!) that our economy, socialist planning, etc., *should be made* (!) into a new (?) *quality* (!?) of law. This is an incorrect position." Even if you beat me, I will understand nothing. Belinskii once wrote in a review: "There is no meaning, but instead, some sort of poetry!" Here I do not even see poetry. But I wished and wish to say simply that so long as the state exists, we will conduct our economic policy through a *legal* order. That is all.

Mistake No. 9. My opinion about the origin of law. I repeat the thoughts of Lafargue. How Cunow is involved here I do not know. Lafargue lived and died a staunch Marxist, recognized as such even by Marx. His hypothesis is based upon the hard facts of terminology of *language* (the word "right" is in all languages). Comrade Angarov "*supposes*" that this is not dialectical. Angarov himself still has not given *his own* conception of law, particularly after Comrade Pashukanis's abjuring his theories.

Mistake No. 10. "Comrade Stuchka speaks of the law of seizure, and directly states that robbery and force are turned into law" (the question is of the first period of law). Comrade Angarov finds that "here the theory of force arises again" and "here we must be especially well armed." Arm yourself, Comrade Angarov, but not only against me. I follow Marx's viewpoint, *incidentally* citing *his words* (pp. 18-19). I can also cite his words on *possession* as seizure and simultaneously the first *right* of ownership.

However I understand the word "force" as Lenin understands it: "law is nothing without an apparatus capable of *enforcing* the observance of the standards of law"[45] [Lenin 1917:471]. And how Lenin literally understands this force is apparent from his comparison between it and the future rules of social life—

"without force, without coercion, without subordination, *without the special apparatus for coercion* called the state"[46] [Lenin 1917:462].

Mistake No. 11. On law in general. "In one place Comrade Stuchka says that law in general *is the fusion* of private and public law" (p. 223). But what is written there in fact is: "Law (*primitive*) *still is not divided* into private and public, civil law; it is law in general." Rather here of course is a transposition: "this is in general law." Or say: simply law, without division into branches. But Comrade Angarov went on to write of the "removal of law from the socialist formation." "Again a *mechanistic* attempt to give a definition of law in general." This is already too much. For I posed the question of *class* law; I have been struggling for this class concept of law for decades. But you, lost in *your own* scholastic, mechanistic, etc. concept of *bourgeois law* namely as law in general, now have arrived nowhere. I wrote a hundred times that I understand the words "social relations" as Marx understood them: in the sense of relations of production (Marx *later added* exchange). And here you joke about the replacement of law with the words "credit," "school," etc. And you call this a "scholarly discussion"? No thanks. I hope that we have at last come out of this web of abstract constructs *incomprehensible to anyone (even yourself)*.

Mistake No. 12. "Comrade Stuchka states that the law of private property is a concept where meaning is the same as the concept of domination and subordination." Again a mechanistic position. I stand firmly on the base of the views of Marx and Lenin on "domination-subordination." Do I need to cite those places? Do I need to repeat the words of Marx that production relations are in legal language relations of ownership, etc.? Still one more argument: Allegedly, I have discarded "civil society." (This again is our Hegelian speaking!) Already in 1918 (1) I adduced Marx's thoughts on *the division in bourgeois society of man into citizen and man*; in my *Treatise on Soviet Civil Law* I devoted several pages to the problem of Marx on *civil society*, its contrast to "political life," etc.

Here are my 12 *sins*, 12 errors as illuminated by Comrade Angarov. After what I have said, let the reader judge if they are *well founded*. I will be told: it was a colossal job—Comrade Angarov read 227 pages. Excuse me, but I must limit this figure: Comrade Angarov *read only pages*: 9, 13, 16, 17, 19, 22, 23, 54, 69, 70, 72, 78, 157, 158, 159, 160, 166, 169, i.e. 18 pages of 227. This means that he did not *study civil law*, but merely *looked for* mistakes either following orders, or on the principle: the more the better. For "quantity is transformed into quality." But into what quality? It is true concluding with the accent on "reconciliation," Comrade Angarov finishes his speech with the inspiring words: "Having overcome the mistakes in our (i.e., my and Pashukanis's) views, we will travel the road of *dialectical synthesis of those correct* positions which are in their works.[47]

In a word, to the struggle—"Toreador, bravely, Toreador, Toreador."

I have finished the reply on *the first series* of my mistakes: "My Way and My Mistakes." The humorist Mark Twain gives the thoughts of an honest candidate in political elections: he went into the electoral struggle an honest man; he came out of the struggle labeled a hoodlum, rapist, bandit, etc.[48] I am not a "scaredy-cat." I was long accustomed to being *alone* in the struggle. But I count on *independently thinking* young people. I will not let myself be deflected from the way I have set out on.

I will end with the words of Dante from Marx's preface to the first edition of *Das Kapital*, "Sequi il tuo corso" . . . and in Russian translation: "go on—go on—go on."

Notes

1. See the editors' note at the end of the article.

2. See *Thirteen Years of Struggle for a Revolutionary Marxist Theory of Law*, p. 34.

3. On May 24, 1921, I received a new assignment from the Orgbureau for *Theory of the State and Constitution of the RSFSR.*

4. So that there will be no new reproaches that I broke off the citations, I ask you to read them yourselves.

5. K. Marx and F. Engels, *Letters*, p. 322, footnote.

6. When the term "proletarian law," as this law *was first called*, is opposed, then one should remember that the article in the collection *The October Revolution and the Dictatorship of the Proletariat* compiled in commemoration of the first anniversary of "October" in fall, 1918, *was written by me on a theme assigned by the Central Committee of the Party.* I must note that the idea of publishing this collection as a popularization of the successes of Soviet power belongs to Lenin. Thereafter Lenin himself *looked over all the manuscripts* before their printing. I do not know if traces (notes, etc.) of his opinion remain in written form, but verbally he expressed a flattering reaction to my article. This was unexpected: the article was written hastily because I had to submit it in a period of 10 days.

7. [Stuchka 1931, p. 148ff].

8. Incidentally, I cited the remarkable pages from Marx's *Capital* where he leads from the "sphere of commerce or commodity exchange, of this true Eden of inborn rights of man," legally speaking, of formal equality, to the world of inequality of economic, hired slavery—to the real world of production.

9. At that time, Goikhbarg appeared to be a legal authority (the German "Kapazität") in communist scholarly circles. At the State Scholarly Council I first proposed to open a legal department attached to the Institute of the Red Professors and, by his own sabotage, Goikhbarg delayed the work for the creation of the program and also for the opening of the department for three years. And the management of the legal section of the *Great Soviet Encyclopedia* was assigned not to our section but to Goikhbarg personally, and so the matter continued until his fall.

10. [Stuchka 1931, p. 106ff and p. 118f].

11. [Stuchka 1931, p. 219].

12. K. Marx and F. Engels, *Letters*, p. 310. Engels' words serve as an answer to the confused conclusions of my "opponents" on the system of Soviet law. In my view, the only regulator is the single dictatorship and its uniform policy, and one or another combined or separate code. This is not, in the expression of Comrade Stalin, "two boxes," etc.

13. I was first among us to apply the term "facilitation," from Marx's *Capital*, to law.

14. I will ignore here the transition period where two types of supply coexist.

15. Compare our application *of the leveling principle* in collective farms, severely condemned by leading comrades (speeches of Comrade Molotov, Comrade Iakovlev, and others).

16. K. Marx and F. Engels, *Letters*, p. 301.

17. Lenin, vol. XIV, pt. 2, p. 372, 374 and others.

18. *Sobranie uzakonenii*, no. 29 (1920):item 143.

19. Note Articles 2, 6, and 7 of the Introductory Law and Article 59 of the draft Civil Code.

20. I can say here only a few words on the struggle against *illegal-municipalization* (i.e., taking without an equivalent) of housing, including by judicial procedure. I quote decrees: "So that hidden municipalization of buildings located on the land is not conducted under the guise of taking of land" (October 10, 1930). "To approve the circular of September 17, 1929" (October 5, 1930), etc. I on several grounds do not cite more of them; you note that the dates indicate the time *after the decree on dekulakization*. (Is not an attack on me under such circumstances irresponsible?)

21. An interesting coincidence: about the attacks of the extremists on the middle peasants, Comrade Stalin incidently wrote "Don Quixote also imagined he was conducting an offensive against his enemies when he attacked a windmill. But we know that he his head broken in this offensive, if one can call if that. Apparently, our 'deft' distorters are envious of the laurels of Don Quixote."

22. Lenin, vol. XIV, pt. 2, p. 373.

23. Lenin, [sic] vol. I, p. 202. [In the text, Stuchka is referring to Part I of his *Treatise on Soviet Civil Law* (Moscow, 1927)—Eds.]

24. To this should be added also the fact that the *labor contract* is regulated by the Code on Labor and not by the Civil Code on which both myself and judicial practice firmly agree, and which also was consented to by Comrade Pashukanis.

25. See also the article by Kalmonovich in *Pravda* and *Izvestia* of April 16, 1931: "These distortions attempted with 'left'-opportunist 'pseudo-ideas' to the effect that *money was already being turned into purely accounting symbols*, that *commodity exchange* must be replaced by direct socialist *product exchange*. Affirmations of this type proceeded from the belief that the growth of planning at the given stage in our economy was incompatible with the basic method of economic operations under conditions of the New Economic Policy—economic accountability."

26. *Treatise*, pt. 2, p. 11.

27. Here is how Comrade Pashukanis describes this movement: "But why has P.I. (i.e., I myself) assigned such huge significance to decree? Because in the *autumn* (suddenly) of dekulakization, liquidation of the kulak as a class, conducted by the mass of poor and middle peasants moving into collective farms, happened contrary to the famous principle of equivalence and before the issuance of a new law." No, dear comrade! I assigned this revolutionary decree such great importance because I am a consistent Leninist. Comrade Pashukanis forgets that a significant part of those "moving" randomly into the collective farms, rushed back just due to the fall of the "*left*" excesses. (See Comrade Stalin, "Dizzy with Success.")

28. Pt. 2 of my *Treatise* was published in 1929, i.e., before those events which of course bring a fundamental break also in civil law. They are noted in the draft of the *Fundamental Principles*.

29. *13 years*, p. 25.

30. *Encyclopedia of State and Law*, vol. II, p. 14ff.

31. K. Marx and F. Engels, *Letters*, p. 310.

32. See in the Russian edition of "The Poverty of Philosophy," the letter from Marx to Annenkov.

33. Note here the unusual transposition: not *the role of class law*, but *the class role of law*. You see how he has turned everything backward to the old concept of law, i.e., away from the *class* nature of all law.

34. *Treatise*, 1:54.

35. See also pp. 19, 158, and 160.

36. Lenin, vol. 13, p. 304–305, 249.

37. The Greek popular epic of Homer even allows its king of the gods—Zeus—to nod at times.

38. A misprint. The word "state" should be here. [The text Stuchka quotes had the Russian word "gospodstvom" (rule) instead of "gosudarstvom" (state)—translator's note.]

39. Imitating Lenin, I wrote on the side here: Guard and added they are cutting in broad daylight.

40. Lenin, vol. 15, p. 529. See this thought and citation of Lenin even in Comrade Pashukanis's paper printed in our journal, no. 1 (1931).

41. *Treatise*, 1:114.

42. *Encyclopedia of State and Law*, 3:438.

43. *Treatise*, 1:158.

44. Lenin, vol. XV, p. 373.

45. Lenin, vol. XIV, p. 377.

46. Ibid., p. 370.

47. The synthesis of two antitheses (of their "correct positions"). I, Stuchka, according to Hegel, am the thesis, the position, Comrade Pashukanis is the antithesis, the negation; while Comrade Angarov is the synthesis, the negation of the negation? Is this it? Or something else?

48. In the first period of struggle, the "whites" slandered the people's judges under my decree as "Stuchka's kids." Now I am being worked over from the other side (of course not Comrade Angarov), defining my way as "Stuchkaism" or a special legal form of "Menshevism." I hand this trick over to the court of public opinion and society. It is beneath my dignity to answer such slanders.

FROM THE EDITORS
[of *Sovetskoe gosudarstvo i revoliutsiia prava*—Ed.]

1. The editors are providing space for the article by Comrade P. I. Stuchka, "My Journey and My Mistakes," because he promised at the Congress of Marxist Specialists on the State to publish an article subjecting his mistakes to self-criticism.

2. The editors must note that in the present article, along with recognition of some of his mistakes—as noted in the resolution of the Congress of Marxist Specialists on the State—Comrade Stuchka nevertheless essentially justifies his disagreement with the decisions of the Congress. This includes the question of labor equivalence and the evaluation of his mistakes.

3. The editors consider it inexpedient to have a discussion on the questions raised by Comrade Stuchka's article. They were decided on by the Congress, and such a discussion would inevitably distract the attention of all those working in the area of the state, Soviet construction, and law from the current problems of socialist construction.

On this basis, the editors have found it necessary to limit themselves to the publication of brief informational replies by Comrade Pashukanis and Comrade Angarov, since Comrade Stuchka puts questions to them or makes statements related to their speeches and the partial publication of the transcript of Comrade Angarov's speech at the session of the directorate on October 12, 1930 on the paper of Comrade Pashukanis (still not yet published anywhere), since Comrade Stuchka cites the latter paper in this article.

Bibliography of Works Cited by Stuchka

Abbreviations

LCW: Lenin, V. I., *Lenin: Collected Works*. Moscow: Progress Publishers.

MESW: Marx, Karl, and Frederick Engels, *Karl Marx and Frederick Engels: Selected Works*. Moscow: Progress Publishers, 3 volumes, 1969.

*　　*　　*

Adoratskii, V.V. "Legal Ideology," *Encyclopedia of State and Law* (Moscow, 3 vols., 1925–27), vol. 2.

Berman, Ia. L. 1923. *Transactions of Sverdlov Communist University*, vol. I.

Bukharin, Nikolai 1920. "The Economics of the Transition Period," in Bukharin, *The Politics and Economics of the Transition Period*, ed. K. T. Tarbuck, tr. O. Field. London: Routledge & Kegan Paul, 1979.

———— 1924. "The Bourgeois Revolution and the Proletarian Revolution," in *Ataka: A Collection of Theoretical Articles*. Moscow.

Dicey, A. V. 1889. *Introduction to the Study of the Law of the Constitution*. London: Macmillan.

Engels, Friedrich 1878. *Anti-Dühring*. London: Lawrence and Wishart, 1975.

———— 1884. "The Origin of the Family, Private Property and the State," *MESW* 3:204–334.

———— 1890. "Letter to C. Schmidt, October 27, 1890." *MESW* 3:489–95.

———— 1890a. "Letter to C. Schmidt, August 5, 1980." *MESW* 3:483–85.

———— 1893. "Letter to F. Mehring, July 14, 1893." *MESW* 3:495–99.

Engels, Friedrich and Karl Kautsky 1887. "Juridical Socialism." *Politics and Society*, 7 (1977):203–20.

Finn-Enotaevskii, A. 1906. "Class and the Party." *Education*, December.

Grin'ko, G.F. 1931. "Speech to the Central Executive Committee of the Soviet Union." January 5, 1931.

Gurvich, G. 1922. *Neue Zeit*, no. 18.

Kautsky, Karl 1902. *Neue Zeit*, no. 31.

Laski, Harold J. 1919. *Authority in the Modern State*. New Haven: Yale University Press.

Lenin, V. I. 1917. *State and Revolution. LCW* 25:381–492.

———— 1917a. "Revision of the Party Programme." *LCW* 26:149–81.

———— (1917b), *Decree No. 1 on the Court.* (Council of People's Commissars). *Decrees,* vol. 1, pp. 124–36.

———— 1918. "The Immediate Tasks of the Soviet Government" *LCW* 27:235–77.

———— 1918a. "The Extraordinary Seventh Congress of the R.C.P. (B.)." *LCW* 27:85–139.

———— 1918b. "Speech to Chairmen of Gubernia Soviets." *LCW* 28:171–78.

———— 1918c. "Third All-Russia Congress of Soviets of Workers', Soldiers' and Peasants' Deputies." *LCW* 26:453–82.

———— 1918d. "Speech at a Joint Session of the All-Russia Central Executive Committee, the Moscow Soviet, Factory Committees and Trade Unions of Moscow." *LCW* 28:17–34.

———— 1918e. "Joint Session of the All-Russia Central Executive Committee, the Moscow Soviet of Workers', Peasants' and Red Army Deputies and the Trade Unions." *LCW* 27:419–43.

———— 1918f. "Report of the Council of People's Commissars." *LCW* 27:507–28.

———— 1919. "A Great Beginning." *LCW* 29:408–34.

———— 1919a. "The Achievements and Difficulties of Soviet Government," *LCW* 29:55–87.

———— 1919b. "Eighth Congress of the R.S.D.P. (B.)," *LCW* 29:141–225.

———— 1920. "A Contribution to the History of the Dictatorship Question," *LCW* 31:314–334.

———— 1920a. "The Tasks of the Youth Leagues." *LCW* 31:283–99.

———— 1920b. "The Trade Unions, The Present Situation and Trotsky's Mistakes." *LCW* 32:1–19.

———— 1921. "The New Economic Policy and the Tasks of the Political Education Departments." *LCW* 33:60–79.

———— 1921a. "The Fourth Anniversary of the October Revolution." *LCW* 33:51–59.

———— 1921b. "Notes for a Report at the Second All-Russia Congress of Political Education Workers." *LCW* 36:549–50.

———— 1922. "Speech at the Fourth Session of the Ninth All-Russia Central Executive Committee." *LCW* 33:390–95.

———— 1922a. "'Dual' Subordination and Legality." *LCW* 33:363–67.

———— 1922b. "Notes for a Speech on March 27, 1922." *LCW* 36:571–75.

———— 1922c. "Eleventh Congress of the R.C.P. (B.)." *LCW* 33:259–326.

———— 1923. "On Co-operation." *LCW* 33:467–71.

Magerovskii, D. (1922), "Law, Socialism and State Capitalism in the Transition Period," *Sovetskoe pravo* [Soviet Law], No. 1, pp. 24–32. Partially translated in Michael Jaworskyj, ed. *Soviet Political Thought: An Anthology.* Baltimore: Johns Hopkins Press, 1967, pp. 93–98.

Marx, Karl 1843. "On the Jewish Question," in *Karl Marx: Early Texts*, ed. D. McLellan. Oxford: Basil Blackwell, 1971. pp. 85–114.

———— 1846. "Letter to P. V. Annenkov." *MESW* 1:517–27.

———— 1848. *The Poverty of Philosophy. Marx-Engels Collected Works*, New York: International Publishers, 1976. 6:105–212.

———— 1849. "Speech at the Trial of the Rhineland District Committee of Democrats," in *Karl Marx: Political Writings*, ed. David Fernbach. New York: Random House, 1973. 1:245–64.

———— 1852. "Marx to J. Weydemeyer in New York," *MESW* 1:528.

———— 1858. *The Grundrisse: Foundations of the Critique of Political Economy.* Tr. Martin Nicolaus. New York: Random House, 1973.

———— 1859. "Preface to A Contribution to the Critique of Political Economy."
MESW 1:502–06.

———— 1862, *Theorien über den Mehrwert*. Berlin: Dietz Verlag, 1956.

———— 1867. *Capital*. International Publishers, New York, 1967. 3 vols.

———— 1869. *The Eighteenth Brumaire of Louis Bonaparte, MESW* 1:398–487.

———— 1871. "Marx to L. Kugelmann in Hanover," *MESW* 2:420–21.

———— 1875. "Critique of the Gotha Programme." *MESW* 3:13–30.

Marx, Karl and Engels, Friedrich. 1845. "Feuerbach. Opposition of Materialistic and Idealistic Outlook." *MESW* 1:16–80.

———— 1845. *The German Ideology*. Moscow: Progress, 1976.

———— 1847–1848. "Manifesto of the Communist Party." *MESW* 1:98–137.

McDougall, William. (1920). *The Group Mind*. New York and London: G. P. Putnam.

Oppenheimer, Franz. *Der Staat*. Frankfurt am Main, 1919.

Pashukanis, E. B. 1924. *The General Theory of Law and Marxism*. In *Pashukanis: Selected Writings on Marxism and Law*. ed. P. Beirne and R. Sharlet, tr. Peter B. Maggs. London: Academic Press, 1980. pp. 40–131.

Radbruch, G. 1914. *Grundzüge der Rechtsphilosophie*. Leipzig: Quelle & Meyer, 1914.

Reisner, M. A. 1920. *Fundamentals of the Soviet Constitution*. Moscow, 1920.

———— 1922, Review of P.I. Stuchka, *Obshchaia teoriia prava* [General Theory of Law]; *Vestnik sotsialisticheskoi akademii* [Herald of the Socialist Academy], 1922, No. 1, pp. 173–81.

———— 1923. "A Critique of the Theory of Stuchka," *Vestnik sotsialisticheskoi akademii* [Herald of the Socialist Academy].

Renner, Karl. 1904, *The Institutions of Private Law and Their Social Functions*. Tr. A. Schwarzchild. London: Routledge and Kegan Paul, 1949.

S "ezdy 1959. S "ezdy Sovetov SSSR, soiuznykh i avtonomnykh SSR [Sessions of Soviets of the USSR, and of the Union and Autonomous Soviet Socialist Republics], Moscow 1959.

Stalin, J. V. 1929a. "The Right Deviation in the C.P.S.U. (B)." *J. V. Stalin: Works*. Moscow: Foreign Languages Publishing House, 1955. 12:1–113.

———— 1929b, "Concerning Questions of Agrarian Policy in the U.S.S.R.," *J. V. Stalin: Works*. Moscow: Foreign Languages Publishing House, 1955. 12:147–78.

———— 1929c. "Reply to Collective-Farm Comrades." *J. V. Stalin: Works*. Moscow: Foreign Languages Publishing House, 1955. 12:207–34.

Stuchka, P. I. 1921. *The Revolutionary Part Played by Law and the State— A General Doctrine of Law*. In John N. Hazard, ed., *Soviet Legal Philosophy*, tr. Hugh W. Babb. Cambridge: Harvard University Press, 1951.

———— 1931. *Thirteen years of the Struggle for a Revolutionary Marxist Theory of Law: A Collection of Articles, 1917–1930*. Moscow.

Tsigen, T. 1893. *Physiological Psychology*.

Veger, V.I. 1922. *Sovetskoe pravo* [Soviet Law], no. 1.

Weber, Max. 1961. *General Economic History*. Tr. Frank H. Knight. New York: Collier Books, 1961.

Wilson, Woodrow. 1900. *Congressional Government: A Study in American Politics*. Cambridge, Mass.: Riverside Press.

Name Index

Subject Index